Race and Ethnicity in Pandemic Times

This edited collection brings together social scientists working on race and ethnicity to address the question of the impact of the Covid-19 pandemic, with a focus on issues linked to racial and ethnic inequalities.

The fourteen chapters that make up this collection were produced during the pandemic in 2020 and are intended to address key facets of the impact of the pandemic in contemporary Europe, the United States, and globally. Individual chapters address the pandemic by drawing both on empirical research and conceptual analysis. They also seek to draw important connections between broader dimensions of racial and ethnic inequalities and the health inequalities that have been highlighted by the sharp impact of the pandemic on particular communities and groups. This volume speaks to the need for researchers working on race and ethnicity to respond to the Covid-19 pandemic through both original research and by reflection on current policy challenges and interventions.

The chapters in this book were originally published as a themed issue of *Ethnic and Racial Studies*.

John Solomos is Professor of Sociology at the University of Warwick. He has researched and written widely on the history and contemporary forms of race and ethnic relations in Britain, theories of race and racism, the politics of race, equal opportunity policies, multiculturalism and social policy, race and football, and racist movements and ideas. His most recent books are *Race, Ethnicity and Social Theory* (2022) and *Race and Racism in Britain* 4th Edition (2022). His most recent edited books are the *Routledge International Handbook of Contemporary Racisms* (2020) and *Theories of Race and Racism: A Reader* Third Edition (co-edited with Les Back) (2022). He is Editor-in-Chief of the international journal *Ethnic and Racial Studies*, composed of sixteen issues and published by Routledge. He is also Co-Editor of the book series *Racism, Resistance and Social Change* for Manchester University Press and General Editor of *The Routledge Encyclopedia of Race and Racism*.

Ethnic and Racial Studies

Series editor:

John Solomos, *University of Warwick, UK*

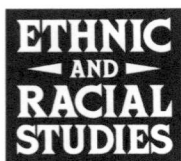

The journal *Ethnic and Racial Studies* was founded in 1978 by John Stone to provide an international forum for high quality research on race, ethnicity, nationalism and ethnic conflict. At the time the study of race and ethnicity was still a relatively marginal sub-field of sociology, anthropology and political science. In the intervening period the journal has provided a space for the discussion of core theoretical issues, key developments and trends, and for the dissemination of the latest empirical research.

It is now the leading journal in its field and has helped to shape the development of scholarly research agendas. *Ethnic and Racial Studies* attracts submissions from scholars in a diverse range of countries and fields of scholarship, and crosses disciplinary boundaries. It is now available in both printed and electronic form. The journal publishes 16 issues per year, three of which are dedicated to *Ethnic and Racial Studies Review* offering expert guidance to the latest research through the publication of book reviews, symposia and discussion pieces, including reviews of work in languages other than English.

The *Ethnic and Racial Studies* book series contains a wide range of the journal's special and themed issues. These special issues are an important contribution to the work of the journal, where leading social science academics bring together articles on specific themes and issues that are linked to the broad intellectual concerns of *Ethnic and Racial Studies*. The series editor works closely with the guest editors of the special issues to ensure that they meet the highest quality standards possible. Through publishing these special and themed issues as a series of books, we hope to allow a wider audience of both scholars and students from across the social science disciplines to engage with the work of *Ethnic and Racial Studies*.

Race and Ethnicity in Pandemic Times

Edited by
John Solomos

Routledge
Taylor & Francis Group

LONDON AND NEW YORK

ETHNIC
AND
RACIAL
STUDIES

First published 2022
by Routledge

2 Park Square, Milton Park, Abingdon, Oxon OX14 4RN
and by Routledge

605 Third Avenue, New York, NY 10158

Routledge is an imprint of the Taylor & Francis Group, an informa business

British Library Cataloguing in Publication Data
A catalogue record for this book is available from the British Library

ISBN: 978-1-032-07352-1 (hbk)
ISBN: 978-1-032-07353-8 (pbk)
ISBN: 978-1-003-20652-1 (ebk)

DOI: 10.4324/9781003206521

Typeset in Myriad Pro
by Newgen Publishing UK

Publisher's Note
The publisher accepts responsibility for any inconsistencies that may have arisen
during the conversion of this book from journal articles to book chapters, namely
the inclusion of journal terminology.

Disclaimer
Every effort has been made to contact copyright holders for their permission to
reprint material in this book. The publishers would be grateful to hear from any
copyright holder who is not here acknowledged and will undertake to rectify any
errors or omissions in future editions of this book.

Printed in the United Kingdom
by Henry Ling Limited

Contents

Citation Information

The chapters in this book were originally published in the *Ethnic and Racial Studies*, volume 44, issue 5 (2021). When citing this material, please use the original page numbering for each article, as follows:

Introduction
Race and ethnicity in pandemic times
John Solomos
Ethnic and Racial Studies, volume 44, issue 5 (2021), pp. 719–734

Chapter 1
Fever dreams: W. E. B. Du Bois and the racial trauma of COVID-19 and lynching
Freeden Blume Oeur
Ethnic and Racial Studies, volume 44, issue 5 (2021), pp. 735–745

Chapter 2
Face mask symbolism in anti-Asian hate crimes
Jingqiu Ren and Joe Feagin
Ethnic and Racial Studies, volume 44, issue 5 (2021), pp. 746–758

Chapter 3
Prejudice and pandemic in the promised land: how white Christian nationalism shapes Americans' racist and xenophobic views of COVID-19
Samuel L. Perry, Andrew L. Whitehead and Joshua B. Grubbs
Ethnic and Racial Studies, volume 44, issue 5 (2021), pp. 759–772

Chapter 4
Race, police, and the pandemic: considering the role of race in public health policing
Adam Dunbar and Nicole E. Jones
Ethnic and Racial Studies, volume 44, issue 5 (2021), pp. 773–782

Chapter 12

Has the Covid-19 pandemic undermined public support for a diverse society? Evidence from a natural experiment in Germany

Lucas G. Drouhot, Sören Petermann, Karen Schönwälder and Steven Vertovec

Ethnic and Racial Studies, volume 44, issue 5 (2021), pp. 877–892

Chapter 13

Cultures of rejection in the Covid-19 crisis

Benjamin Opratko, Manuela Bojadžijev, Sanja M. Bojanić, Irena Fiket, Alexander Harder, Stefan Jonsson, Mirjana Nećak, Anders Neegard, Celina Ortega Soto, Gazela Pudar Draško, Birgit Sauer and Kristina Stojanović Čehajić

Ethnic and Racial Studies, volume 44, issue 5 (2021), pp. 893–905

Chapter 14

Race, immigration and health: the Hostile Environment and public health responses to Covid-19

Giorgia Donà

Ethnic and Racial Studies, volume 44, issue 5 (2021), pp. 906–918

For any permission-related enquiries please visit:
www.tandfonline.com/page/help/permissions

Notes on Contributors

Jehonathan Ben, Centre for Resilient and Inclusive Societies, Alfred Deakin Institute for Citizenship & Globalisation, Deakin University, Melbourne, Australia.

Manuela Bojadžijev, Institute of Sociology and Cultural Organization, Leuphana University of Lüneburg, Lüneburg, Germany.

Sanja M. Bojanić, Center for Advanced Studies of Southeastern Europe, University of Rijeka, Rijeka, Croatia.

W. Carson Byrd, National Center for Institutional Diversity, University of Michigan, Ann Arbor, Michigan, USA.

Kristina Stojanović Čehajić, Center for Advanced Studies of Southeastern Europe, University of Rijeka, Rijeka, Croatia.

Ryon J. Cobb, University of Georgia, USA.

Giorgia Donà, Centre for Migration, Refugees and Belonging, University of East London, London, UK.

Gazela Pudar Draško, Institute for Philosophy and Social Theory, University of Belgrade, Belgrade, Serbia.

Lucas G. Drouhot, Department of Socio-Cultural Diversity, Max Planck Institute for the Study of Religious and Ethnic Diversity, Göttingen, Germany.

Adam Dunbar, Department of Criminal Justice, University of Nevada-Reno.

Amanuel Elias, Centre for Resilient and Inclusive Societies, Alfred Deakin Institute for Citizenship & Globalisation, Deakin University, Melbourne, Australia.

Jennifer Elrick, Department of Sociology, McGill University, Montreal, Canada.

Christy L. Erving, Department of Sociology, Vanderbilt University, Nashville, Tennessee, USA.

Joe Feagin, Department of Sociology, Texas A&M University, College Station, Texas, USA.

Irena Fiket, Institute for Philosophy and Social Theory, University of Belgrade, Belgrade, Serbia.

Joshua B. Grubbs, Department of Psychology, Bowling Green State University, Bowling Green, Ohio, USA.

Alexander Harder, Institute of Sociology and Cultural Organization, Leuphana University of Lüneburg, Lüneburg, Germany.

Emma Hill, University of Edinburgh, School of Social and Political Sciences, Edinburgh, UK.

Maike Isaac, Department of Sociology, McGill University, Montreal, Canada.

Nicole E. Jones, Department of Sociology and Criminology & Law, University of Florida, Florida, USA.

Stefan Jonsson, Institute for Research on Migration, Ethnicity and Society, Linköping University, Linköping, Sweden.

Fethi Mansouri, Centre for Resilient and Inclusive Societies, Alfred Deakin Institute for Citizenship & Globalisation, Deakin University, Melbourne, Australia.

Nasar Meer, University of Edinburgh, School of Social and Political Sciences, Edinburgh, UK.

Mirjana Nećak, Institute for Philosophy and Social Theory, University of Belgrade, Belgrade, Serbia.

Anders Neegard, Institute for Research on Migration, Ethnicity and Society, Linköping University, Linköping, Sweden.

Freeden Blume Oeur, Department of Sociology, Tufts University, Medford, Massachusetts, USA.

Benjamin Opratko, Department of Political Science, University of Vienna, Vienna, Austria.

Yin Paradies, Centre for Resilient and Inclusive Societies, Alfred Deakin Institute for Citizenship & Globalisation, Deakin University, Melbourne, Australia.

Timothy Peace, University of Glasgow, School of Social and Political Sciences, Glasgow, UK.

Samuel L. Perry, Department of Sociology, University of Oklahoma, Norman, USA.

Sören Petermann, Social Science Faculty, Sociology, Ruhr-Universität Bochum, Bochum, Germany.

Yue Qian, Sociology, University of British Columbia, Vancouver, Canada.

Jingqiu Ren, Department of Sociology, Texas A&M University, College Station, Texas, USA.

Karina Santellano, Department of Sociology, University of Southern California, Los Angeles, USA.

Birgit Sauer, Department of Political Science, University of Vienna, Vienna, Austria.

Karen Schönwälder, Department of Socio-Cultural Diversity, Max Planck Institute for the Study of Religious and Ethnic Diversity, Göttingen, Germany.

Angela Simms, Department of Sociology, Barnard College, New York, USA.

John Solomos, Department of Sociology, University of Warwick, Warwick, UK.

Celina Ortega Soto, Institute for Research on Migration, Ethnicity and Society, Linköping University, Linköping, Sweden.

Steven Vertovec, Department of Socio-Cultural Diversity, Max Planck Institute for the Study of Religious and Ethnic Diversity, Göttingen, Germany.

Leslie Villegas, University of Edinburgh, School of Social and Political Sciences, Edinburgh, UK.

Andrew L. Whitehead, Department of Sociology, Indiana University–Purdue University Indianapolis, Clemson, USA.

Rima Wilkes, Sociology, University of British Columbia, Vancouver, Canada.

Cary Wu, Sociology, York University, Toronto, Canada.

Race and ethnicity in pandemic times

John Solomos

ABSTRACT

Social scientists working on race and ethnicity are facing up to the challenge of how the Covid-19 pandemic is impacting on their research agendas. In this introduction, we discuss the emerging evidence about the impact of Covid-19 in terms of race and ethnicity, on migrants and refugees, and on research agendas. By focusing on the discussion that has developed about these issues during 2020 we aim to provide some of the broader background to the specific concerns to be found in the rest of this themed issue. We move on from this overview of key developments to a discussion of the key themes that are explored by the fourteen papers that follow.

There can be little doubt that the Covid-19 pandemic has provided a major challenge to all academic disciplines and sub-fields, across the social sciences, humanities and sciences. Within the social sciences, the shock of the pandemic's impact on societies across the globe has led to intense discussion about how social scientists can contribute to a rounded analysis of the social, cultural and political consequences of Covid-19. For those working in the interdisciplinary field of race and ethnicity, the impact of the pandemic has been evident from the beginning, particularly as from the very early stages of its global spread questions were raised about the impact on racialized minority communities and vulnerable groups within them.

Although there is a wealth of both historical and more recent academic discussion about the historical and contemporary impact of pandemics, particularly in relation to influenza and more recently AIDS, in practice the social and political impact of Covid-19 forced many disciplines to reflect on what they had to say about a real-world health crisis that had the potential to impact on the future of the whole of humanity (Bassett 2020; Napier and Fischer 2020). It is of course far too early to say what the medium or long-term consequences of this period of reflection will be, although it seems plausible to say that in future questions about global public health and viral pandemics are likely to feature more prominently in the development of future research agendas across not just the sciences but also increasingly the social sciences and humanities. This is already to some extent happening, but it is likely to become more evident over the next few years, particularly as the impact of the pandemic is reassessed on the basis of new research on its social impact in a wide range of different societies and community settings.

If we take the specific case of sociology, we have already seen the embryonic expression of this shift in research agendas. Writing about sociology's response to the pandemic Raewyn Connell has argued forcefully that "sociology as we know it is not very good in handling a historical moment, unpacking a conjuncture, let alone grasping a radically new situation like this" (Connell 2020, 5). In this environment, it has become evident that both as researchers and as members of specific societies and communities, sociologists have had to engage very directly with questions about the likely impact of the pandemic on the issues that were the focus of their research as well as on wider aspects of the contemporary situation. In doing so they have had to reassess both the conceptual frames that sociologists use to make sense of the social world around them and the empirical focus of their research.

Those sociologists who are focused on research on race and ethnicity have faced this challenge even more directly, particularly since from the very earliest stages of the pandemic questions about its impact on black and minority communities came to the fore both in media discourses and in scholarly debates. It was with this in mind that *Ethnic and Racial Studies* issued a call for short rapid response papers that addressed the broad question of the impact of Covid-19 on questions about race and ethnicity. As the leading international journal in our field, we felt that there was a need for us to bring together a wide range of short papers, based on both original research and critical thinking, that explored key facets of the impact of the Covid-19 pandemic on questions about race, racism and ethnicity. Although there had been much discussion about questions of race and ethnicity as the pandemic evolved in the form of mass media coverage and online blogs, we felt there was a need for journals such as *Ethnic and Racial Studies* to provide space for more reflective pieces that draw on research and scholarship more directly. In order to respond as quickly as possible to the pandemic, we asked our authors to submit contributions to a very tight deadline and our referees to help us by providing their comments more rapidly than we usually request. We are grateful to both authors and referees for responding to our call and hope that the resulting themed issue will be of interest to them as well as the wider readership of the journal.

We received thirty submissions after we published the call and we processed them by following the standard peer review procedures that we follow as a journal. Since the call for papers was open and did not specify particular areas of interest the submitted papers differed significantly in terms of both substantive focus and empirical and conceptual framing. The fourteen papers that we have been able to include here have been revised as a result of the peer review process and cover key facets of the impact of the pandemic on questions about race and ethnicity. In practice, there are inevitably facets of the current pandemic that are not covered in this themed issue and we hope that in future issues we shall be able to include regular research papers that address these. We hope to be able to cover these aspects of the impact of pandemic as research develops and covers issues that have been relatively neglected in the immediate aftermath.

Having said that, it is also important to emphasize that the papers we have been able to include in this issue are an important first step in trying to make sense of the complex ways in which the pandemic has impacted on questions about race and ethnicity. We see the papers included in this themed issue as the start of a conversation that has been shaped by the need to respond to the challenges of the Covid-19 pandemic, but which will evolve to take account of broader questions about questions of health, global governance, poverty and social inequality and related questions.

Historical comparisons and the present

Before moving on to discuss the impact of Covid-19 on questions about race and ethnicity it is interesting to note that almost as soon as the pandemic became a global issue an important facet of responses to it has been the search for historical comparisons with the ways in which societies responded to earlier pandemics. Given the aftershocks that followed the global response to Covid-19, it is perhaps not surprising that one line of response has been to look back at the history of pandemics and disease in shaping human history. This is partly because there is a wealth of scholarship that has highlighted the role of viruses and bacteria in shaping human history and societies (Kucharski 2020; Snowden 2019; Stepan 2011; Winegard 2019). But much of this body of work has remained outside of the mainstream of sociological research and social research more generally. In the aftermath of the spread of Covid-19 on a global scale, some of this historical knowledge has become a point of reference both in academic research and in popular media coverage of the pandemic. Good examples of this search for historical comparisons are the renewed interest in the impact of the influenza outbreak on 1918–19 and the AIDS epidemic from the 1980s onwards (Bassett 2020). Although both of these pandemics had attracted interest even before Covid-19 (Barry 2010; Kazanjian 2014), there seems little doubt that one of the consequences of the current situation is that there has been renewed interest in looking back at the role of pandemics in previous historical conjunctures in shaping societies.

Part of the reason for this has been a concern to look for earlier examples of pandemics in order to understand how a pandemic on this scale is likely to impact on social and political institutions both in the short-term and from a longer-term perspective. Another important reason for these comparisons seems to lie in the search for routes beyond the pandemic, both through scientific responses such as the search for a vaccine and through social and economic interventions aimed at managing the social costs of the pandemic. More generally, the search for historical points of reference seems to be at least partly the outcome of the growing sense that we can learn something from the past in this time of fear and uncertainty. The search for historical comparisons has been partly framed by the need to ask questions about how societies manage the process of recovery from globalized pandemics.

Some of the comparisons have looked back on the response to the AIDS pandemic from the 1980s onwards. Although there have been panics about other pandemic in the period since AIDS came onto the scene, such as bird flu, mad cow disease and zika (Abeysinghe 2013; Barry 2010; Lakoff 2015, 2017), the social and medical response to AIDS has provided an important point of reference partly because of its global scale as well as the fears that it gave rise to. It has drawn comparisons with the medical and social responses in the early stages of both pandemics, when little was known about both the biological origins of either AIDS or Covid-19, or the ways in which they were transmitted. Nelkin and Gilman use the AIDS pandemic to highlight how devastating diseases are often accompanied by fears and blame:

> Perplexing medical questions have always generated fear, prejudice, and hostility. Thus, any disease that is poorly understood is freighted with social meaning. The patterns of blame that prevail in different periods reflect the social stereotypes, fears, and political biases that are associated with threats of social or political change. (Nelkin and Gilman 2020, 347)

As a number of the papers in this issue note one of the features of the Covid-19 pandemic has been the use of narratives that seek to put the blame for the spread of the disease on particular countries or communities. This has been reflected in the efforts by some to name the virus as the "China virus", an approach that has also impacted on perceptions of Chinese diasporic communities in the West. From this perspective, an important reason for scholars exploring comparisons lies in efforts to make sense of both the social and cultural consequences that follow from pandemics as well as to provide an insight into how societies may be able to move on and manage the health, social and cultural consequences of pandemics.

Whatever the merits of recent efforts to search for historical comparisons between Covid-19 and earlier pandemics there seems little doubt that as the current pandemic progresses there will be more research that attempts to situate it within a broader time frame that explores what we can learn from analysing the present situation in relation to previous pandemics. In this sense, Connell and others are surely right in arguing that sociology, and other social science disciplines, will never be the same in the post-Covid-19 era as they seek to make sense of an event that challenges them like no other in recent times.

Race, ethnicity and Covid-19

Turning now to the impact of Covid-19 within the sub-field of race and ethnic studies. It became clear from the very earliest stages of public debate about the Covid-19 pandemic that its impact on racialized communities, migrants and refugees was an area of public concern. This is perhaps not surprising given the wealth of research pre-dating the pandemic that analysed the complex connections between race, immigration, poverty and inequalities in health (Gómez et al. 2013; Karlsen and Nazroo 2010; Nazroo 2010; Obaso-gie, Headen, and Mujahid 2017). Indeed, one of the Special Issues we had published in 2012, edited by Patricia Fernandez-Kelly and Alejandro Portes, had addressed the complex connections between health care and immigration from a range of angles (Fernández-Kelly 2012; Fernández-Kelly and Portes 2012). We have also published other papers over the past decade that have addressed both directly and indirectly questions about the relationship between health and racial and ethnic inequalities.

But what became clear in the period following the spread of Covid-19 on a global scale from early 2020 onwards is that issues around race, class and poverty were seen as intimately linked to the impact of the pandemic on specific communities. This was particularly the case in the discussion that developed in the U.S. about the differential impact of the pandemic in terms of patterns of residence, locality and socio-economic deprivation. As one study notes about the situation in the U.S.:

> In the United States, race-ethnic disparities in COVID-19 cases emerged rapidly. Although data remain woefully incomplete, the proportion of cases and deaths among Black, Latino, and Indigenous Americans ranges from twofold to four-fold higher than the presence of those groups in the population. And deaths for people of color are occurring at younger ages. (Bassett 2020, 230)

Similar trends have been reported in other countries. In the UK, for example, there was intense discussion throughout 2020 about what seemed to be the disproportionate impact of the pandemic on relatively poor racialized communities who were already seen as suffering from poor health outcomes, both in terms of physical and mental health. There was also an on-going discussion in the UK and other European countries about the likely impact of the pandemic on vulnerable migrant and refugee groups.

At the same time, there was intense discussion in the UK about the impact of the pandemic on frontline health professionals and support workers in the National Health Service, many of whom were from minority or migrant backgrounds. Such concerns were expressed both within minority communities and in official reports such as those produced by Public Health England (Paton et al. 2020; Public Health England 2020). These concerns were partly linked to the long-established reliance of the National Health Service on a labour force with a high number of doctors, nurses and support workers from a range of ethnic and racial backgrounds. A similar pattern could be traced in the context of care homes for the elderly.

More generally, there emerged evidence from the very early stages of the pandemic that it was impacting particularly heavily on minority communities. Given previous research on disparities in health in relation to race and ethnicity, this was perhaps not a surprising development. For example, there is a wealth of research over the past few decades in the broad research field of race, ethnicity and health that has highlighted the intersections between social divisions and health outcomes (Stewart, Cobb, and Keith 2020; Yang, Park, and Matthews 2020). In relation to conditions such as diabetes and hypertension, there is a strong body of research that has focused on the often messy and complex relationship between social and economic disadvantage and differences in health outcomes based on race and ethnicity. But what this research has also emphasized is that there is need to take fully into account not just the interplay between race and ethnicity and the wider environment that helps to shape social divisions and inequalities and how they are experienced.

It is also important to explore more fully but factors such as geographical location and access to, and quality of, health services, heterogeneity within ethnic groups and the social nature of ethnicity and the negative impact on health of experiences of racism and discrimination. A wide range of studies in the U.S. have over the past few decades have sought to disentangle the interplay between residential segregation and health outcomes. In an overview of these studies, Kathryn Anderson has helpfully highlighted the complex ways in which forms of residential segregation can play an important role in shaping adverse health outcomes for both African American and Latino communities over time (Anderson 2017). More recently research in the UK has also highlighted the need to focus more attention on the role of structural inequalities in shaping health outcomes for minority communities. A good example of this body of research can be found in a study by James Nazroo and colleagues on the phenomenon of severe mental illness, which highlights the important role that racial and ethnic inequalities structured by institutional racism play in shaping mental health outcomes for particular communities (Nazroo, Bhui, and Rhodes 2020).

Part of the difficulty faced in addressing this dimension of the pandemic is that it is difficult to disentangle the legacies of discrimination and exclusion from the situation faced by particular minority communities in which entrenched patterns of segregation and social exclusion have become the norm. This is an issue that forms a core theme in a number of the papers in this issue and is a recurrent point of reference in both academic debates and in popular media coverage of the pandemic. Additionally, a number of scholars have drawn attention to the important role that gender plays in this area. Research by Denise Obinna in the U.S. has drawn attention to the complex ties between class, race and gender in shaping the health of African American women (Obinna 2020). Although Obinna argues that such inequalities have a deep historical context, she also forcefully makes the case that the Covid-19 pandemic has accentuated an already deeply problematic position for black women:

> For African Americans, inequality manifests in different forms with race-related health disparities being some of the starkest and most resistant to change. Being African American and female amplifies these disparities –a reality which COVID-19 has brought into clearer focus. (Obinna 2020, 3)

From this perspective, the impact of Covid-19 is significant and important, but it cannot be separated from the historically shaped structural inequalities that both pre-dated the pandemic and are likely to continue to be a key facet of the everyday realities of African American communities in the period to come (Chandler et al. 2020; Yang, Emily Choi, and Sun 2020).

At this stage of the pandemic, it is difficult to draw firm conclusions about the impact of Covid-19 on racialized communities, but it is worth noting that a number of preliminary studies have already begun to shed some light on this issue. One study of structurally vulnerable neighbourhoods and racial-ethnic inequalities has noted that:

> The consequences of the pandemic reach far beyond COVID-19 morbidity and mortality. The effects of social and economic insecurity and the trauma of massive loss of life will continue to impact societies around the world for generations. Just as we are seeing during the pandemic, residents of colour in structurally vulnerable neighbourhoods are at risk of bearing the brunt of these long-term consequences if nothing is done. (Berkowitz et al. 2020, 3)

Indeed, what became evident from early 2020 onwards was that one of the features of the Covid-19 pandemic is that although it has impacted on all societies at a global level it has also been experienced differently by black and minority communities, by migrants, by refugees and other vulnerable groups more generally (The New Yorker 2020). What is needed in the future is a body of research that seeks to address the complex social, health and related issues that can help us to make sense of this situation.

We still know relatively little about the everyday processes that have led to this situation in societies with a diverse social make-up, health systems and economic institutions. It will be important in the coming period to develop research, and policy interventions that are to some extent shaped by it, that addresses the role of both social and economic inequalities in shaping the impact of the pandemic.

Global migration, race and the pandemic

Another key facet of the pandemic has been the growing body of scholarly evidence that it has had a profound impact on both the movement of migrants and refugees in various geopolitical environments and on the perception of these groups and how they are portrayed in both popular and media discourses. This is perhaps not surprising, since over the past two decades questions about migration and refuge have been a key political issue in various parts of the globe. In 2015, the so-called "refugee crisis" had impacted on many European countries both in a political and societal sense (Lucassen 2017; Pruitt 2019). In the United States, the issue of migration became one of the central preoccupations of the 2016 Election, leading to the election of Donald Trump (Durand and Massey 2019; Waldinger 2018). In this conjuncture questions about immigration and refugees were both heavily politicized and divisive in many societies.

As Wemyss and Yuval-Davis (2020) have noted in their discussion of bordering practices during the pandemic

> Some of the bordering practices operating during the crisis reflect continuing and intersecting political projects of governance and of belonging. Very few states have recognised all migrants as fully entitled members of society during the pandemic; only a few states have recognised the right of all members of societies for minimum income during the pandemic; and policies aimed at the exclusion and deprivation of all those who live in national and global grey limbo zones are endangering the lives of millions across the globe. (Wemyss and Yuval-Davis 2020, 15)

Perhaps the most obvious impact of the pandemic has been the tendency for nation-states to use bans on travel and controls at the border as one of the mechanisms for responding to Covid-19, with obvious consequences for migrants and refugees. The impact of the pandemic has, if anything, tended to accentuate the difficulties already faced by migrants and refugees. Whether specifically because of measures introduced to tackle the spread of Covid-19 or initiatives that were introduced on the basis of fears and concerns about migration more generally there seems little doubt that the pandemic has impacted on global migration in a wide range of ways. Given the changing rules about travel that were put in place as a result of the pandemic, the most direct consequence for many migrants and refugees was the search for routes that would allow them to move even at a time where lock-downs had become the norm.

Given the already vulnerable position of many groups of irregular migrants and refugees, there is now growing evidence, including in some of the papers included in this themed issue, that Covid-19 is likely to increase their sense of insecurity. A report by the Organisation for Economic Co-operation and Development on the management of migration during the Covid-19 pandemic highlighted the almost complete closure of borders to most migrants and refugees. But it also noted that "it is important to recognize the bigger question of how COVID-19 may fundamentally change migration overall" (Organisation for Economic Co-operation and Development 2020, 9). What seems evident is that as the situation evolves after the pandemic is under control the impact on migrants and refugees will in all likelihood remain significant in various parts of the world.

This is likely to be the case both for migrants who are looking to move, even at such as difficult time, as well as for those who are settled but who will face questions about their access to rights and resources. In the context of the pandemic much of the attention has been focused on controls at the border but of equal importance are the increasing economic and social pressures faced by settled minority communities. Even before the pandemic became the focus of so much political and policy debate the previous decade had witnessed intense debate in many countries about the position of racialized minorities in terms of their rights as citizens and their position within national cultures. This was exemplified in the U.S. in the role of immigration and the border with Mexico in the 2016 Presidential Election, which in many ways provided the launching pad for Donald Trump's successful campaign. In the British context, the Brexit Referendum in 2016 also brought together concerns about immigration with preoccupations about the impact of race and multiculturalism on "Britishness" (Kellner 2017; Sayer 2017). Given these trends were already part of the political context even before the impact of the pandemic it remains to be seen how it helps to shape the development of future policies about migration, refuge and citizenship. Will the pandemic help to give voice to populist pressures to close borders and narrow the boundaries of who has rights to citizenship and belonging? Or will it allow for other voices that articulate ideas about a common humanity and the need to "welcome others"? These are questions that are likely to be faced even more directly in the aftermath of the pandemic.

Rethinking research agendas

It is perhaps too early, while we are still in the midst of the pandemic, to make a reasoned judgement about the longer-term impact of the pandemic on both current and future research agendas about race, racism and ethnic relations. Even at this early stage, however, it is worth noting that as a consequence of the pandemic it seems likely that scholars and researchers in the field of race and ethnicity will have to at least engage in conversations about how they can begin to rethink their on-going research agendas. Although, as we have noted above, there is a reasonably long-standing body of research on race, ethnicity and health there has been relatively little focus on this dimension of race and ethnic studies within the mainstream research agendas in this field. Rather, it has been left to researchers in the sociology of health and public health to address questions about health in relation to race and ethnicity.

Given the on-going discussion about race and health disparities in the context of Covid-19, it is particularly noticeable that the mainstream of research on the sociology of race and ethnicity has been relatively slow to respond to the challenges posed by including health as a core issue in research. Although journals such as *Ethnicity & Health* have done much to broaden scholarly research agendas over the past three decades it remains the case that in much of the theoretical and empirical research on race and ethnicity questions about health and well-being remain at best a marginal. *Ethnic and Racial Studies* has been interested since its inception in broadening the boundaries of research on race and ethnicity and responding to new challenges as they arise. We have sought to provide a space for cutting edge research that crosses academic disciplinary boundaries and seeks to provide new understandings of the role of race and ethnicity in contemporary societies. In the current conjuncture, there can be little doubt that over the next few years one of the questions we shall need to address more fully in the pages of the journal is how to understand the role of the Covid-19 pandemic in the context of race and ethnic relations. We very much look forward to playing a role in the coming period in publishing high-quality research-based papers that address the wide-ranging implications of Covid-19 for scholarship and research in the core areas that we cover as a journal. Although the papers in this themed issue are almost exclusively focused on the situation in the U.S. and in parts of Europe, we very hope that there will be other contributions in the future that provide us with an insight into the impact of Covid-19 in other parts of the globe. We offer this themed issue in the spirit of initiating conversations and debates that will no doubt continue in the period to come.

The fourteen short papers we have been able to include in this themed issue are best seen as the beginning of a conversation, and one that will be of interest to our readers and the wider communities of researchers, scholars and students that we serve. We also look forward in the future to receiving standard research papers that explore key facets of the impact of the Covid-19 pandemic on issues linked to the broader aims and objectives of our journal. We feel that an important role for a journal such as *Ethnic and*

Racial Studies is to provide a space for responding rapidly to evolving social issues and to reflect emerging areas of scholarship and research as well as to set out possible avenues for future scholarly investigation. Although it is almost impossible to make predictions about the future impact of the Covid-19 pandemic it does seem to be the case that it will continue to help shape social and economic relations in the coming period. Given this situation, scholars and researchers working on race, ethnicity, migration and related issues will have to remain responsive to the ways in which it will help to frame the issues that we research in the coming period.

More generally, the pandemic has brought to the fore the need to bring questions about health much more centrally into research agendas on race and ethnicity. How this can be achieved in the short-term remains unclear, but the discussions that have begun to take shape in the immediate aftermath of the pandemic have at least highlighted important gaps in knowledge that need to be addressed through investment in responsive research programmes that encourage researchers to tackle them through research focused on particular national contexts as well as through comparative and collaborative research. It is only through addressing these noticeable gaps in knowledge that researchers in this field will be able to engage fully with the public debates about the impact of the pandemic on black and minority communities, and the links between geospatial poverty and the differential impact Covid-19 in terms of race (Ward 2020). These are major challenges for scholars of race and ethnic relations but given advances over the past decade or so in the field as a whole we should be well placed to bring the empirical and conceptual tools needed to address them.

It is also important to note that during the period of the pandemic we have also seen another crisis come to the fore, namely the issue of police violence against black communities. The killing of Breonna Taylor and George Floyd at the hands of the police in the U.S. became the symbolic spark that ignited a series of both national and international mobilizations under the banner of *Black Lives Matter*. While the issues surrounding the role of the police and more generally of extrajudicial killings can be traced back over a longer period the degree of anger that grew out of the deaths of Taylor and Floyd led to a series of public protests that continued through the summer of 2020 and focused attention on a broader debate about the continuing role of deep-seated inequalities faced by African Americans, and other minority communities, and the failure to address their root causes. It is not surprising in this context that scholars such as Alyasah Sewell and Jean Beaman have argued that there is a need to explore the ties between the Covid-19 pandemic and police violence against black individuals through the lens of the systemic racism that structures the everyday experiences of deprived communities, both in the U.S. and globally (Beaman 2020; Sewell 2020). This is an issue that is also taken up in a number of the papers included in this themed issue.

It will also be important for researchers of race and ethnicity to become an integral part of conversations outside of academia about these very same issues. This is particularly the case in relation to the conversations about how best to develop policies to deal with the differential impact of the pandemic. Much of the discussion that has developed through 2020 has been shaped by researchers from other fields who have had little or no engagement with the wider research and scholarly literature in race and ethnicity. This is not to say, of course, that their interventions are not relevant or important. But it will be important for race and ethnic scholars to engage more fully with the policy networks that have emerged in the aftermath of the pandemic in order to ensure that their key findings about the differential impact of Covid-19 on ethnic minority communities become part of the policy debates that will help to shape distribution of resources both at the national and the local level. It is only by engaging with these policy debates that the voices of researchers working on race and ethnic relations will be heard in the public sphere.

Key themes in this issue

The fourteen papers that make up this themed issue cover a range of facets of the impact of the Covd-19 pandemic in relation to race and ethnicity. Given the on-going nature of the health crisis that has been caused by the pandemic, the papers are inevitably interventions that seek to shed light on both specific dimensions of the pandemic as well as on broader questions that take us somewhat beyond the immediate impact of the pandemic. We have grouped them around some key themes in order to help readers explore some of the connections that run across them and to allow readers to make some connections as they go through individual papers. We begin the issue with three papers that address some of the broader ideological and political constructions of the pandemic. The first paper, by Freeden Blume Oeur, explores the changing dynamics of race relations during and beyond the Covid-19 pandemic. Drawing on Du Bois reflections on disease and extrajudicial killings the paper endeavours to situate the current pandemic against the broader historical background of slavery and racialized exclusion. Although it is perhaps too early to come to definitive conclusions the issues raised in this paper raise important points for reflection. This is followed by Joe Feagin's and Jingqiu Ren's account of anti-Asian hate crimes as a result of the pandemic. The third paper in this part, by Samuel Perry, Andrew Whitehead and Joshua Grubbs explores the relationship between white Christian nationalism and views about Covid-19. Both of these papers raise important questions about the ways in which cultures of fear and blame have taken root in the aftermath of the pandemic.

The next two papers are concerned more specifically, and largely from a conceptual angle, with the interrelationships between racism and xenophobia and the pandemic. In the paper by Adam Dunbar and Nicole Jones, the focus is on the ways in which the policing of public health guidelines may in practice be racialized through the reproduction of stereotypes about minority communities. This is followed by the paper by Amanuel Elias, Jehonathan Ben, Fethi Mansouri and Yin Paradies that takes up the idea that the articulation of forms of "Covid-racism" may have consequences for the ways in which racism and xenophobia are articulated in the post-pandemic world.

The impact of the pandemic on minority communities forms the main thematic frame for the next four papers. Karina Santellano's paper focuses on the difficulties experienced by Latinos and African Americans in accessing support from the Paycheck Protection Program that was set up in the aftermath of the pandemic. Ryon Cobb, Christy Erving and Carson Byrd provide an account of the psychological distress experienced by Black Americans. The impact of the pandemic on psychological distress has been an important undercurrent in public debate. This is followed by a paper in which Cary Wu, Yue Qian and Rima Wilkes analyse the impact of the pandemic on Asian Americans and Asian immigrants. The final paper in this part, by Angela Simms, uses data from specific local settings to analyse how layers of racial disadvantage help to shape the impact of the pandemic. The issues covered by this paper are likely to be an important point of reference in developing future research agendas.

The final five papers are focused on various dimensions of the impact of the pandemic on migrant and refugee communities. The first paper, by Maika Isaac and Jennifer Elrick, explores how the labelling of migrant workers as essential in the context of the pandemic may have an unintended consequence in terms of pressures for improved legal status. This links up with some of the themes addressed in the paper by Nasar Meer, Emma Hill, Timothy Peace and Leslie Villegas, which investigates the impact of the pandemic in terms of pressures to enforce controls on immigration and refuge. In their paper Lucas Drouhot, Soren Petermann, Karen Schönwalder and Steven Vertovec seek to explore the impact of the pandemic on attitudes to diversity in Germany. After the decision by Angela Merkel in 2015 to admit up to one million refugees to Germany the issue of attitudes to cultural and religious diversity became an important issue of public debate, and this paper looks back on this on-going conversation from the perspective of the pandemic. The penultimate paper by Benjamin Opratko et. al. outlines the notion of "cultures of rejection" in order to explore the impact of the post-pandemic environment on ideas about rejection and welcoming in relation to attitudes to migrants and refugees. The final paper by Giorgia Dona is focused on the experience of gendered and racialized migrants in the context of the pandemic and hostile environment to immigration created by successive British governments. Dona's paper engages with an issue that is very much at the heart of public discourse in post-Brexit British society and provides an insight into how the pandemic may shape future policy debates.

Taken together the papers included in this themed issue provide a snapshot of some of the key areas of debate about the impact of Covid-19 on race and ethnic relations. Although we are aware that there are necessarily some gaps that result from our efforts to bring this themed issue together over a relatively short time period, we very much hope that our readers will agree that these papers provide an important insight into both the impact of Covid-19 and highlight key areas that require further research, analysis and discussion. *Ethnic and Racial Studies* is committed to providing a forum for high-quality research into the on-going impact of the pandemic on race and ethnic relations and therefore giving voice to a wide range of scholars and researchers from all over the world. In the meantime, we hope our readers will find this themed issue helps them to think through some of the key issues that have been raised by Covid-19.

Disclosure statement

No potential conflict of interest was reported by the author(s).

References

Abeysinghe, Sudeepa. 2013. "When the Spread of Disease Becomes a Global Event: The Classification of Pandemics." *Social Studies of Science* 43 (6): 905–926.

Anderson, Kathryn Freeman. 2017. "Racial Residential Segregation and the Distribution of Health-Related Organizations in Urban Neighborhoods." *Social Problems* 64 (2): 256–276.

Barry, John M. 2010. "The Next Pandemic." *World Policy Journal* 27 (2): 10–12.

Bassett, Mary T. 2020. "First AIDS, Now COVID-19: Another Plague Shows Us Who We Are." *Social Research: An International Quarterly* 87 (2): 229–232.

Beaman, Jean. 2020. "Underlying Conditions: Global Anti–Blackness Amid COVID–19." *City & Community* 19 (3): 516–522.

Berkowitz, Rachel L., Xing Gao, Eli K. Michaels, and Mahasin S Mujahid. 2020. "Structurally Vulnerable Neighbourhood Environments and Racial/Ethnic COVID-19 Inequities." *Cities & Health*, 1–4.

Chandler, R., D. Guillaume, A. G. Parker, A. Mack, J. Hamilton, J. Dorsey, and N. D. Hernandez. 2020. "The Impact of COVID-19 among Black Women: Evaluating Perspectives and Sources of Information." *Ethnicity & Health*, 1–14.

Connell, Raewyn. 2020. "COVID-19/Sociology." *Journal of Sociology* 56 (5): 745–751.

Durand, Jorge, and Douglas S Massey. 2019. "Debacles on the Border: Five Decades of Fact-Free Immigration Policy." *The Annals of the American Academy of Political and Social Science* 684 (1): 6–20.

Fernández-Kelly, Patricia. 2012. "Rethinking the Deserving Body: Altruism, Markets, and Political Action in Health Care Provision." *Ethnic and Racial Studies* 35 (1): 56–71.

Fernández-Kelly, Patricia, and Alejandro Portes. 2012. "Health Care and Immigration – Understanding the Connections." *Ethnic and Racial Studies* 35 (1): 1–2.

Gómez, Laura E., Nancy López, R. Burciaga Valdez, and Jonathan Kahn. 2013. *Mapping 'Race': Critical Approaches to Health Disparities Research*. New Brunswick, NJ: Rutgers University Press.

Karlsen, Saffron, and James Y. Nazroo. 2010. "Religious and Ethnic Differences in Health: Evidence from the Health Surveys for England 1999 and 2004." *Ethnicity & Health* 15 (6): 549–568.

Kazanjian, Powel. 2014. "The AIDS Pandemic in Historic Perspective." *Journal of the History of Medicine and Allied Sciences* 69 (3): 351–382.

Kellner, Douglas. 2017. "Brexit Plus, Whitelash, and the Ascendency of Donald J. Trump." *Cultural Politics: an International Journal* 13 (2): 135–149.

Kucharski, Adam. 2020. *The Rules of Contagion: Why Things Spread – And Why They Stop*. London: Profile Books.

Lakoff, Andrew. 2015. "Real-Time Biopolitics: The Actuary and the Sentinel in Global Public Health." *Economy and Society* 44 (1): 40–59.

Lakoff, Andrew. 2017. "A Fragile Assemblage: Mutant Bird Flu and the Limits of Risk Assessment." *Social Studies of Science* 47 (3): 376–397.

Lucassen, Leo. 2017. "Peeling an Onion: The 'Refugee Crisis' from a Historical Perspective." *Ethnic and Racial Studies* 41 (3): 383–410.

Napier, A. David, and Edward F. Fischer. 2020. "Misunderstanding a Viral Pandemic: The Social and Cultural Contexts of COVID-19." *Social Research: An International Quarterly* 87 (2): 271–277.

Nazroo, James Y. 2010. "Health and Health Care." In *Race and Ethnicity in the 21st Century*, edited by A. Bloch, and J. Solomos, 112–137. Basingstoke: Palgrave Macmillan.

Nazroo, James Y., K. S. Bhui, and James Rhodes. 2020. "Where Next for Understanding Race/Ethnic Inequalities in Severe Mental Illness? Structural, Interpersonal and Institutional Racism." *Sociology of Health & Illness* 42 (2): 262–276.

Nelkin, Dorothy, and Sander L. Gilman. 2020. "Placing Blame for Devastating Disease." *Social Research: An International Quarterly* 87 (2): 335–351.

The New Yorker. 2020. "Dispatches from a Pandemic." *The New Yorker* April 13, 34–50.

Obasogie, Osagie K., Irene Headen, and Mahasin S. Mujahid. 2017. "Race, Law, and Health Disparities: Toward a Critical Race Intervention." *Annual Review of Law and Social Science* 13 (3): 313–329.

Obinna, D. N. 2020. "Essential and Undervalued: Health Disparities of African American Women in the COVID-19 Era." *Ethnicity & Health*, 1–12.

Organisation for Economic Co-operation and Development. 2020. *Managing International Migration Under COVID-19*. Paris: Organisation for Economic Co-operation and Development.

Paton, Alexis, Gary Fooks, Gaja Maestri, and Pam Lowe. 2020. *Submission of Evidence on the Disproportionate Impact of COVID 19, and the UK Government Response, on Ethnic Minorities and Women in the UK*. Birmingham: Aston University.

Pruitt, Lesley J. 2019. "Closed Due to 'Flooding'? UK Media Representations of Refugees and Migrants in 2015–2016 – Creating a Crisis of Borders." *British Journal of Politics and International Relations* 21 (2): 383–402.

Public Health England. 2020. *Disparities in the Risk and Outcomes of COVID-19*. London: Public Health England.

Sayer, Derek. 2017. "White Riot-Brexit, Trump, and Post-Factual Politics." *Journal of Historical Sociology* 30 (1): 92–106.

Sewell, Alyasah Ali. 2020. "Policing the Block: Pandemics, Systemic Racism, and the Blood of America." *City & Community* 19 (3): 496–505.

Snowden, Frank M. 2019. *Epidemics and Society: From the Black Death to the Present*. New Haven, CT: Yale University Press.

Stepan, Nancy. 2011. *Eradication: Ridding the World of Diseases Forever?* Ithaca, NY: Cornell University Press.

Stewart, Q. T., R. J. Cobb, and V. M. Keith. 2020. "The Color of Death: Race, Observed Skin Tone, and All-Cause Mortality in the United States." *Ethnicity & Health* 25 (7): 1018–1040.

Waldinger, Roger. 2018. "Immigration and the Election of Donald Trump: Why the Sociology of Migration Left us Unprepared … and Why We Should Not Have Been Surprised." *Ethnic and Racial Studies* 41 (8): 1411–1426.

Ward, Paul R. 2020. "A Sociology of the Covid-19 Pandemic: A Commentary and Research Agenda for Sociologists." *Journal of Sociology* 56 (4): 726–735.

Wemyss, Georgie, and Nira Yuval-Davis. 2020. "Bordering During the Pandemic." *Soundings: A Journal of Politics and Culture* 75: 13–17.

Winegard, Timothy C. 2019. *The Mosquito: A Human History of our Deadliest Predator*. New York: Dutton.

Yang, T. C., S. W. Emily Choi, and F. Sun. 2020. "COVID-19 Cases in US Counties: Roles of Racial/Ethnic Density and Residential Segregation." *Ethnicity & Health* 14 (6): 1–32.

Yang, Tse-Chuan, Kiwoong Park, and Stephen A. Matthews. 2020. "Racial/Ethnic Segregation and Health Disparities: Future Directions and Opportunities." *Sociology Compass* 14: 6.

Fever dreams: W. E. B. Du Bois and the racial trauma of COVID-19 and lynching

Freeden Blume Oeur ⓘ

ABSTRACT
In 1899, diphtheria claimed the life of W. E. B. Du Bois's son, Burghardt. How can Burghardt's death help us to understand the racialized consequences of the present coronavirus pandemic? This article considers what Du Bois described as the "phantasmagoria" that ensnares racial structures. I examine COVID as the latest iteration of a distinctly racialized American trauma narrated in the grammar of Du Bois's reflections on disease, extrajudicial killings, and kinship. This *fever dream* of conflagration and asphyxiation has haunted Black lives since slavery. Du Bois gave meaning to this racial spectre in religious terms as a story of perpetual death but eventual emancipation. By situating Du Bois in relation to the work of Christina Sharpe (2016. *In the Wake: On Blackness and Being*. Durham, NC: Duke University Press), this essay ruminates on the orthography of slavery's inheritances with regard to disease and its symbiotic relationship with lynching. I conclude by considering Du Bois's invocation to *darkwater* as a demand for Black healing.

An early milestone in social epidemiology, W. E. B. Du Bois's book *The Philadelphia Negro* (1899) reinterpreted the well-known epidemiological triad and identified systemic racism as an infectious social germ (Jones-Eversley and Dean 2018). It is a tragic irony that diphtheria receives scant mention in its pages. Once known as "the strangling angel of children", diphtheria was a leading cause of youth mortality worldwide until immunization became widespread in the 1920s (Hammonds 1999). In the same year that *The Philadelphia Negro* was published, the disease claimed the life of Du Bois's first child, Burghardt, not long after Du Bois had moved with his family to Atlanta, Georgia in the Jim Crow South.

How can Burghardt's death as a result of diphtheria help us to understand the racialized consequences of the coronavirus pandemic? In the United States, the loss of human life to the disease has been staggering. According to the APM Research Lab (2020), African Americans suffer the highest death rate of any group, at a rate over twice that of whites. African American communities in the South have been hit especially hard. Two of the five counties with the nation's highest COVID death rates are in Georgia (The COVID Tracking Project 2020).[1] Both are predominantly African American. Given these realities of concentrated suffering, scholars emphasize the "injuries of inequality" that make groups more vulnerable to disease (Watkins-Hayes 2019). An early analysis of COVID maintains that racial capitalism – the co-constituting logics of capital accumulation, white supremacy, and colonialism – is the "fundamental cause" of the virus (Laster Pirtle 2020). In *Black Reconstruction in America* Du Bois ([1935] 1998, 698) himself described this cause as the "foundation stone" of American society, and that the "widespread physical results" of caste structure were "disease and death".

My essay turns from the political economy of health disparities to what Du Bois described as the "phantasmagoria" that ensnares racial structures: those grotesque spectres that are seemingly illusory but have devastating material, somatic, and psychological consequences. I elucidate the "cultural classification" (Alexander 2004; Eyerman 2001) of COVID as the latest iteration of a distinctly racialized American trauma narrated in the grammar of Du Bois's reflections on disease, extrajudicial killings, and kinship. Disease, in this view, is not simply a "routine harm" (Onwuachi-Willig 2016), but a ritualized form of terrorism. Drawing on Du Bois's reflections on "the nature of the pain" (Alexander 2004, 13), I conceive of the racial trauma of COVID as a *fever dream* that has haunted Black lives since slavery. Du Bois gave meaning to this racial spectre in religious and mythological terms as a story of perpetual death but eventual rebirth and emancipation. This essay situates Du Bois in relation to what Sharpe (2016) has called the orthography of slavery's inheritances, and ruminates especially on the symbiotic relationship between disease and lynching. I then illustrate this symbiosis with a discussion of the May 2020 police killing of George Floyd in Minneapolis, Minnesota. I conclude by reflecting on Du Bois's invocation to *darkwater* as a call for healing in the face of white supremacist terrorism.

Children of trauma

Cultural sociologists describe trauma as a process where intellectuals broadly defined articulate the suffering of a population and help ingrain that suffering into the collective memory (Alexander 2004). For Eyerman (2001), the memory of slavery and its traumatic legacies are the *sine qua non* of Du Bois's text *The Souls of Black Folk* (1903). Yet Du Bois was no ordinary narrator of shared memory. He had used the occasion of his 25th birthday in 1893 to position himself as a Moses for his people; his life's intention was to "raise my race" (Du Bois 1985, 29).[2] From this perspective, Du Bois was traumatized by the deaths of two "children" – his kinfolk – in 1899: his own son, Burghardt; and Sam Hose. By giving meaning to this trauma and its "reticences" and "repressions", Du Bois helped chart the "intricate jungle of ideas conditioned on unconscious and subconscious reflexes of living things" (2007, xxxiii).

The most personally traumatic essay in *Souls* is the volume's shortest: the elegy for Burghardt, "Of the Passing of the First-Born". It anchors the book's spiritual preoccupations with birth, death, and rebirth; the volume's Forethought refers to "buried" memories in the collective psyche while the Afterthought pleads that Du Bois's cries not go "stillborn". Burghardt Gomer Du Bois died at 19-months of age from diphtheria. White doctors refused to treat Burghardt and the elder Du Bois tried in vain to find one who was Black. Medical care for Black children at the time was especially limited in the South, and Burghardt would have had a better chance of survival in New England, where he was born (and a slightly better chance in Philadelphia) (Karp and Gearing 2015). Du Bois (2003, 206) would later assert that higher rates of "infantile diseases" afflicting African Americans were an "index of a social condition" and not due to biological traits. Diphtheria is a bacterial infection that enters the respiratory tract and produces a horrible fever. It coats the back of the throat with a thick "pseudomembrane" that greatly restricts breathing. Burghardt was tortured and asphyxiated. His death reprised a reality of slavery where enslaved children died in large numbers from the same disease (Kiple and Kiple 1980).

So, while COVID may be *novel* in the sense that it was unknown before 2019, epidemics have, in fact, historically been a regular feature of the Black experience (Onwuachi-Willig 2016). Though a virus and not a bacterium, COVID infects in much the same way as diphtheria, invading the respiratory tract and producing inflammation in the lungs. Unnervingly recalling the "Shadow of Death" that claimed Burghardt ([1903] 2017, 203), this inflammation appears as shadowy patches on computerized tomography (CT) scans, with the scientific name of "ground-glass opacity" (Fiore 2020). In cases of respiratory failure, patients require intubation, an emergency procedure first introduced in the treatment of diphtheria (Hammonds 1999).

During his time in Philadelphia, there is a good chance that Du Bois met Jacob R. Johns, a physician based in the city and a leading expert on diphtheria.[3] In 1898, Johns reported that the disease had recently devastated the city's "Shelter for Colored Orphans". The following year, in a Philadelphia medical journal published the month before Burghardt's death, Johns provided a more comprehensive scientific report on diphtheria. He characterized the disease as "a bacterial fire, kindling itself into the respiratory mucous membrane and burning into the tissues … The longer [the bacilli] burn or the hotter the flame, the deeper, more far reaching, the damage resulting" (Johns 1899, 193). Johns also shared the Spanish name for the disease, with allusions to lynching: *garrotillo,* derived from *garrote,* a mode of execution where victims are "strangled with a rope" (180).

Just as his first-born had burned and been strangled *from the inside,* horrible fires were also kindling themselves all around Du Bois. Just weeks before Burghardt died, Sam Hose was lynched near Atlanta. There were an estimated 6400 lynchings in the U.S. between the Civil War and mid-twentieth century (Equal Justice Initiative 2020). Hose had been burned alive and his body dismembered by the white mob. The familiar story is that when Du Bois saw Hose's burned knuckles on display in a store window, he was motivated to leave strictly scientific endeavors and to pursue a life of political activism (Mathews 2018). Also well-known is Du Bois's devastating early commentary on the menace of lynching. I wish to bring focus to how, in keeping watch beside the dead (Burghardt and Hose), Du Bois drew out an orthography of Black trauma (Sharpe 2016): a language to articulate the racial terror of the *burning* and *asphyxiation* of Black children. While Burghardt was a child and Hose an adult, Du Bois positioned African Americans as God's children in "Children of the Moon" from *Darkwater* ([1920] 1999). Du Bois's poem is a "transfiguring" of White Christianity (referring to the religion but also a metaphor for white supremacy) in the image of Black Christian nationalism. The wings of White Christianity had veiled the "limitless potential" of the children of the moon, or their "blazing Blackness" (Blum 2013, 163). Diphtheria was a scourge for Black children, and COVID is proving especially fatal for Black adults; but together they preserve a systemic racism defined as "the state-sanctioned ... vulnerability to premature death" (Gilmore 2007, 247).

Historians have described the trauma of lynching a "contagion" that has a "*multiplier effect*" across families, communities, and generations (Mathews 2018, 6; emphasis in original). Yet Du Bois had come to understand that it was limiting to use disease as a mere metaphor for lynching.[4] Deep metaphors, however, underscore shared sociopolitical and corporeal effects in slavery's wake (Sharpe 2016). When Du Bois portrayed racial terror as an "engulfing and choking" force in *Souls* ([1903] 2017, 18), he is alluding most obviously to lynchings. Yet his semi-veiled testimonials on disease – the grammar of a "politics of a lower frequency" (Hartman 1997, 35) – are sutured to his public condemnations of lynchings perpetrated by "white folk", or "the modern Prometheus" as he calls them in *Darkwater.* This designation references Frankenstein, here intended as a metaphor for monstrous white supremacy; as well as the Greek titan who made humans powerful by giving them fire and, thus, the power of destruction.[5] In Du Bois's interpretation, the *art of warfare* makes whites fully human and dehumanizes Blacks. The Black Panthers, whose own efforts to fight medical discrimination were inspired by Du Bois's writings, would later refer to a *germ warfare* targeted at Blacks (Nelson 2011). This biological terrorism directed at African Americans has since been unrelenting. In the Greek myth, Zeus punishes

Prometheus for his act of stealing fire by pinning him against a rock. Each day, an eagle tortured Prometheus by eating his liver – the organ that detoxifies and promotes health – which would regenerate overnight. To symbolize the return "toward slavery" after the failure of Reconstruction, Du Bois reinterprets the myth once again, describing a "black Prometheus bound to the Rock of Ages" and who "has his vitals eaten out", or made perpetually ill from white supremacy ([1935] 1998, 670). Du Bois adapted this language from a political cartoon by M. Crump in the July 1927 issue of *The Crisis* magazine.[6] In it, a Black man is lynched by "Uncle Sam" – representing the false patriotism of white supremacy – who sends eaglets to tear at the man's heart. The vulture representing Georgia is hovering over the victim.

Allegory and mythology were among the arsenal of cultural tools – those "spirals of signification" embedded in the "multivalent symbolic process" of articulating the nature of collective pain (Alexander 2004, 12) – that Du Bois used to narrate a fever dream. These are colloquially known as unsettling dreams brought on by fever. Drawing on Du Bois's writings, I conceptualize a fever dream as the collective Black trauma of conflagration and asphyxiation. Steeped in religious symbolism, fire and water are dueling elements in Du Bois's oeuvre, and each come to represent both healing and destructive forces. Yet Du Bois reserved natural combustion to represent the terror of white violence. White mobs have historically weaponized fire to terrorize Black bodies and Black property, from the use of molotov cocktails to cross-burning (Parry 2020). When Sam Hose was lynched that Sunday in 1899, his murderers – many who had come straight from church – shouted, *"Glory be to God!"* In the white Protestant South, lynchings were perceived as a racial cleansing intended to restore the moral order. Religion was not simply a justification for lynching, but "lynching *was* religion" (Mathews 2018, 2; emphasis in original). Fire, in Du Bois's view, did not represent God so much as the ritualistic obedience to the "religion of whiteness" (Hughey 2020). And ultimately white society would stand in judgment for its sins, for it had *crucified* both Hose and Burghardt.[7] Du Bois's social autopsy had elevated his son's death to the "blood ritual" of lynching (Blum 2013).

The lynching pandemic

Du Bois's trauma narrative casts light on how the traumas of disease and lynching continue to incubate one another in a climate of white supremacy. On May 25, 2020, a white Minneapolis police officer, Derek Chauvin, pinned his knee on the back of George Floyd's neck for eight minutes as Floyd lay prone. Extralegal police violence constitutes modern-day lynchings (Embrick 2015); they "are the inheritors of the history of the spirometer that produced Black bodies as defective and monstrous" (Sharpe 2016, 112). By *kneeling* – a traditional act of religious deference – on Floyd's body, Chauvin recreated "an act of worship that honors the demons of racist hate" (Gilkes 2020). Autopsy reports ruled that Floyd's death was caused by cardiopulmonary arrest and revealed he had suffered from "underlying conditions" (itself an apt term for systemic racism) that facilitated his death. This included heart disease, the leading cause of death in the U.S., but an especially acute problem for Black Americans (U.S. Department of Health and Human Services 2020). Eric Garner, who like Floyd uttered "I can't breathe" when he was killed by New York City police in 2014, had also suffered from this condition. Du Bois (1903) himself wrote that a history of colonization and slavery had given Africa "heart disease". In Du Bois's account, the sum of violence, resource deprivation, and forced migrations had suffocated the continent.

Sharpe (2016, 111) calls this "the weather", or the "totality of the environments" that exhausts the lungs; in the language of the SARS-CoV-2 pandemic, a perpetual forecast of *severe, acute, respiratory* distress. "Fool that I was to think", Du Bois ([[1903] 2017, 205–206) cried, that Burghardt "should grow choked … within the Veil!" Diseases and lynching have existed historically in a synergetic relationship; indeed, as the autopsies revealed, shortly before his respiratory failure at the hands of Officer Chauvin, Floyd had contracted COVID. The 14 states in the Southeast U.S. (which had legalized chattel slavery) that saw the vast majority of lynchings through mid-twentieth century today have among the highest Black death rates due to COVID.[8] The symbiosis of disease and lynching becomes clearer if the definition of lynching is expanded to include deadly police encounters. Adequate health care, insurance, and nutritional foods are choked off from low-income Black communities just as a gluttonous carceral state feeds itself on these same communities. Frequent and aggressive police contact in turn nurtures higher levels of distress, depression, and suicidal tendencies (Herd 2020). While the United Nations warns of police overreach "under the guise of … emergency measures" ("UN Raises Alarm" 2020), police contact with Blacks during the pandemic has continued unabated in the U.S. Wearing government-mandated face masks puts Black citizens at greater risk of being perceived as dangerous. Police used tear gas – a chemical agent banned in war – to choke protesters who took to the streets after George Floyd's killing.

Lynching and disease exist in a symbiotic relationship as forms of extrajuridical violence that promote premature death. In broad terms, a lynching is the hypervigilant enforcement of racial caste through extrajudicial violence (Equal Justice Initiative 2020). By adopting the language of terrorism, "arguably understood as the ultimate form of victimhood", the racial trauma of lynching has been elevated to America's national trauma (Simko 2020, 56). The domestic terrorism of disease – a germ warfare that terrorizes and controls Black populations – similarly plagues American democracy. The Civil War and Reconstruction unleashed a germ warfare on families from which the African American population has never recovered. Malaria, smallpox, and other diseases tormented Black soldiers, freed slaves seeking a new life, and women and children left on their own in dirty encampments; they all had been made "sick from freedom" (Downs 2012). In this reading, sickness is not merely a "routine harm" (Onwuachi-Willig 2016), but a morally-sanctioned *ritual* that affirms intergenerationally the supremacy of white humanity and the disposability of Black lives.

An extralegal killing involves not only people taking justice into their own hands (e.g. through civilian-empowered "Stand Your Ground" laws). It is also *extrajuridical* in the sense of a lack of formal legal protection from gross abuses of power. Take, for example, how state and federal authorities have buckled under pressure to "reopen the country". Here COVID, like lynchings, makes death a public spectacle. In May 2020, a White House advisor announced that the "human capital stock" was ready to get back to work, a dehumanizing term fueled by neoliberal logic and reminiscent of taxonomies of enslaved Blacks (Democracy Now 2020). By reopening Georgia, Governor Brian Kemp defied public health officials and claimed that state residents could determine for themselves what risks they were willing to accept (McCrummen 2020). But this extrajuridical move both absolves the state from responsibility and reveals that "risk assessment" is really no choice at all for the Black workers who are disproportionately labelled as "essential", and who endanger their health and that of their families in order to meet consumer demand. Since slavery, Black kinship has been a volatile category as "*it can be invaded at any … moment by the property relations*" (Spillers 1987, 4; emphasis in original). The weather seizes control over one's breathing; while the labour that COVID demands fatigues the lungs, the pseudoscience behind chattel slavery "operationalized" forced labour "as that which kept breath in and vitalized the Black body" (Sharpe 2016, 112). Moreover, COVID's necropolitics devolves risk onto Black Americans and feeds the perception that the virus is a "Black disease". As a white patron at a high-end mall near Atlanta told a reporter in May, "When you start seeing where the cases are coming from and the demographics – I'm not worried" (McCrummen 2020).

Just as the risk of contracting COVID spirals for Black Americans on the frontlines, they are also more likely than others to suffer privately. Today, a discriminatory penal system hides and anonymizes Black death. COVID outbreaks in prisons endanger African Americans at alarming rates; in May, a Black woman in New Jersey died from COVID in solitary confinement after begging for help (Speri 2020). Others are quarantined in hospitals and die alone. Du Bois was left with the grave consolation that his son had been spared a life behind the veil. George Floyd used his final breaths to call out for his dead mother, whose name, Cissy, was tattooed just below his heart.

The healing of darkwater

The day after his crucifixion in 1899, a newspaper wrote of the "terrible expiation which Sam Hose was forced to pay" (Mathews 2018, 263). Yet the "swarthy spectre" (Du Bois [1903] 2017) haunts the present, leading a growing chorus demanding that the country atones for its history of lynching. The murders of George Floyd and other Black Americans during the COVID pandemic (including Breonna Taylor, Ahmaud Arbery, and Walter Wallace, Jr.) have increased pressure on Congress to make formal policy proposals for reparations. In the face of persistent racial terror, the anti-hero of the Black Prometheus "lives and fights" (Du Bois [1935] 1998, 670) with the aid of fire. As the caption to M. Crump's illustration reads, "Up from Slavery to that fire of freedom, which the Souls of Black Folk brought down from heaven!"

Water, too, is a source of revolutionary fire. Du Bois's polysemous image of *darkwater* is commonly interpreted as a rejection of the era's racist fears in the "rising tide" of racial propagation (Waligora-Davis 2006). I want to sit with the image's motif of reproduction. Darkwater is a kind of "amniotic fluid" (Mullen 2003); in the context of Black trauma, it represents the protective lifeforce of "newborn", progressive forms of healing. Du Bois's own personal tragedy – a grief that is unspeakable in his later writings (e.g. 2007) – gave meaning to the collective trauma of African Americans. My analysis has drawn out the symbiotic relationship between disease and lynchings in Du Bois's trauma narratives, and amplifies Du Bois's appeals for reparations for the "presence of the slave past" (Balfour 2003, 33). Reparations would prioritize healing for African American survivors of the disease, for the immediately-endured suffering and for the still-unknowable consequences of "long COVID". But there is more than the proximity to death. Sharpe's own polysemeous rendering of slavery's "wake" urges another interpretation of the darkwater *in the path of a ship:* the need to buoy forms of care that imagine ways of living and "keeping and putting breath in the Black body" (2016, 130). In COVID's wake, darkwater might just catch fire.

Notes

1. All figures in this paragraph as of 20 October 2020.
2. In *Souls* ([1903] 2017), Du Bois famously calls Black Americans "the seventh son".
3. Johns's publications indicate his Philadelphia office was located a short distance from the Seventh Ward, the location of Du Bois's study.
4. There is a danger in using the language of biology and pathology to explain race (Thomas and Byrd 2016). Biological metaphors therefore should be viewed as the persuasive language of speech acts which articulate collective injury and seek "reparation and reconstitution" (Alexander 2004, 11). At the same time, "dysgraphia" (Sharpe 2016) places limits on language for telling coherent stories about suffering in slavery's wake.

5. The subtitle of Mary Shelley's 1818 classic is *or, The Modern Prometheus*. The Prometheus myth has inspired many anti-slavery writings.
6. See Hawkins (2019), figure 1.
7. Menzel (2019) has rightfully critiqued the paternalism in Du Bois's lynching narratives. They indeed reflected a desire to protect a violated Black manhood. Lynching victims were castrated for the alleged charge of making sexual advances toward white women.
8. Data from the APM Research Lab (2020) shows the over-representation of Black deaths relative to their state population size.

Acknowledgements

I am grateful for generous comments from James M. Thomas, Jeffrey Guhin, and Phillip Luke Sinitiere, as well as from the anonymous reviewers. This article also benefited from feedback I received from audience members and other panelists at the Center for Humanities at Tufts University, the annual meeting of the American Sociological Association, the School of Sociology at the University of Arizona, and the W. E. B. Du Bois Center at the University of Massachusetts, Amherst.

Disclosure statement

No potential conflict of interest was reported by the author(s).

ORCID

Freeden Blume Oeur 🅘 http://orcid.org/0000-0002-9442-9144

References

Alexander, Jeffrey C. 2004. "Toward a Theory of Cultural Trauma." In *Cultural Trauma and Collective Identity*, edited by J. Alexander, R. Eyerman, B. Giesen, N. J. Smelser, and P. Sztompka, 1–30. Berkeley: University of California Press.
APM Research Lab. 2020. https://www.apmresearchlab.org/covid/deaths-by-race.
Balfour, Laurie. 2003. "Unreconstructed Democracy: W. E. B. Du Bois and the Case for Reparations." *The American Political Science Review* 97 (1): 33–44.
Blum, Edward J. 2013. *W. E. B. Du Bois: American Prophet*. Philadelphia: University of Pennsylvania Press.
The COVID Tracking Project. 2020. https://covidtracking.com/
Democracy Now. 2020. "COVID Racial Data Tracker: Ibram X. Kendi on How Better Data Reveals the True Toll of the Pandemic." May 27. https://www.democracynow.org/2020/5/27/the_covid_racial_data_tracker.
Downs, Jim. 2012. *Sick from Freedom: African American Illness and Suffering During the Civil War and Reconstruction*. New York: Oxford University Press.
Du Bois, W. E. B. 1899. *The Philadelphia Negro: A Social Study*. Philadelphia: University of Pennsylvania Press.
Du Bois, W. E. B. 1903. *The Negro Church*. Atlanta, GA: Atlanta University.
Du Bois, W. E. B. [1920] 1999. *Darkwater: Voices from within the Veil*. Mineola: Dover.
Du Bois, W. E. B. 1985. "Celebrating His Twenty-Fifth Birthday (1893)." In *Against Racism: Unpublished Essays, Papers, Addresses, 1887-1961*, edited by H. Aptheker, 26–29. Amherst: University of Massachusetts Press.

Du Bois, W. E. B. 2003. "The Health and Physique of the Negro American." *American Journal of Public Health* 93 (2): 272–276.

Du Bois, W. E. B. 2007. *Dusk of Dawn: An Essay Toward an Autobiography of a Race Concept*. Edited by. H. Louis Gates, Jr. New York: Oxford University Press.

Du Bois, W. E. B. [1903] 2017. *The Souls of Black Folk*. Amherst: University of Massachusetts Press.

Du Bois, W. E. B. [1935] 1998. *Black Reconstruction in America, 1860-1880*. New York: The Free Press.

Embrick, David. 2015. "Two Nations, Revisited: The Lynching of Black and Brown Bodies, Police Brutality, and Racial Control in 'Post-Racial' Amerikkka." *Critical Sociology* 41 (6): 835–843.

Equal Justice Initiative. 2020. "Reconstruction in America: Racial Violence after the Civil War, 1865-1876." https://eji.org/report/reconstruction-in-america/.

Eyerman, Ron. 2001. *Cultural Trauma: Slavery and the Formation of African American Identity*. Cambridge: Cambridge University Press.

Fiore, Kristina. 2020. "Hazy on Ground-Glass Opacities? Here's What They Are." *MedPage Today*, June 24. https://www.medpagetoday.com/pulmonology/generalpulmonary/86751.

Gilkes, Cheryl Townsend. 2020. "Kneeling to Venerate Hate: The Meaning of a Police Killing in Minnesota." *Religious News Service*, May 28. https://religionnews.com/2020/05/27/kneeling-to-venerate-hate-the-meaning-of-a-police-murder-in-minnesota/?fbclid=IwAR0omKYRxqk3nDSa3b0IU5n8WFZbMss9F8ijmDnWdKaeno0HozC7I9OiZws.

Gilmore, Ruth Wilson. 2007. *Golden Gulag: Prisons, Surplus, Crisis, and Opposition in Globalizing California*. Berkeley: University of California Press.

Hammonds, Evelynn Maxine. 1999. *Childhood's Deadly Scourge: The Campaign to Control Diphtheria in New York City, 1880-1930*. Baltimore, MD: Johns Hopkins University Press.

Hartman, Saidiya. 1997. *Scenes of Subjection: Terror, Slavery, and Self-Making in Nineteenth-Century America*. New York: Oxford University Press.

Hawkins, Tom. 2019. "The Veil, the Cave and the Fire-Bringer." *International Journal of the Classical Tradition* 26: 38–53.

Herd, Denise. 2020. "Cycles of Threat: *Graham v. Connor*, Police Violence, and African American Health Inequities." *Boston University Law Review* 100: 1047–1067.

Hughey, Matthew W. 2020. "'The Souls of White Folk' (1920–2020): A Century of Peril and Prophecy." *Ethnic and Racial Studies* 43 (3): 1–26.

Johns, Jacob R. 1898. "Immunization and Formaldehyde Disinfection in the Stamping out of Epidemics." *The Philadelphia Monthly Medical Journal* 1: 606–608.

Johns, Jacob R. 1899. "Clinical Diphtheria: A Summary of Investigations Concerning the Diphtheria-Bacillus, the Toxin and the Anti-Toxin of Diphtheria, Including the Diagnosis, Prognosis, and Treatment of the Disease." *The Philadelphia Monthly Medical Journal* 1: 179–212.

Jones-Eversley, Sharon D., and Lorraine T. Dean. 2018. "After 121 Years, It's Time to Recognize W. E. B. Du Bois as a Founding Father of Social Epidemiology." *The Journal of Negro Education* 87 (3): 230–245.

Karp, Robert J., and Bobby Gearing. 2015. "The Death of Burghardt Du Bois, 1899; Implications for Today." *Journal of the National Medical Association* 107 (1): 68–74.

Kiple, Kenneth, and Virginia Kiple. 1980. "The African Connection: Slavery, Disease and Racism." *Phylon* 41 (3): 211–222.

Laster Pirtle, Whitney. 2020. "Racial Capitalism: A Fundamental Cause of Novel Coronavirus (COVID-19) Pandemic Inequities in the United States." *Health Education & Behavior* 47 (4): 504–508.

Mathews, Donald G. 2018. *At the Altar of Lynching: Burning Sam Hose in the American South*. New York: Cambridge University Press.

McCrummen, Stephanie. 2020. "'This Feels Great': A Preview from Georgia about How America Might Reemerge from the Coronavirus." *Washington Post*, May 17. https://www.washingtonpost.com/nation/2020/05/17/coronavirus-reopening-shopping-mall-georgia/?arc404=true.

Menzel, Annie. 2019. "'Awful Gladness': The Dual Political Rhetorics of Du Bois's 'Of the Passing of the First-Born.'" *Political Theory* 47 (1): 32–56.

Mullen, Bill. 2003. "Du Bois, *Dark Princess*, and the Afro-Asian International." *Positions: East Asia Cultures Critique* 11 (1): 217–239.

Nelson, Alondra. 2011. *Body and Soul: The Black Panther Party and the Fight Against Medical Discrimination*. Minneapolis: University of Minnesota Press.

Onwuachi-Willig, Angela. 2016. "The Trauma of the Routine: Lessons on Cultural Trauma from the Emmett Till Verdict." *Sociological Theory* 34 (4): 335–357.

Parry, Tyler. 2020. "A Meditation on Natural Light and the Use of Fire in United States Slavery." *Black Perspectives*, January 13. https://www.aaihs.org/a-meditation-on-natural-light-and-the-use-of-fire-in-united-states-slavery/.

Sharpe, Christina. 2016. *In the Wake: On Blackness and Being*. Durham, NC: Duke University Press.

Simko, Christina. 2020. "Marking Time in Memorials and Museums of Terror: Temporality and Cultural Trauma." *Sociological Theory* 38 (1): 51–77.

Speri, Alice. 2020. "A Woman Died of Covid-19 in a New Jersey Prison After Begging to Be Let Out of a Locked Shower." *The Intercept*, May 11. https://theintercept.com/2020/05/11/new-jersey-prisons-coronavirus-death/.

Spillers, Hortense. 1987. "Mama's Baby, Papa's Maybe: An American Grammar Book." *Diacritics* 17 (2): 65–81.

Thomas, James M., and W. Carson Byrd. 2016. "The 'Sick' Racist: Racism and Psychopathology in the Colorblind Era." *Du Bois Review* 13 (1): 181–203.

"UN Raises Alarm about Police Brutality in COVID-19 Lockdowns.". 2020. *Aljazeera*, April 28. https://www.aljazeera.com/news/2020/04/raises-alarm-police-brutality-covid-19-lockdowns-200428070216771.html.

U.S. Department of Health and Human Services. 2020. "Heart Disease and African Americans." https://www.minorityhealth.hhs.gov/omh/browse.aspx?lvl=4&lvlid=19.

Waligora-Davis, Nicole A. 2006. "W. E. B. Du Bois and the Fourth Dimension." *The New Centennial Review* 6 (3): 57–90.

Watkins-Hayes, Celeste. 2019. *Remaking a Life: How Women Living with HIV/AIDS Confront Inequality*. Oakland: University of California Press.

Face mask symbolism in anti-Asian hate crimes

Jingqiu Ren and Joe Feagin

ABSTRACT
This article examines the intersectional locations of Asian Americans facing hate crimes during the COVID-19 pandemic by assessing the racial, gender, and related symbolism involved in many attacks on those wearing face masks. We demonstrate that a one-dimensional assessment of xenophobia is necessary but insufficient, as it elides the broader power of the societal majority in numerous contexts within US structural domains shaped by the dominant white racial framing. Considering solutions, we propose identification and formation of a broader coalition of Asian Americans with those who share comparable social intersectional locations and identities. Active promotion of a collective ethic and shared humanness is required to counter discrimination, cultural individualism, and socio-racial inequality.

During their entire settlement in California they have never adapted themselves to our habits, modes of dress or our educational system, have never learned the sanctity of an oath, never desired to become citizens, or to perform the duties of citizenship.... Impregnable to all the influences our Anglo-Saxon life, they remain the same stolid Asiatics that have floated on the rivers and slaved in the fields of China for thirty centuries of time. (California., and Haymond 1878, 63)

Racialized national discourse and "Model minority" mythologizing

These white-framed words were uttered in an 1878 report by the California State Senate's Special Committee on Chinese Immigration. A number of late nineteenth century developments contributed to white villainizing of Chinese Americans in a national xenophobic and racist campaign. In this era a predominantly white United States saw a string of events fracturing its racial, economic, and nationalistic unity, including major economic contractions, abolishment of slavery, restoration of southern white Democrats to Congress after Reconstruction, aggressive white westward expansion, and California's development as a swing state in presidential elections. Chinese immigrants' racialized foreignness became a major and convenient white-framed scapegoat for economic and social ills: "Presidential candidates of both parties in 1876 and 1880 featured platforms that declared the racial incompatibility and inferiority of Chinese – as marked by their status as unfree, heathen, coolie labourers; the undermining of white, working-class family men through unfair economic competition" (Hsu 2015, 27).

This anti-Asian perspective was related to the emergence of the era's eugenics movement, led by white intellectuals and politicians portraying immigrants who were not white Anglo-Saxon Protestants as inherently diseased, morally disabled, and criminally dangerous (Dolmage 2018). This view contrasted with a conception of superior "whiteness", which was central to the dominant white framing that legitimized the US's aggressive nation-building process in this era (Guess 2006; Williams 2005; Brown and Webb 2007; Feagin and Ducey 2019). This overarching white racial worldview features at its centre a positive subframe emphasizing white virtuousness, and is contrasted with anti-nonwhite subframes portraying the racialized "others" as unvirtuous – including in negative stereotypes and images, false narratives, hostility and other negative emotions, and inclinations to discriminate (Feagin 2020). In a society where conceptualization of virtuous "whiteness" not only denotes racial superiority but powerfully imprints its racialized interpretations of historical, social, and political values on the public's collective consciousness, the US today has clearly not moved on from its early white/nonwhite binary paradigm to a colour-blind "post racial society" (Bonilla-Silva 2015). Despite the increasing demographic significance of Americans of colour, this white racial framing is still dominant in shaping contemporary societal values, policies, and structures. The consequences of such racialized national history and contemporary discourse are reflected in the historical and present-day experiences of Asian Americans discussed herein.

By the 1960s, a new title of "model minority" was bestowed by whites upon Asian Americans, first coined by demographer William Pettersen in a *New York Times Magazine* article on Japanese American success in quietly overcoming discrimination (Pettersen 1966). Numerous media articles followed with success stories of Asian Americans, often contrasted with then vociferously protesting African Americans in the era's civil rights movement. The white-approved kind of Asian Americans are portrayed as well-educated, good-mannered, and financially successful through their skills and work ethic. Examined through the societal lens of white racial framing, this imagery of Asian Americans may seem positive, but in fact is laden with strong racist implications. It involves stereotyping of Asian Americans as homogenous and bequeathed with certain inherent racial qualities *almost* equal to whites. The interpretive concept associated with terms such as "model minority" and "honorary white" confers a distinction setting Asian Americans apart from other racial groups considered more inferior by whites. Their westernized education, hard-working ethic, and conflict-avoidance values positioned them as a poster child for the persisting "American Dream". Yet, this white-framed narrative ignores the structural and institutional mechanisms that have systematically privileged the white throughout the country's discriminatory history against all groups of colour. It provides justifications for collective elevation or victimization of particular groups that benefits those at the racial hierarchy's summit. In late 2019, when the COVID-19 pandemic happened to break out first in Asia and soon emerged in the racially fractured US society ripen with growing health, economic, and political tensions, it took no time and little pretense for the "real whites" to throw "honorary whites" back to being "racial inferiors." Asian Americans were again seen as culturally uncivilized, physically inferior, and hygienically backward. We turn to a detailed analysis of this reality.

Anti-Asian hate crimes

For many decades the US has seen thousands of hate crimes annually directed at Americans of colour. The most recent FBI report (2018) put the number at 7,120, although it is a well-known underestimate because a majority of police departments do not report hate crime numbers (FBI 2018). Other sources put the number as high as 200,000 per year (US Bureau of Justice Statistics 2017). In the 2018 FBI report, 57 per cent of known offenders targeting Asians were white, with the next largest group (27 per cent) being black. Additionally, the most recent National Crime Victimization Survey reveals that a majority of offenders were men (US Bureau of Justice Statistics 2017, 7). From the general pattern revealed by these data sources, it is logical to reason that recent anti-Asian hate crimes might also disproportionately involve white men.

More substantial documentation of hate crimes, including those targeting Asian Americans, has been left to private organizations. The Stop AAPI Hate reporting centre, a website developed by Asian American organizations,[1] received nearly 1,900 reports of coronavirus-related discrimination against Asian Americans between March 19 and May 15, 2020. These incidents ranged from boycotting Asian restaurants, to bullying Asian American school children, to verbal and physical assaults of Asian Americans in public places. Here we are particularly interested in examining certain intersectional dimensions and distinctive symbolism involved in attacks on Asians wearing face masks during the first months of the US pandemic. Granted access to the Stop AAPI Hate's discrimination incident database in mid-April,[2] we selected from the numerous reports 82 anti-Asian incidents with information indicating that the discriminatory actions had directly resulted from Asians wearing or not wearing face masks.

Face mask symbolism and its significance in Stop AAPI hate data

Of these 82 incidents with data on perpetrators' racial characteristics (33), 61 per cent involved white perpetrators and 39 per cent involved black perpetrators. This white-dominance pattern is roughly similar to that in the aforementioned FBI data. Given the well-recorded tendency of most Americans to note the racial identity of a person of colour, especially of black Americans, in describing conflictual and other social situations yet rarely advert to it when a key person is white (Feagin and Ducey 2019, 93–94), we also suspect that the actual white perpetrator percentage in our face-mask cases, including those where perpetrator identity is unrecorded, may be significantly higher than 61 per cent.

Coding the content of these face-mask incidents, we discovered several important racial and cultural dimensions. The largest categories emerging in the analysis consisted of the racialized marking of masked Asian individuals as diseased and framing them as the source of the pandemic (63 per cent), portraying them as particularly weak or sickly individuals (15 per cent), and generally asserting Asian groups' foreignness or inherent socio-racial inferiority (12 per cent). Most perpetrators openly indicated or strongly implied a racialization of their Asian targets. Furthermore, a small percentage (4 per cent) also involved mocking of mask-wearing individuals. Let us illustrate the central themes of what face mask discrimination reveals with a few key examples.

As foreign, racialized, and source of disease

Most of the incidents involve the attackers viewing Asian Americans as racially foreign and dangerous in bringing with them diseases like COVID-19. One Chinese American woman gave this troubling account:

> At the hospital for a bone marrow donor screening (I'm the donor). Was asked to wear a facemask by the nurse. Man sitting next to me said loudly into his cell phone, "I'm going to get sick because of all these Chinese with face masks on." I was the only non-white person in the room.

On her way to work, another Chinese American woman recounted a serious physical threat:

> I was crossing the street to get into my work. I was wearing a face mask due to my being immuno-compromised. A man walked past me and yelled "take that

mask off, you fucking brought it here in the first place" and menaced at me. I
was stunned and unable to respond and just went inside to my work building.

A Korean American woman described her experience of being verbally
abused and seen as a disease-carrying Chinese:

> We were wearing masks in Target to protect ourselves while shopping for
> essentials and three African Americans walked by and said in passing extra
> loudly: "I don't even know whys they're wearing masks. They're the ones who
> brought it over— motherfucking cat, dog, rat-eating Chinese mothafuckers."

One Asian American man was accosted by someone echoing President
Donald Trump's characterization of the coronavirus as "Chinese virus":

> While I was trying to pick a bike at the dock station, a Bay Wheels operations
> employee who was changing the batteries on ebikes yelled at me and said
> "Spray that shit" (meaning I need to spray the bike with disinfectant after
> riding.) This employee went on and said "the Chinese invented the virus and
> Donald Trump knows it." I'm Asian and was wearing a mask at the time of
> the incident.

Clearly, Asian Americans wearing face masks are viewed here as diseased and
as the source of COVID-19. While white offenders account for most incidents in
the larger sample, the last example here involves African Americans as the perpetrators. Their racist framing reveals that some people of colour can also
utilize anti-Asian stereotypes – such as *diseased* rat-eaters – originally crafted
in the nineteenth century by whites. Asian Americans interviewed in the
media have understandably expressed fear that wearing protective masks publicly *marks* them as "diseased". For example, an opinion article in one *New York
Times'* Chinese edition summarized views of many Chinese Americans that they
often chose not to wear masks due to this concern (Ma 2020), including prominent people like Hollywood producer Janet Yang (Sheer and Yang 2020).

Xenophobia is born out of fear for things unfamiliar, and one finds this
response in many countries as the most serious global pandemic in
memory threatens people's sense of safety, security, and normalcy everywhere. This deadly and unprecedented pressure undoubtedly distorts how
they interpret social reality and express fears. In this perspective, xenophobia
does not necessarily need to be racially motivated. However, these examples
distinctly signal the operation of a dominant white frame explicitly blaming
the "non-whiteness" when considered within the context of America's racialized history. Singling out disease-carrying foreigners has been part of the
standard US anti-immigrant perspective, historically targeting numerous
immigrant groups, including the Irish in the early 1800s and European Jews
in the mid-to-late 1800s. Many groups, especially immigrants not northern
European, have been debased as physically unclean, dangerously diseased,
and culturally immoral. Although xenophobic discrimination has often
emphasized immigrant stereotypes, understanding how this "foreignness"

has regularly been linked to "non-whiteness" in the dominant white frame over US history helps to contextualize recent manifestations of anti-Asian xenophobia. As Kincheloe (1999) points out, as "with any racial category, whiteness is a social construction in that it can be invented, lived, analyzed, modified and discarded ... (It) begins to reveal itself when we understand that the Irish, Italians, and Jews have all been viewed as non-white in particular places at specific moments in history". "Whiteness" is so inextricably bound with socio-political dominance that whites arbitrarily impose a "non-white" identity on immigrant groups perceived as foreign and inferior. Consequently, Asian Americans being perceived as dangerous and diseased foreigners by hate-crime perpetrators involves more than irrational xenophobic fear. It links clearly to a highly racialized US history and collective white racial consciousness over generations. This white framing works to reveal that the inferior societal location of Asian Americans is similar to many immigrant groups coming earlier, as defined by their material and symbolic placement in both historical and contemporary US racial hierarchies.

As revealing underlying weakness and suitable racial targets

A second main theme in the incidents exposes how mask-wearing Asian Americans are viewed as physically weak and sickly, and how perceived weakness often provokes attacks. One Asian American respondent underscored a white grocery employee's reaction to her mask that threatened physical attack. The perpetrator's hostility seemed to assess the respondent as distinctively *weak*:

> While washing my hands in the bathroom with my N95 mask on, a white . . . female employee came out of the stall. She came up behind me & started gesticulating in an aggressive tone: "Look at this woman here wearing a mask." Then she moved close to my right side and leaned forward into my personal space with an aggressive stance and threatened, "I could cough all over you now and your mask would do you no good." Then, she rushed out of the bathroom.

Other Asian Americans were similarly cognizant about perceived weakness and related threats in their experience:

> While I was walking ... a man of light complexion (Caucasian or Hispanic background) decided to spit in my direction as I walked past him. He did not have a face mask on while I wore a face mask. I was dumbfounded and afraid and opted to get away from this assailant as quickly as possible for fear of physical violence. I believe he did this "hate crime" due to my gender, ethnic background, and my face mask because I looked like an easy and weak victim. He was taller and bigger than me.

> I was trying to line up at the self-checkout counters. A white woman in front of me turned around and asked me to keep 6-feet away from her and said "I might cough on you." In the meanwhile, she made coughing noises at me. She didn't

wear a mask but I did. She didn't keep distance with people in front of her, or ask anyone else to keep 6-feet distance with her.

During the morning, I was purchasing toilet paper at a Safeway. I wore a face mask to avoid being a potential vector for disease. An older while male yelled at me for having two packs of toilet paper while ignoring [white] people passing by with carts full of toilet paper.

Moreover, a few reported being aggressively attacked for *not* wearing masks. In these cases, a similar sickly and diseased identity was imposed on the Asian victim. Repeatedly, the face mask becomes a symbolic and physical barrier to separate the racially inferior from the superior.

One Korean American woman noted:

I was jogging … on late Sunday morning. I had decided to walk back as the jog tired me out. One white male, in his early to mid-20s runs towards me, and screams "where is your mask, fuck you!!" and runs past me.

Similarly, another Asian female reported:

I was stopped at a red light in my car when some white man smiled maliciously at me and pointed at me to his wife while gesturing me to put a mask on. He wasn't wearing a mask.

Note that these hate-crime incidents are often not only racialized but *gendered*. Of the incidents with data on victims' gender (64), 80 per cent of those targeted were female. Moreover, 73 per cent of perpetrators were male in the 66 incidents with perpetrators' gender reported. This perpetrator pattern is similar to the aforementioned National Crime Victimization Survey data. Additionally, in the larger sample of coronavirus-related discriminatory incidents analysed by the Asian Pacific Policy and Planning Council in its 2020 report, a similar proportion (69 per cent) of the racial targeting was directed at women (Jeung and Nham 2020).

What this theme uncovers is the negative Western stigmatization of sickly/weak individuals. Americans with various health conditions and disabilities have also been viewed and discriminated against in the same individualized sickly/weak framework. This framing is linked to a long US eugenics tradition that insists on excluding or subordinating eugenically "weak" or "diseased" people (Dolmage 2018). The relevant dominant majority in this context can be more than a racial majority, for it can include all who consider themselves healthy and vigorous – though the latter in the US are disproportionately associated with higher racial and socioeconomic statuses. Thus, a health hierarchy overlaps substantially with racial/class hierarchies. Moreover, the fact that Asian American women have been very disproportionally attacked reveals not only a racial framing, but also a male-sexist framing of women as a distinctively weak population segment.

This sickly-individual framing has become increasingly apparent as the face mask requirement has been implemented in more places in the US in response to the ongoing pandemic. Discrimination against mask-wearing has been encountered by more people beyond Asian Americans. A recent survey study (Liu et al. 2020) confirmed that mask-wearing was interacting with respondents' working status as the pandemic started forcing nonessential workers to stay home. People who had to work outside of homes and wear face masks experienced more discrimination just due to mask wearing, regardless of racial identity. Nevertheless, without comprehensive longitudinal data and detailed comparative study, especially in the US context of the politicization and disinformation of mask wearing, it is hard to specify how face-mask-related discrimination may actually differ in nature and scope between whites, Asian Americans, and other groups.

Divergent cultural heritages

Overall, these hate crime incidents also suggest significant cultural differences between Asian and Western societies. Many Americans refuse face masks for individualistic reasons. Major political leaders have declined to wear them, asserting that is a sign of individual weakness or lack of virility, especially for men (Karni 2020). Top state and federal officials have also acted against enforcing mask wearing, siding with some people's "mistaken belief the requirement is unconstitutional" and ignoring the reality that "these people, while exercising their believed rights, put others at risk" (Tensely 2020).

Yet, cross-cultural assessments by scholars and investigative journalists have found that Asian countries such as China and Japan have had a strong communal tradition of using protective masks during public health crises, at least since the early twentieth century (Lynteris 2018). As Judy Yuen-man Siu, a Hong Kong anthropologist, noted, "if you do not use a face mask in public areas, you will be stigmatized and discriminated against, not just because people would [be] afraid of you as a potential virus-spreader, but [because] it can mean you have low civic responsibility" (Friedman 2020). This Asian and Asian American perspective on wearing face masks goes beyond individual protection to valuing *collective* ethical ideals and civic action to achieve common good through cooperation. This collective ethic was articulated strongly by Chinese scholar-diplomat P.C. Chang who was instrumental in helping the United Nations draft its 1948 Universal Declaration of Human Rights. In contrast to Western-centric individualism, it emphasized collective brotherhood, moral growth, tolerance of ideas, community duties balancing individual rights, and the right of all peoples to self-determination (Columbia University 2016; Twiss 2010, 110–112). Individual rights in Asian thoughts are unalienably connected to collective responsibilities. This is evident in the immediate, voluntary, and nearly universal compliance of mask wearing in places like China, Japan,

Korea, Hong Kong and Taiwan from the onset of current and previous pan-demics. Appreciation of this non-Western cultural heritage is missing in how mask-wearing Asian Americans have been viewed and attacked by some Amer-icans during the current pandemic.

For example, one Vietnamese American traveller reported:

> Two white males on the flight sitting next to me laughed, tried to take photos and videos of me wearing a face mask because I'm Asian.

A Chinese American female student described her experience:

> I wore a face mask out of consideration because I had caught a cold. A student, as he walked by talking to his friend, laughed and pointed to me saying "now THAT looks like coronavirus."

Another incident was reported on public transportation:

> I was wearing a mask, got on a subway car that had two women-one white and one black. The white woman began coughing, laughing and said aloud that she was going to start coughing and continued to do so. I turned to look at her and said "yeah, real funny," and moved to another subway car. The woman the yelled out that I'm only supposed to wear a mask if I'm sick.

One Asian American victim made his point plainly about a mask:

> While entering store, woman made disgust noise and spitting motion at me. I was wearing a face bandana presumably to protect others from MY germs.

Face covering as cultural symbol is also negatively associated with decades-old US entertainment and news media portrayals of criminals wearing masks. White producers, who control most media presentations, often operate out of a racial framing of nonwhite Americans (Feagin 2020), assuming a dispropor-tionate criminality on the latter's part. Thus, Americans of colour publicly wearing masks can trigger negative responses from those having absorbed the presumption of such veiled criminality through persistent media depic-tions, however unconsciously it may be. Such historical framing was likely amplified in media portrayals of coronavirus issues in the pandemic's early months. Reviews of US media coverage in numerous cities showed a dispropor-tionate percentage of pandemic related photos depicting people of Asian descent wearing masks. One noted the common photo is of an "Asian person in a face mask looking alone, solemn, often wandering around some urban dys-topia" (Burton 2020). What the public absorbs from this imagery, likely histori-cally linked, is an impalpable but unmistakably racialized signal of viral danger.

Anti-hate coalitions: towards universal humanness

Analysing the intersectionality of racial and gender identities, scholars Patricia Hill Collins and Sirma Bilge have focussed on effecting social change by going beyond racial identities to social dimensions intersecting with them. Utiliz-ation of intersectionality as an analytical tool "creates space for coalitional possibilities among individuals, as well as new directions for understanding groups" (Collins and Bilge 2016, 133–134). Thus, although face-mask-related attacks strongly suggest Asian Americans' racial identity as a major cause, they frequently reflect more than a one-dimensional framing, such as to include gender and nativity. To make sense of attackers' motivations, we need "a multifaceted perspective acknowledging the richness of the mul-tiple socially-constructed identities" (Lind 2010, 3). The importance to recog-nize other causes of face-mask discrimination lies in the revelation that there is much in common between Asian Americans and other groups in this regard. Analysis through a comparative intersectional lens helps uncover dimensions of oppression by dominant groups in yet other US structural and cultural arenas. Thus, the dominating power may take the form of white neighbours viewing masked people of colour suspiciously, of proud native-born people regarding immigrants as foreign and dangerous, of busi-nesspeople discriminating against disabled or sick employees, or of govern-ment policymakers espousing "free market" neoliberalism and exalting decontextualized individualism over collective responsibilities and the public good. The identity of Asian Americans as a racial group can be seen as intersecting with other societal categories such as gender, class, disability, nationality, and cultural heritage – thereby underscoring their connections with these important groups. In our view, recognizing such group intersec-tions and connections is highly relevant to creating a multi-group identity coalition to combat not only all types of societal discrimination but also US society's hyper-individualistic ethical values.

In conclusion, our review of face-mask discrimination targeting Asian Amer-icans helps *unmask* much of the reality and complexity of the underlying racial-power hierarchy and continuing dominance of white racial framing in regard to intersectional identity construction. The 1960s' white framing of Asian Americans as a "model minority" helped separate Asian Americans from other Americans of colour, weakening the coalitional efforts and power of people of colour as a whole. Similarly, decrying hate crimes against Asian Americans today just with respect to their racialized identity *alone* will not likely help build a broader coalition among all Americans of colour, and indeed with authentic white allies. From this perspective, a broad coalition of people that values collective ethics, human rights, and group equality seems required to counter dominant groups that trample others' individual and collective rights in asserting their own unjust powers. As poignantly pointed out by the executive board of the American Anthropological Associ-ation in a 1947 letter to UN Commission on Human Rights, the "rights of Man in the Twentieth Century cannot be circumscribed by the standards of any single culture, or be dictated by the aspirations of any single people"

(Liu 2014). What we are suggesting for the *twenty-first century* is not just "Asian American" rights, but equal human rights for all groups and peoples who are, in different eras and times, subjugated to and disenfranchised by hate crimes and other discrimination of oppressive dominant groups.

Notes

1. These groups are Chinese for Affirmative Action, the Asian Pacific Policy and Planning Council, and San Francisco State University Department of Asian American Studies.
2. Face-mask discrimination incidents we analyzed are from the Stop AAPI Hate database (March 19 to April 15, 2020). The Stop AAPI Hate website is a voluntary reporting site for people with first-hand experience or as witnesses of anti-Asian and Pacific Islander discrimination. We thank Chinese for Affirmative Action, Asian Pacific Policy and Planning Council, and San Francisco State University's Department of Asian American Studies for launching the center and providing access to their database. Names and places are anonymous.

Disclosure statement

No potential conflict of interest was reported by the author(s).

References

Bonilla-Silva, Eduardo. 2015. "The Structure of Racism in Color-Blind, "Post-Racial" America." *American Behavioral Scientist* 59 (11): 1358–1376.

Brown, David, and Clive Webb. 2007. *Race in the American South: From Slavery to Civil Rights*. Gainesville: University Press of Florida.

Burton, Nylah. 2020. "Why Asians in Masks Should Not be the 'Face' of the Coronavirus." *Vox*, March 6. https://www.vox.com/identities/2020/3/6/21166625/coronavirus-photos-racism.

California. and Haymond, Creed. 1878. "Chinese Immigration; Its Social, Moral, and Political Effect." Sacramento: F.P. Thompson, supt. state printing. Accessed May 1, 2020. file://catalog.hathitrust.org/Record/007104526.

Collins, Particia H., and Sirma Bilge. 2016. *Intersectionality*. Cambridge, England: Polity Press.

Columbia University Weatherhead East Asian Institute. *"Professor Lydia H. Liu on Human Rights Pioneer and Columbia Alum P.C. Chang*. New York: Columbia University. Accessed April 23, 2020. http://weai.columbia.edu/professor-lydia-h-liu-on-human-rights-pioneer-and-columbia-alum-p-c-chang/.

Dolmage, Jay T. 2018. *Disabled Upon Arrival: Eugenics, Immigraton, and the Construction of Race and Disability*. Columbus, OH: Ohio State University Press.

FBI. 2018. Hate Crime Statistics. Accessed April 27, 2020. https://ucr.fbi.gov/hate-crime/2018/topic-pages/tables/table-5.xls.

Feagin, Joe R. 2020. *The White Racial Frame: Centuries of Racial Framing and Counter-Framing*. 3rd Ed. New York: Routledge.

Feagin, Joe R., and Kimberly Ducey. 2019. *Racist America*. New York: Routledge.

Friedman, Uri. 2020. "Face Masks Are In." *The Atlantic*, April 2. https://www.theatlantic.
com/politics/archive/2020/04/america-asia-face-mask-coronavirus/609283/.

Guess, T. J. 2006. "The Social Construction of Whiteness: Racism by Intent, Racism by
Consequence." *Critical Sociology* 32 (4): 649–674.

Hsu, Madeline Y. 2015. *The Good Immigrants: How the Yellow Peril Became the Model
Minority*. Princeton, New Jersey: Princeton University Press.

Jeung, Russell, and Kai Nham. 2020. *Incidents for Coronavirus Related Discrimination*.
Chinese for Affirmative Action, the Asian Pacific Policy and Planning Council, and
San Francisco State University Department of Asian American Studies. Accessed
May 1, 2020. http://www.asianpacificpolicyandplanningcouncil.org/wp-content/
uploads/STOP_AAPI_HATE_MONTHLY_REPORT_4_23_20.pdf.

Karni, Annie. 2020. "Pence Tours Mayo Clinic and Flouts Its Rule That All Visitors Wear a
Mask," *New York Times*, April 28. https://www.nytimes.com/2020/04/28/us/politics/
coronavirus-pence-mask.html.

Kincheloe, Joe L. 1999. "The Struggle to Define and Reinvent Whiteness: A Pedagogical
Analysis." *Collegelit College Literature* 26 (3): 162–194.

Lind, Rebecca Ann. 2010. "A Note From the Guest Editor." *Journal of Broadcasting &
Electronic Media* 54: 3–5.

Liu, Lydia H. 2014. "Shadows of Universalism: The Untold Story of Human Rights
Around 1948." *Critical Inquiry* 40 (4): 385–417. doi:10.1086/676413.

Liu, Ying, Brian Karl Finch, Savannah G. Brenneke, Kyla Thomas, and PhuongThao D. Le.
Perceived Discrimination and Mental Distress Amid the COVID-19 Pandemic:
Evidence From the Understanding America Study." *American Journal of Preventive
Medicine (Jul, 2020).*, http://www.pubmedcentral.nih.gov/articlerender.fcgi?artid=
7336127&tool=pmcentrez&rendertype=abstract

Lynteris, Christos. 2018. "Plague Masks: the Visual Emergency of Anti-Epidemic
Personal Protection Equipment." *Medical Anthropology: Cross Cultural Studies in
Health and Illness* 37 (6): 442–457. doi:10.1080/01459740.2017.1423072.

Ma, Kailin. 2020. ""To Wear or Not Wear Face Mask: Chinese American's Dilemma 戴不戴口
罩, 美国华人的两难选择(Chinese)." *New York Times, March 19*. Accessed May 4, 2020.
https://cn.nytimes.com/opinion/20200319/chinese-american-coronavirus-mask.

Pettersen, William. Success Story, Japanese-American Style." The New York Times,
January 9, 1966. http://inside.sfuhs.org/dept/history/US_History_reader/Chapter1
4/modelminority.pdf.

Power, Gerard J. 1995. "Media Dependency, Bubonic Plague, and the Social
Construction of the Chinese Other." *Journal of Communication Inquiry* 19 (1): 89–
110. doi:10.1177/019685999501900106.

Sheer, Richard, and Janet Yang. "The Power and Pain of Being Asian American During
the Coronavirus Crisis,"April 17, 2020, in *Sheer Intelligence*, produced by Joshua
Scheer, podcast, https://scheerpost.com/2020/04/23/janet-yang-the-power-and-
pain-of-being-asian-american-during-the-coronavirus-crisis/.

Tensely, Brandon. 2020. "Coronavirus, Face Masks and America's New Fault Line". *CNN*,
May 5. https://www.cnn.com/2020/05/04/politics/coronavirus-face-masks-new-
fault-line-trnd/index.html.

Twiss, Sumner B. 2010. "Confucian Contributions to the Universal Declaration of Human
Rights: A Historical and Philosophical Perspective." In *The World's Religions: A
Contemporary Reader*, edited by Arvind Sharma, 105–114. Minneapolis, MN:
Fortress Press.

U.S. Bureau of Justice Statistics. "Hate Crime Victimization, 2004-2015." Washington D.C.: Bureau of Justice Statistics, 2017. Accessed May 4, 2020. https://www.bjs.gov/index.cfm?ty=pbdetail&iid=5967.

Williams, Eric Eustace. 2005. *Capitalism & Slavery*. Chapel Hill: University of North Carolina Press.

Prejudice and pandemic in the promised land: how white Christian nationalism shapes Americans' racist and xenophobic views of COVID-19

Samuel L. Perry ⓘ , Andrew L. Whitehead ⓘ and Joshua B. Grubbs ⓘ

ABSTRACT
During the COVID-19 crisis in March/April of 2020, far-right American political leaders and pundits proffered xenophobic explanations for the pandemic while ignoring that poorer, Black Americans and prison populations were being disproportionately infected. We propose such xenophobic and racist evaluations of COVID-19 drew from and appealed to a pervasive and politically strategic ethnoreligious ideology—white Christian nationalism. Panel data fielded before and during the COVID-19 crisis show that Christian nationalism was invariably the strongest predictor that Americans felt it was not racist to call COVID-19 "the Chinese virus", blamed minorities for their own disproportionate infection rate, favoured immigration restrictions to solve the pandemic, and minimized or justified the infections of prison inmates. Racial identity also moderated Christian nationalism's effect such that it was typically a more powerful influence among whites compared to Blacks. Findings affirm that racist and xenophobic views promulgated during the COVID-19 crisis were undergirded by white Christian nationalism.

At the height of the COVID-19 crisis in the United States during March and April of 2020, far-right American political leaders (including the President) and pundits repeatedly publicized on social media and in national interviews various xenophobic explanations and solutions for the pandemic. This included making a point of referring to COVID-19 as "the China virus" or "the Chinese virus" (Somvichian-Clausen 2020) or reiterating the need for a border wall between the United States and Mexico (Rosenberg and Rogers 2020). At the same time, GOP leaders also ignored or dismissed that poorer, Black Americans and other disadvantaged minority groups were being disproportionately infected, as well as those within prison populations

(Barragan 2020; Kendi 2020). Some opined that persons in poorer, minority communities themselves were to blame for failing to wash their hands (Chiu 2020; Kendi 2020), while others suggested that some racial minorities were biologically more susceptible to COVID-19 (Thomas 2020), and still others stated outright that prison inmates (a disproportionate number of whom are racial minorities and are often assumed to be Black by white Americans; see Yancy 2016) did not deserve the same sorts of protective measures others received to prevent infection (Paxton 2020).

We propose that what unites these various xenophobic and racist interpretations of COVID-19, from Trump to many of his surrogates and supporters, is a pervasive and politically-strategic ethnoreligious ideology that equates national belonging and membership with ethnocultural markers including race, nativity, and religious background—what we call white Christian nationalism. Building on previous research showing that white Christian nationalism is one of the foremost drivers of contemporary racist and xenophobic views in the US (Dahab and Omori 2019; Davis and Perry 2019; McDaniel, Nooruddin, and Faith Shortle 2011; Perry and Whitehead 2015; Perry, Whitehead, and Davis 2019), as well as one of the leading factors driving continued support for Donald Trump and his policies (Baker, Perry, and Whitehead 2020; Whitehead, Perry, and Baker 2018), we theorize that recent racist and xenophobic interpretations of COVID-19 were driven largely by Christian nationalism, and particularly among white Americans. Concretely, we predict that Christian nationalist ideology will be among the leading predictors of holding the various racist and xenophobic views described above, over and above traditional measures of religious and political conservatism. Moreover, because interpretations of religion and nation are highly racialized (Perry and Whitehead 2019; Shelton and Emerson 2012), we expect Christian nationalism will be a particularly powerful predictor of racist and xenophobic interpretations of COVID-19 for white Americans, among whom "Christian" becomes a dog-whistle term meaning "people like us". Below we describe our data, methods, and findings.

Methods

Data

We analyze data from 3 waves of the Public and Discourse Ethics Survey (Perry, Whitehead, and Grubbs 2020). Waves 1 and 2 were fielded in August 2019 and February 2020, respectively. In April 2020, a supplemental third wave was collected to gather data on experiences and interpretation of the coronavirus pandemic. The authors designed the survey instruments and each were fielded by YouGov, an international research data and analytics company. See Perry, Whitehead, and Grubbs (2020) for more information about the

YouGov recruitment and sampling strategy. Sample weights are employed so as to ensure that the survey sample aligns with nationally representative numbers for gender, race, education, age, and region of the country. The original survey sample at Wave 1 included 2,519 American adults that were matched and weighted. Because of sample attrition between waves and a small number of missing cases, our final samples for analyses contain between 1,252 and 1,257 cases in full multivariate models. See Table 1 for descriptive statistics of each measure included in the analyses.

Racist or xenophobic perspectives on COVID-19

An emergency Wave 3 of the PDES was fielded in April 2020 in order to assess experiences and interpretations of COVID-19 among the panel of respondents. We designed questions in light of common racist or xenophobic narratives that were pervasive during the height of the COVID-19 crisis in March and April of 2020 (Chiu 2020; Kendi 2020; Paxton 2020; Rosenberg and Rogers 2020; Thomas 2020). Respondents were asked to indicate their level of agreement with nine questions that were either explicitly race/ethnicity-related or racially-coded. The statements included:

- It is racist to refer to COVID-19 as "the Chinese virus".
- The fact that poor, minority communities are more likely to be infected with COVID-19 is a symptom of our unjust society.
- Black Americans are being infected with COVID-19 at higher rates largely because they are not behaving responsibly.
- Some racial minority groups may have a biological susceptibility to COVID-19.
- Our lax immigration laws are partly to blame for the COVID-19 crisis.
- All immigration should be halted at least temporarily to protect American jobs during this time.
- One way to prevent further pandemics in the United States would be to build the wall along our Southern border.
- The fact that COVID-19 is spreading rapidly among prison inmates should be the least of our concerns.
- If prison inmates are being infected with COVID-19 at higher rates, that could be a form of divine justice.

All measures were (re)coded so that higher scores indicated more racist or xenophobic views. The three immigration measures were combined into an averaged scale reflecting Americans' belief that restricting immigration is a solution to the COVID-19 crisis (Cronbach's alpha = .85). All seven outcomes ranged in values from 1 to 5 and we used ordinary least squares (OLS) regression as our model estimation strategy.

Table 1. Descriptive statistics.

Variables	Wave	Range	Mean/%	SD	Total	Correlation with Christian Nationalism				
						White	Black	Latino	Asian	Other
Disagree it is racist to call COVID-19 "the Chinese Virus".	3	1–5	2.9	1.7	**.66**	**.64**	**.23**	**.53**	.31	**.51**
Disagree higher minority infections are symptom of unjust society	3	1–5	2.3	1.5	**.64**	**.59**	**.18**	**.58**	**.44**	**.63**
Blacks infected with COVID-19 because of irresponsibility	3	1–5	2.2	1.2	**.36**	**.38**	**.18**	**.30**	**.45**	**.52**
Racial minorities may be biologically susceptible to COVID-19	3	1–5	2.8	1.2	**.26**	**.31**	.11	**.21**	**.23**	.11
Immigration Restriction As Solution to COVID-19 (Avg. Scale)	3	1–5	2.6	1.3	**.69**	**.76**	**.27**	**.63**	**.58**	**.72**
Lax immigration laws partly to blame for COVID-19 crisis	3	1–5	2.4	1.4	**.57**	**.66**	.13	**.51**	**.36**	**.51**
All immigration should be halted temporarily to protect jobs	3	1–5	3.3	1.5	**.61**	**.70**	**.25**	**.45**	**.67**	**.59**
Southern border wall will help prevent further pandemics	3	1–5	2.3	1.4	**.62**	**.68**	**.27**	**.60**	**.46**	**.58**
COVID-19 spreading among prisoners is least of our concerns	3	1–5	2.4	1.3	**.42**	**.47**	.05	**.42**	**.52**	**.46**
Prisoners infected with COVID-19 could be divine justice	3	1–5	2	1.2	**.38**	**.39**	**.24**	**.38**	**.56**	**.42**
Christian nationalism	2	0–24	11.1	7.2	.03					
White	1	0–1	66%		-.05					
Black	1	0–1	12%		.04					
Latino	1	0–1	14%		.03					
Asian	1	0–1	3%		-.02					
Other Race	1	0–1	5%		.03					
Age	1	19–90	52.8	15.9	**.22**	**.28**	.12	.10	.29	-.06
Male	1	0–1	47%		-.08	-.07	-.16	-.09	-.14	-.07
Married	1	0–1	62%		.11	.12	.07	.13	.14	.16
Kids under 18	1	0–1	23%		.00	-.02	.15	.06	.28	-.27
Education	1	1–6	3.3	1.5	-.25	-.29	-.05	-.27	.08	-.17
Income $0–29,999	1	0–1	25%		.07	.05	-.04	**.15**	-.08	.17
Income $30,000–99,999	1	0–1	50%		.00	.03	**.18**	-.04	-.04	-.43
Income $100,000 or more	1	0–1	15%		-.06	-.09	-.06	-.09	.10	**.24**
Income did not report	1	0–1	10%		-.03	-.02	-.17	-.05	.05	.08
Southern	1	0–1	38%		.10	.10	.09	.07	.07	.01
Republican	1	0–1	26%		**.44**	**.55**	-.02	**.34**	**.48**	.18
Political Conservative	1	1–5	3	1.2	**.67**	**.75**	**.30**	**.63**	**.48**	**.51**
Born-Again Protestant	1	0–1	22%		**.42**	**.43**	**.34**	**.42**	**.41**	**.52**
Liberal Protestant	1	0–1	13%		.03	.03	-.10	.09	**.38**	.05
Catholic	1	0–1	17%		**.06**	.11	-.03	-.06	.11	.03

Other Christian	1	0–1	3%	.02	.01	.02	.10		.10
Other Religion	1	0–1	12%	–.04	**–.07**	.12	–.08	–.21	
Secular	1	0–1	32%	**–.43**	**–.44**	**–.35**	**–.35**	**–.36**	**–.57**
Religiosity Scale	1	–5.9–3.9	–.14	2.6	**.59**	**.61**	**.52**	**.54**	**.56**	**.62**

Source: 2019–2020 Public Discourse Ethics Survey, Waves 1–3 (N = 1,256).

* $p < .05$; ** $p < .01$; *** $p < .001$ (two-tailed tests).

Christian nationalism

Research on Christian nationalism has employed a variety of measures to capture the construct, each with similar findings (e.g. Dahab and Omori 2019; McDaniel, Nooruddin, and Faith Shortle 2011; Perry and Whitehead 2015, 2019). Our analyses utilize a scale created from combined measures originally used in the Baylor Religion Surveys (see Whitehead and Perry 2020). The survey asked Americans to respond to six level-of-agreement questions: "The federal government should advocate Christian values", "The federal government should declare the United States a Christian nation", "The federal government should allow prayer in public schools", "The federal government should allow religious symbols in public spaces", "The success of the United States is part of God's plan", and "The federal government should enforce strict separation of church and state (reverse coded)". Consistent with previous studies, we create an additive scale from these six measures ranging from 0 to 24. Higher scores indicate greater agreement with Christian nationalist ideology (Cronbach's alpha = .90). In order to ensure temporal precedence to the Wave 3 outcomes, we use Christian nationalism measures from Wave 2 of the PDES.

Controls

Analyses also included a variety of controls theorized to be both related to racist or xenophobic attitudes and Christian nationalist ideology (Perry and Whitehead 2015). Control variables are all from Wave 1 of the PDES. Racial identity was measured with five categories: White (reference group), Black, Latino, Asian, and Other Race. The Other Race category is unfortunately a catch-all group making interpretation nearly impossible. Thus, it is left uninterpreted throughout. The four minority group categories are used in interaction terms with Christian nationalism in order to discern how racial identity potentially moderates Christian nationalism's influence on racist or xenophobic perspectives on COVID-19.

Analyses include sociodemographic controls for age (in years), gender (female = 0, male = 1), marital status (unmarried = 0, married = 1), parental status (other = 0, children under 18 = 1), educational attainment (1 = less than high school, 6 = postgraduate degree), household income (0 = zero to $29,000 per year, 1 = $30,000–99,000 per year, 1 = $100,000 or more, 1 = did not report), and region of residence (other = 0, lives in the South = 1).

Because Christian nationalism could serve as a proxy for political and/or religious conservatism (Whitehead and Perry 2020), it is also critical to consider respondents' political and religious characteristics. Political controls include party affiliation (other = 0, Republican = 1), and political ideology (1 = very liberal, 5 = very conservative). Controls for religious characteristics include religious affiliation and religiosity. Religious affiliation is measured with six categories: Born-again Protestant, liberal Protestant, Catholic, Other Christian, Other Religion, and Seculars (including the unaffiliated, atheists, and agnostics). Born-again Protestants are the reference category. Religiosity is an additive scale constructed from three measures (religious service attendance, prayer frequency, and religious importance), each of which was standardized (Cronbach's alpha = .85).

Plan of analysis

The analysis proceeds as follows. In Table 1, we present bivariate correlations between each of the seven racist/xenophobic interpretations of COVID-19 and Christian nationalism for the full sample and for each racial category separately. Table 2 presents findings from OLS regression models predicting the seven racist/xenophobic interpretations of COVID-19 (Wave 3) on Christian nationalism (Wave 2) with all controls in place (Wave 1). In order to discern how racial identity potentially moderates the influence of Christian nationalism on Americans' racist/xenophobic interpretations of COVID-19, Table 3 presents findings from OLS regression models with interaction terms for Christian nationalism × Black, Latino, Asian, and Other Race. Both unstandardized and standardized coefficients are presented in all models in order to assess substantive significance as well as statistical significance.

Results

Bivariate correlations presented in Table 1 indicate that, for the full sample and white Americans in particular, Christian nationalism is significantly associated with each racist or xenophobic statement, with all but one correlation ranging in size from moderate (r = above .30) to quite strong (r = above .70). For non-white racial minorities, the correlations between Christian nationalism and racist or xenophobic interpretations of COVID-19 are slightly weaker than that of whites, but most of them still statistically significant and in the direction suggesting that even among racial minorities Christian nationalism is associated with holding more racist or xenophobic interpretations of COVID-19. The correlations are the weakest among Black Americans, all of which are either small in size (r = below .28) or non-significant.

Turning the multivariate models, Table 2 indicates that even after accounting for sociodemographic, religious, and political characteristics, Christian nationalism is not only significantly associated with holding each racist or xenophobic interpretation of COVID-19, but it is the strongest predictor, followed by political conservatism, and occasionally, being secular (rather than born-again Protestant) or Republican.

Table 2. Indicators of racist or xenophobic evaluations or interpretations of COVID-19.

Predictors	Disagree it is racist to call COVID-19 "the Chinese Virus".		Disagree higher minority infections are symptom of unjust society.		Blacks infected with COVID-19 because of irresponsibility.		Racial minorities may be biologically susceptible to COVID-19		Immigration Restriction As Solution to COVID-19 (Scale)		COVID-19 spreading among prisoners is least of our concerns.		Prisoners infected with COVID-19 could be divine justice.	
	b	β	b	β	b	β	b	β	b	β	b	β	b	β
Christian nationalism	.09***	.39	.08***	.38	.05***	.28	.03***	.21	.09***	.54	.06***	.34	.06***	.37
Black	-.59***	-.12	-.43***	-.09	-.26*	-.07	—	—	-.25*	-.06	-.31**	-.08	—	—
Latino	-.22**	-.05	—	—	—	—	—	—	—	—	—	—	.18*	.05
Asian	—	—	—	—	—	—	—	—	.25*	.05	—	—	.37*	.05
Other Race	.42**	.06	—	—	—	—	—	—	—	—	—	—	—	—
Age	—	—	.01**	.08	—	—	—	—	—	—	-.01**	-.08	-.01***	-.11
Male	.36***	.11	—	—	—	—	—	—	.18***	.07	.18**	.07	—	—
Married	—	—	—	—	—	—	—	—	—	—	—	—	—	—
Kids under 18	—	—	—	—	—	—	—	—	—	—	—	—	.16*	.06
Education	—	—	—	—	—	—	—	—	—	—	—	—	-.05*	-.07
Income $30,000-99,999	—	—	—	—	—	—	-.23**	-.10	—	—	—	—	—	—
Income $100,000+	.41**	.09	—	—	—	—	-.31**	-.09	—	—	—	—	-.25*	-.08
Income did not report	.29*	.05	—	—	—	—	-.28*	-.07	—	—	—	—	—	—
Southern	—	—	—	—	—	—	—	—	—	—	—	—	—	—
Republican	.49***	.13	—	—	.21***	.21	—	—	.31***	.11	—	—	.15***	.16
Political Conservative	.42***	.31	.37***	.32	—	—	—	—	.29***	.28	.30***	.28	.30**	.09
Liberal Protestant	—	—	.27*	.06	—	—	—	—	.21*	.06	.30*	.08	.34**	.11
Catholic	—	—	.29**	.08	.27*	.08	—	—	.20*	.06	.25*	.07	.45*	.06
Other Christian	—	—	—	—	—	—	—	—	.31*	.04	—	—	.38**	.11
Other Religion	.30*	.06	.25*	.06	.28*	.08	—	—	.38***	.10	.30*	.08	.03*	.10
Secular	.32*	.09	.35***	.11	.34***	.13	—	—	.28*	.10	.28*	.10	—	—
Religiosity Scale	-.05*	-.08	-.04*	-.07	—	—	—	—	-.04*	-.08	-.05*	-.10	-.06**	-.12
Intercept	—		—		1.12***		2.57***		.51**		.86***		1.22***	
Adjusted R^2	.470		.403		.165		.074		.572		.259		.207	
N	1,257		1,257		1,254		1,257		1,257		1,255		1,252	

Source: 2019–2020 Political and Ethics Discourse Survey, Waves 1–3

Note: reference categories are White, Income from $0 to 29,999 per year, and Born-Again Protestant. Outcomes are from Wave 3 (April 2020), while all predictors are from Wave 1 (August 2019) except for Christian nationalism, which is from Wave 2 (February 2020).

* $p < .05$; ** $p < .01$; *** $p < .001$ (two-tailed tests).

Table 3. Interactions between christian nationalism and racial identity on racist or xenophobic evaluations/interpretations of COVID-19.

Predictors	Disagree it is racist to call COVID-19 "the Chinese Virus".		Disagree higher minority infections are symptom of unjust society.		Black Americans infected with COVID-19 because of irresponsibility.		Racial minorities may be biologically susceptible to COVID-19		Immigration Restriction As Solution to COVID-19 (Scale)		COVID-19 spreading among prisoners is least of our concerns.		Prisoners infected with COVID-19 could be divine justice.	
	b	β	b	β	b	β	b	β	b	β	b	β	b	β
Christian nationalism	.10***	.42	.08***	.38	.04***	.26	.04***	.25	.10***	.60	.06***	.35	.05***	.33
Black	—	—	—	—	—	—	—	—	.38*	.10	—	—	—	—
Latino	—	—	—	—	—	—	—	—	—	—	—	—	—	—
Asian	—	—	—	—	—	—	—	—	—	—	—	—	—	—
Other Race	-.04*	-.10	-.04*	-.10	-.59*	-.11	—	—	—	—	—	-.15	—	—
CN × Black	—	—	—	—	—	—	—	—	-.06***	-.19	-.05**		—	—
CN × Latino	—	—	—	—	—	—	—	—	-.02*	-.08	—	—	—	—
CN × Asian	—	—	.05*	.10	.05*	.12	—	—	—	—	—	—	.06*	.10
CN × Other Race	—	—	—	—	—	—	—	—	—	—	—	—	-.01***	-.11
Age	—	—	.01***	.09	—	—	—	—	.17***	.07	-.01**	-.08	—	—
Male	.35***	.11	—	—	—	—	—	—	—	—	.18**	.07	.16*	.06
Married	—	—	—	—	—	—	—	—	—	—	—	—	-.05*	-.07
Kids under 18	—	—	—	—	—	—	—	—	—	—	—	—	—	—
Education	—	—	—	—	—	—	—	—	—	—	—	—	—	—
Income $30,000-99,999	.42**	.09	—	—	—	—	-.23**	-.10	—	—	—	—	-.26*	-.08
Income $100,000+	.29*	.05	—	—	—	—	-.30**	-.09	—	—	—	—	—	—
Income did not report	—	—	—	—	—	—	-.29*	-.07	—	—	—	—	—	—
Southern	—	—	—	—	—	—	—	—	—	—	—	—	—	—
Republican	.47***	.12	.37***	.31	.22***	.22	—	—	.27***	.09	.29***	.27	.16***	.17
Political Conservative	.41***	.31	.27*	.06	—	—	—	—	.27***	.27	.28*	.07	.30**	.09
Liberal Protestant	—	—	.30**	.08	—	—	—	—	.20*	.05	.24*	.07	.35**	.11
Catholic	—	—	—	—	.27*	.09	—	—	.18*	.06	—	—	.45*	.06
Other Christian	—	—	—	—	—	—	—	—	.33*	.04	—	—	.39**	.11
Other Religion	.31*	.06	.26*	.06	.28*	.08	—	—	.39***	.10	.32*	.08	.26*	.10
Secular	.32*	.09	.36***	.11	.35**	.13	—	—	.28*	.10	.28*	.10	—	—

(Continued)

Table 3. Continued.

Predictors	Disagree it is racist to call COVID-19 "the Chinese Virus".		Disagree higher minority infections are symptom of unjust society.		Black Americans infected with COVID-19 because of irresponsibility.		Racial minorities may be biologically susceptible to COVID-19		Immigration Restriction As Solution to COVID-19 (Scale)		COVID-19 spreading among prisoners is least of our concerns.		Prisoners infected with COVID-19 could be divine justice.	
	b	β	b	β	b	β	b	β	b	β	b	β	b	β
Religiosity Scale	-.05*	-.08	-.04*	-.07	—	—	—	—	-.04**	-.09	-.05*	-.09	-.06**	-.12
Intercept	—		—		1.11***		2.55***		.42**		.83***		1.25***	
Adjusted R^2	.472		.407		.169		.074		.580		.265		.209	
N	1,257		1,257		1,254		1,257		1,257		1,255		1,252	

Source: 2019–2020 Political and Ethics Discourse Survey, Waves 1–3.
Note: reference categories are White, Income from $0 to 29,999 per year, and Born-Again Protestant. Outcomes are from Wave 3 (April 2020), while all predictors are from Wave 1 (August 2019) except for Christian nationalism, which is from Wave 2 (February 2020).
* $p < .05$; ** $p < .01$; *** $p < .001$ (two-tailed tests).

Importantly, and consistent with previous research on Christian national-ism and various racial or ethnic attitudes (Dahab and Omori 2019; McDaniel, Nooruddin, and Faith Shortle 2011; Perry and Whitehead 2015; Perry, White-head, and Davis 2019; Whitehead and Perry 2020), for five out of seven racist or xenophobic interpretations of COVID-19, religiosity seemed to influence Americans' views in the opposite direction as Christian nationalism. That is to say, while Christian nationalism is associated with more racist or xenopho-bic views on these issues, higher levels of religiosity (attendance, prayer fre-quency, importance) seemed to incline Americans in the opposite direction.

How is Christian nationalism's influence potentially moderated by racial/ethnic identity? Table 3 presents full models from Table 2 with interaction terms for Christian nationalism × each racial minority group. The statistically significant interactions are all illustrated in Figure 1. For four out of the seven

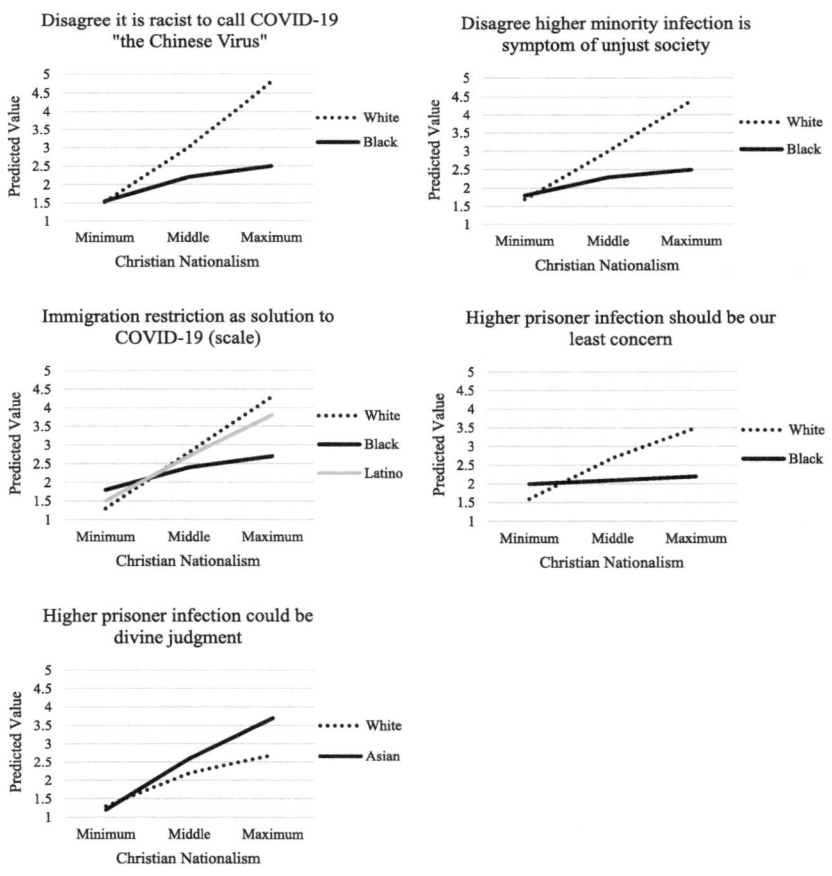

Figure 1. Predicted values of each racist or xenophobic evaluation/interpretation of COVID-19 by race/ethnicity across values of christian nationalism.

outcomes, the interaction term for Christian nationalism × Black American is statistically significant and negative. Plotting out the predicted values for each dependent variable in Figure 1 shows that Christian nationalism influences Black Americans' racialized perspectives on COVID-19 in a direction that is shallower compared to whites. Thus, it is not the opposite direction (Christian nationalism does not seem to make Black Americans more anti-racist) from Whites, but Christian nationalism does not seem to influence their racist or xenophobic attitudes nearly as strongly. For Latinos, the interaction term for Christian nationalism × Latino is only statistically significant for one outcome (the immigration restriction scale), though it is in the same direction as for Black Americans, suggesting a similar pattern.

For Asian respondents, the interaction term for Christian nationalism × Asian is curiously only statistically significant for one outcome and it is positive. As Christian nationalism increased, Asian respondents were more likely to agree that higher rates of COVID-19 infection among prison populations could be divine justice. Lastly, though there are also two positive and significant associations between Christian nationalism × Other Races, because this category represents a catch-all, we do not interpret it here. Overall, it seems that Christian nationalism often (except for Asian respondents) tended to influence white Americans toward more racist or xenophobic interpretations of COVID-19 compared to non-white minorities.

Discussion and conclusion

What underlying ideologies help to account for the far-right's repeated xenophobic explanations and solutions to the COVID-19 crisis and the callous indifference or victim-blaming against disproportionately infected poorer minorities and prison populations? Using numerous measures of racist and xenophobic interpretations regarding COVID-19 and a panel design that allowed us to determine temporal ordering between the theorized variables of interest, we document that Christian nationalist ideology was far and away the leading predictor of Americans' holding racist and xenophobic interpretations of COVID-19. This is true even after considering a host of sociodemographic, religious, and political characteristics.

Importantly, and consistent with previous research on Christian nationalism and racist or xenophobic attitudes (Davis and Perry 2019; McDaniel, Nooruddin, and Faith Shortle 2011; Perry and Whitehead 2015; Perry, Whitehead, and Davis 2019; Whitehead and Perry 2020), religious commitment appears to incline Americans toward more progressive views on race, immigration, and COVID-19. The key finding, in other words, is not that devout Americans necessarily interpret the COVID-19 crisis through a racist or xenophobic lens. Rather, once we account for Americans' desire to institutionalized ethnoreligious identity markers and practices in the public sphere (i.e. Christian nationalism), religious devotion may incline Americans toward more progressive and pro-social views.

Last, interactions with racial identity show that Christian nationalism is a particularly powerful predictor of white Americans holding racist or xenophobic views, almost always more so than Black Americans. This is especially consequential considering over 55 percent of white Americans in our sample score above the mean on our Christian nationalism scale; it is not a fringe ideology. This also affirms previous research showing white and Black Americans merge religion and nation in different ways depending on structural location within the racial hierarchy (Perry and Whitehead 2019; Shelton and Emerson 2012). While for white Americans Christian nationalism clearly defines exclusionary boundaries of "us" and "them", for Black Americans the link between Christianity and American group membership is far less likely to predispose them to see historical "outsiders" (minorities and immigrants) as culpable and/or less worthy of aide, in this case, regarding COVID-19 infections.

Disclosure statement

No potential conflict of interest was reported by the author(s).

Funding

Data collection for this study was supported by research grants from the Charles Koch Foundation and the Society for the Scientific Study of Religion. Neither granting agency exercised any influence whatsoever in designing the survey, analyzing data, or reporting the results.

ORCID

Samuel L. Perry ⓘ http://orcid.org/0000-0002-6398-636X
Andrew L. Whitehead ⓘ http://orcid.org/0000-0001-6587-0996
Joshua B. Grubbs ⓘ http://orcid.org/0000-0002-2642-1351

References

Baker, Joseph O., Samuel L. Perry, and Andrew L. Whitehead. 2020. "Keep America Christian (and White): Christian Nationalism, Fear of Ethnoracial Outsiders, and Intention to Vote for Donald Trump in the 2020 Presidential Election." *Sociology of Religion* 81(3): 272–293.
Barragan, James. 2020. "'Like We Don't Exist.' Black Lawmakers Say Their Pleas About COVID-19's Impact Have Been Ignored." https://www.dallasnews.com/news/politics/2020/06/07/like-we-dont-exist-black-lawmakers-say-their-pleas-about-covid-19s-impact-have-been-ignored/.

Chiu, Allyson. 2020. "Ohio GOP Lawmaker Fired from ER Job Over Remarks About 'Colored Population' and Covid-19." https://www.washingtonpost.com/nation/2020/06/11/black-coronavirus-ohio-gop/.

Dahab, Ramsey, and Marisa Omori. 2019. "Homegrown Foreigners: How Christian Nationalism and Nativist Attitudes Impact Muslim Civil Liberties." *Ethnic and Racial Studies* 42: 1727–1746.

Davis, Joshua T., and Samuel L. Perry. 2019. "White Christian Nationalists and Relative Political Tolerance for Racists." *Social Problems*. doi:10.1093/socpro/spaa002.

Kendi, Ibram. 2020. "Stop Blaming Black People for Dying of the Coronavirus." https://www.theatlantic.com/ideas/archive/2020/04/race-and-blame/609946/.

McDaniel, Eric L., Irfan Nooruddin, and Allyson Faith Shortle. 2011. "Divine Boundaries: How Religion Shapes Citizens' Attitudes Toward Immigrants." *American Politics Research* 39 (1): 205–233.

Paxton, Ken. 2020. "AG Paxton Applauds Fifth Circuit for Prioritizing the Health and Safety of Medical Professionals Combating COVID-19 Crisis Over Demands of Prisoners." https://www.texasattorneygeneral.gov/news/releases/ag-paxton-applauds-fifth-circuit-prioritizing-health-and-safety-medical-professionals-combating.

Perry, Samuel L., and Andrew L. Whitehead. 2015. "Christian Nationalism and White Racial Boundaries: Examining Whites' Opposition to Interracial Marriage." *Ethnic and Racial Studies* 38 (10): 1671–1689.

Perry, Samuel L., and Andrew L. Whitehead. 2019. "Christian America in Black and White: Racial Identity, Religious-National Group Boundaries, and Explanations for Racial Inequality." *Sociology of Religion* 80 (3): 277–298.

Perry, Samuel L., Andrew L. Whitehead, and Joshua T. Davis. 2019. "God's Country in Black and Blue: How Christian Nationalism Shapes Americans' Views About Police (Mis)Treatment of Blacks." *Sociology of Race and Ethnicity* 5 (1): 130–146.

Perry, Samuel L., Andrew L. Whitehead, and Joshua B. Grubbs. 2020. "Culture Wars and COVID-19 Conduct: Christian Nationalism, Religiosity, and Americans' Behavior During the Coronavirus Pandemic." *Journal for the Scientific Study of Religion* 59 (3): 405–416.

Rosenberg, Matthew, and Katie Rogers. 2020. "For Charlie Kirk, Conservative Activist, the Virus is a Cudgel." https://www.nytimes.com/2020/04/19/us/politics/charlie-kirk-conservatives-coronavirus.html.

Shelton, Jason E., and Michael O. Emerson. 2012. *Blacks and Whites in Christian America: How Racial Discrimination Shapes Religious Convictions*. New York: NYU Press.

Somvichian-Clausen, Austa. 2020. "Trump's use of the Term 'Chinese Virus' for Coronavirus Hurts Asian Americans, Says Expert." https://thehill.com/changing-america/respect/diversity-inclusion/489464-trumps-use-of-the-term-chinese-virus-for.

Thomas, Rashaad. 2020. "The COVID-19 Pandemic Response is a Covert War Against Black People." https://www.azmirror.com/2020/05/26/the-covid-19-pandemic-response-is-a-covert-war-against-black-people/.

Whitehead, Andrew L., and Samuel L. Perry. 2020. *Taking America Back for God: Christian Nationalism in the United States*. New York: Oxford University Press.

Whitehead, Andrew L., Samuel L. Perry, and Joseph O. Baker. 2018. "Make America Christian Again: Christian Nationalism and Voting for Donald Trump in the 2016 Presidential Election." *Sociology of Religion* 79 (2): 147–171.

Yancy, George. 2016. *Black Bodies, White Gazes: The Continuing Significance of Race in America*. 2nd ed. Lanham, MD: Rowman & Littlefield.

Race, police, and the pandemic: considering the role of race in public health policing

Adam Dunbar and Nicole E. Jones

ABSTRACT

As cities and states implement social distancing guidelines to mitigate the effects of COVID-19, one concern is that the social construction of race, and the privileges inherent to those constructions, influence how and when to enforce social distancing. In this theoretical paper, we discuss why Black people may be at a greater risk for police intervention when not abiding by public health guidelines. We also describe the importance of considering how Whiteness, in addition to anti-Blackness, may influence how and when public health guidelines are enforced. Finally, we consider how disparate public health policing related to COVID-19 is situated in a broader historical and global context.

As cities and states develop strategies to mitigate the effects of the Coronavirus disease 2019 (hereafter, COVID-19), one commonly utilized approach is social distancing. To facilitate social distancing, law enforcement officers disrupt large clusters of citizens, in some cases going as far as issuing citations and making arrests. This new role for law enforcement officials – that of "public health policing" – raises questions about how race might inform the enforcement of social distancing. One critical question is explored here: Does race affect the policing of public health similarly to the policing of crime? Given the extensive research on racial disparities in criminal justice outcomes, research needs to explore the relationship between race and efforts aimed at stemming the spread of COVID-19.

Given the swift onset of the pandemic and lengthy nature of the research process, research has yet to fully explore the relationship between race and public health enforcement practices, particularly regarding the policing of social distancing violations. However, early data indicate that Black citizens are disproportionally arrested for not adhering to state and county guidelines. For example, arrest data (mid-March to early May) from the New York Police Department indicate that approximately 68% of citizens receiving summonses for social distancing violations were Black (Southall 2020), even though only 24% of that city identifies as Black (U.S. Census Bureau 2019). In Brooklyn, New York, the district attorney's office reported that 87% of people arrested for social distancing violations were Black; more than a third of the arrests were made in Brownsville, a predominantly Black neighborhood (Southall 2020). Similar reports detail widespread racial disparities throughout Chicago (Evans and Bauer 2020) and Ohio (Kaplan and Hardy 2020). For example, in several counties, Black residents in Ohio are disproportionately arrested and charged for violating stay-at-home orders relative to their total population in those counties. Although penalties for violating social distancing orders vary across the country, these preliminary reports suggest that decisions about how and when to enforce social distancing may be heavily influenced by race.

As researchers continue studying the consequences of the pandemic for marginalized communities, the current article highlights the need for a broader examination of the relationship between race/ethnicity and social control, particularly related to the enforcement of public health guidelines. For example, research still largely focuses on the causes and consequences of crime committed by young Black men (Zuberi and Bonilla-Silva 2008). However, the pandemic has raised questions about how race may shield Whites from criminal reproach generally and, more specifically, in the context of a public health crisis in ways that perpetuate racial inequality more broadly. In the remainder of the article, we first describe the well-established literature demonstrating the existence of anti-Black stereotypes, paying particular attention to how these stereotypes might help explain varied responses to social distancing violations. Next, we discuss emergent research on pro-White biases, which provide a complementary framework for understanding disparities in the enforcement of social distancing violations, and have implications for all non-White populations. Finally, we consider the broader global and historical implications of racialized public health policing during the current pandemic.

Policing of black bodies

Although research has yet to fully explore how the current enforcement of public health guidelines reflect broader racial dynamics within the United States, past research provides potential insight. For example, a well-established body of research has highlighted how racialized concerns about crime contribute to the production of racial inequality, even amid a decrease in more overt expressions of racial animus. Research on implicit racial criminalization, or unconscious racialized assumptions about crime, finds that Blacks, compared to Whites, are viewed as more suspicious (Levinson and Young 2009) and are more easily associated with weapons by the public (Eberhardt et al. 2004). Implicit racial criminalization also has implications for policing outcomes. Research reveals that a suspect's race affects numerous behaviors that police regularly engage in, such as visual surveillance and armed response (e.g. Correll et al. 2002; Eberhardt et al. 2004; Payne 2001). The racialization of crime also has real-world consequences, including disproportionate rates of physical contact with police for Blacks and Latinxs compared to Whites (Fryer 2016; Goff et al. 2016; Nix et al. 2017).

Research also indicates that implicit racial criminalization contributes to racial disparities in punishment. When controlling for legally relevant factors, such as criminal record, young Black males are sentenced more severely than other racial or ethnic groups (Crawford, Chiricos, and Kleck 1998; Spohn 2017; Steffensmeier, Ulmer, and Kramer 1998). Findings from prior studies suggest that these disparities occur, in part, because a Black defendant (compared to White) is more likely to be perceived as guilty (Levinson, Cai, and Young 2010), as less easily rehabilitated (Bridges and Steen 1998), and in greater need of severe punishment (Lynch and Haney 2011). Furthermore, studies reveal that defendants are likely to receive longer prison sentences if they look more stereotypically Black—regardless of whether they identify as Black (Eberhardt et al. 2006) or White (Pizzi, Blair, and Judd 2004).

Research exploring the policing of social distancing violations needs to consider the relationship between anti-Black stereotypes about crime and the enforcement of public health guidelines. For example, decades of research has called attention to the over-policing of Black communities, where predominately Black neighborhoods experience heightened surveillance from law enforcement (Alexander 2010). Increased patrols and police-citizen interactions in these communities may also place police officers in greater proximity to Black citizens who do not follow social distancing guidelines. Disproportionate arrests of Black Americans during a stay-at-home order may also be explained by the fact that Blacks are more likely to work in essential services and, therefore, may have less opportunity to avoid police attention (U.S. Bureau of Labor Statistics, 2019; Olivarius 2020). Given decades of racialized violence against Black communities, early reports indicate some may not wear masks to avoid being perceived as more threatening, resulting in increased police attention for violating social distancing guidelines (Alonso III 2020; Natividad 2020). These explanations, in one way or another, all highlight how the pandemic can amplify ongoing disproportionate minority contact with law enforcement, increasing the need for research on the role of anti-Black stereotypes in enforcement decisions.

Protection of white bodies

Although preliminary reports document how Black Americans are dispropor-tionately policed for social distancing violations, it is also important to con-sider how Whiteness can act as a protective factor from police reproach, especially as videos continue to surface of White Americans openly defying mask policies. Critical race theorists, for example, have suggested that, in addition to attitudes about Black criminality, race may also act as a protective factor for Whites. Smith, Levinson, and Robinson (2014) suggest that "implicit white favoritism," or "the automatic association of positive stereotypes and attitudes with members of a favored group" (874), has contributed to legal, political, and social advantages for Whites. These advantages are evident in, for example, immigration laws (Calavita 2007) and the enforcement of drug laws (Beckett 2012).

More broadly, scholars note the dearth of research addressing the causes and consequences of White privilege in the context of criminal justice pro-cesses and the social construction of crime (Smith and Linnemann 2015). In response, an emerging body of research has begun to explore how social constructions of crime and related criminal justice responses account for what Eastman (2015) terms "white innocence," or processes that "rationalize, excuse, and overlook White deviance" (239). Some of this research explores how mug shots of White women are viewed with empathy (Dirks, Heldman, and Zack 2015), how White militant radicalization is often associ-ated with aspirations for individualism rather than violence (Wood, Jakubek Jr, and Kelly 2015), and how mass shootings committed by young White men are often attributed to mental health factors rather than a predisposition to violence (Heitzeg 2015). Related research has also found that Whites are overrepresented as victims of crime as well as law enforcement officers in local television news (Dixon 2017).

Research also demonstrates how both the public and law enforcement officials have a harder time associating Whiteness with criminality. Eberhardt et al. (2004), for example, find pro-White biases related to the detection of crime-relevant items such as guns and knives. When presented with images of guns and knives that start as "fuzzy" but become increasingly easier to identify, participants are slower to identify those items if they were primed with White faces. A more recent study finds that police are less likely to use force when suspects are perceived to be more stereotypically White (Kahn et al. 2016).

As this emerging body of research suggests, racial disparities in the enfor-cement of public health guidelines may be a product of pro-White biases in addition to anti-Black biases. That is, research is needed to examine the impli-cations of, for example, "implicit white favoritism" (Smith, Levinson, and Robinson 2014) and "white innocence" (Eastman 2015) for public health policing. It may be the case that law enforcement is more likely to rationalize, overlook, or excuse public health violations committed by White Americans, consequently affording them the ability to protest public health guidelines without fear of police intervention. It is also important to consider how race relations with law enforcement may have different implications during a public health crisis. Efforts to understand the consequences of public health interventions must consider how White identity, as well as the advantages ascribed to that identity, can insulate some individuals from the enforcement of public health guidelines, while also allowing for those individuals to still benefit from the guidelines.

Conclusion

In sum, the extant research highlights how the social construction of race, and the resulting privileges, may result in varied responses to social distancing violations among individuals of different races and ethnicities. On the one hand, it may be the case that Blacks remain at greater risk for police intervention when not abiding by social distancing guidelines, in part, because of anti-Black stereotypes about criminality. On the other hand, Whites may experience less criminal reproach for social distancing violations, which may allow for greater pushback against efforts to ease the effects of COVID-19. Thus, it is important to consider how anti-Black stereotypes and pro-White stereotypes may influence the policies that are implemented, which can then go on to shape the experiences of all racialized groups insofar as they are perceived or situated as more proximal to Whiteness or Blackness (Bonilla-Silva 2004).

Given that public health crises can amplify inequality, it is imperative to explore how the current pandemic has done so. As Smith and Linnemann (2015) explain, research must consider the role race plays, more broadly, and not merely treat Whiteness as a "reference category." As such, research on the relationship between White privilege and the policing of the current pandemic can continue illuminating the varied ways in which responses to public crises can be more advantageous for Whites while, at the same time, negatively impacting Black communities (Katznelson 2005; Olivarius 2019). Beyond research on anti-Black concerns about crime, it is also important to consider how disparate public health policing might affect other groups like Latinxs or Asian Americans amid documented xenophobia (e.g. Tessler, Choi, and Kao 2020). For example, historically, Asian-Americans have been detained and interrogated due to concerns that China represents a public health threat (Chang 2003). Relatedly, some have recently noted resistance to mask-wearing among Asian-Americans due to a fear of evoking anti-Asian stereotypes (Ao 2020; Ruiz, Horowitz, and Tamir 2020), yet less is known about how this affects enforcement of social distancing guidelines in Asian-American communities.

Although restrictions on social distancing guidelines have eased across the United States (Tolbert, Kates, and Levitt 2020), racial disparities in the enforcement of public health guidelines still highlight a broader problem. Previously, researchers have documented how public health crises related to, for example, venereal diseases (Brooks 2020), yellow fever (Olivarius 2019), and HIV (Espinoza-Madrigal 2020) contribute to the over-policing of Black communities while benefitting some White communities. For example, Olivarius (2020) articulates how current responses to COVID-19 reflect a similar logic to yellow fever responses in the nineteenth century Deep South; Whites had greater ability to socially distance themselves while Blacks generally faced increased pressure to remain in the labor market. Thus, responses to COVID-19 reflect broader racialized patterns of public health policing that we have seen in the past, and should changes not occur, may continue in the future.

Racialized policing practices during the pandemic also potentially highlight a broader global issue. That is, reports from Australia (Blakkarly 2020), Canada (Deshman, McClelland, and Luscombe 2020), Eastern Europe (Amnesty International 2020; Walker, 2020), and sub-Saharan Africa (Finn and Kobayashi 2020) describe how law enforcement is being used to enforce coronavirus-related public health regulations in marginalized communities. Thus, more research needs to consider the causes and consequences of racialized public health policing during a pandemic and, in particular, the implications for enduring social inequality. In the U.S., pro-White and anti-Black biases have clear implications for social inequality, and for other racialized groups insofar as they are positioned as more proximal to Whiteness or Blackness (Bonilla-Silva 2004). Multinational analyses, however, may help to highlight which of these racialized dynamics are endemic to the U.S., and which are manifestations of more global ideologies and patterns of racialized public health policing.

Public health interventions are intended to improve the health of all populations. However, the current pandemic raises questions about the unintended consequences of those interventions, consequences which may limit the benefits of those interventions for people of color. When considering the consequences of this pandemic for Black Americans, it is important to remember that structural racism is not limited to health; it also permeates "our legal, social, and political systems that enable police officers to disproportionately stop people of color, often without cause, and who do so with greater use of force without any repercussions" (Jee-Lyn García & Sharif, 2015, e28). It is also important to consider how race can afford some the privilege to remain safely distant from the pandemic and out of the eye of police surveillance generally. Therefore in the context of public health policing amid COVID-19, racially disparate social distancing guidelines become a byproduct of broader racial dynamics that permeates our legal institutions.

Acknowledgments

We want to thank Charis Kubrin, Nicholas Vargas, Vanessa Gonlin, and Tristan Ivory for their thoughtful input on an earlier draft of this article. We are also grateful for the constructive suggestions from our anonymous reviewers.

Disclosure statement

No potential conflict of interest was reported by the author(s).

References

Alexander, M. 2010. *The new Jim Crow: Mass Incarceration in the Age of Colorblindness.* New York, NY: The New Press.

Alonso III, F. 2020, April 7th. Why some people of color say they won't wear home-made masks. *CNN.* Accessed August 22, 2020 from https://www.cnn.com/2020/04/07/us/face-masks-ethnicity-coronavirus-cdc-trnd/index.html.

Amnesty International. 2020, June 24th. Europe: COVID-19 lockdowns expose racial bias and discrimination within police. Amnesty International. Accessed October 11, 2020. https://www.amnesty.org/en/latest/news/2020/06/europe-covid19-lockdowns-expose-racial-bias-and-discrimination-within-police/.

Ao, B. 2020, April 22nd. Asian Americans already face a mental health crisis. Coronavirus racism could make it worse. *Philadelphia Inquirer.* Accessed October 11, 2020, from https://www.inquirer.com/health/coronavirus/coronavirus-racism-asian-americans-mental-health-20200422.html.

Beckett, K. 2012. "Race, Drugs, and Law Enforcement: Toward Equitable Policing." *Criminology & Public Policy* 11: 641–654.

Blakkarly, J. 2020, April 12th. Concerns police using coronavirus powers to target marginalised communities in Australia. *SBS News.* Accessed October 11, 2020, from https://www.sbs.com.au/news/concerns-police-using-coronavirus-powers-to-target-marginalised-communities-in-australia.

Bonilla-Silva, E. 2004. "From bi-Racial to tri-Racial: Towards a New System of Racial Stratification in the USA." *Ethnic and Racial Studies* 27 (6): 931–950.

Bridges, G. S., and S. Steen. 1998. "Racial Disparities in Official Assessments of Juvenile Offenders: Attributional Stereotypes as Mediating Mechanisms." *American Sociological Review* 63 (4): 554–570. http://www.jstor.org/stable/2657267.

Brooks, E. 2020, August 10th. The Problem with Asking Police to Enforce Public Health Measures. Washington Post. Accessed October 11, 2020. https://www.washingtonpost.com/outlook/2020/08/10/problem-with-asking-police-enforce-public-health-measures/.

Calavita, K. 2007. "Immigration Law, Race, and Identity." *Annual Review of Law and Social Science* 3: 1–20. doi:10.1146/annurev.lawsocsci.3.081806.112745.

Chang, I. May 21, 2003. Fear of SARS, Fear of Strangers. *New York Times.* Accessed October 12, 2020. https://www.nytimes.com/2003/05/21/opinion/fear-of-sars-fear-of-strangers.html.

Correll, J., B. Park, C. M. Judd, and B. Wittenbrink. 2002. "The Police Officer's Dilemma: Using Ethnicity to Disambiguate Potentially Threatening Individuals." *Journal of Personality & Social Psychology* 83 (6): 1314–1329. doi:10.1037/0022-3514.83.6.1314.

Crawford, C., T. Chiricos, and G. Kleck. 1998. "Race, Racial Threat, and Sentencing of Habitual Offenders." *Criminology; An interdisciplinary Journal* 36 (3): 481–512. doi:10.1111/j.1745-9125.1998.tb01256.x.

Deshman, A., A. McClelland, and A. Luscombe. 2020. Stay off the grass: COVID-19 and law enforcement in Canada. *Canadian Civil Liberties Association and The Policing the Pandemic Mapping Project.* Accessed October 13th, 2020. https://ccla.org/cclanewsite/wp-content/uploads/2020/06/2020-06-24-Stay-Off-the-GrassCOVID19-and-Law-Enforcement-in-Canada.pdf.

Dirks, D., C. Heldman, and E. Zack. 2015. "'She's White and She's Hot, So She Can't Be Guilty': Female Criminality, Penal Spectatorship, and White Protectionism." *Contemporary Justice Review* 18 (2): 160–177. doi:10.1080/10282580.2015.1025626.

Dixon, T. L. 2017. "Good Guys are Still Always in White? Positive Change and Continued Misrepresentation of Race and Crime on Local Television News." *Communication Research* 44 (6): 775–792. doi:10.1177/0093650215579223.

Eastman, J. T. 2015. "The Wild (White) Ones: Comparing Frames of White and Black Deviance." *Contemporary Justice Review* 18 (2): 231–247. doi:10.1080/10282580.2015.1025634.

Eberhardt, J. L., P. G. Davies, V. J. Purdie-Vaughns, and S. L. Johnson. 2006. "Looking Deathworthy: Perceived Stereotypically of Black Defendants Predicts Capital-Sentencing Outcomes." *Psychological Science* 17 (5): 383–386. doi:10.1111/j.1467-9280.2006.01716.x.

Eberhardt, J. L., P. A. Goff, V. J. Purdie, and P. G. Davies. 2004. "Seeing Black: Race, Crime, and Visual Processing." *Journal of Personality and Social Psychology* 87 (6): 876–893. doi:10.1037/0022-3514.87.6.876.

Espinoza-Madrigal, I. 2020, April 16th. Don't Criminalize The Coronavirus. *WBUR.* Accessed October 11, 2020. https://www.wbur.org/cognoscenti/2020/04/16/police-coronavirus-ivan-espinoza-madrigal.

Evans, M., and K. Bauer. 2020, May 26th. Chicago Police Only Arrested People For Social Distancing Violations On The South And West Sides, Data Shows. *Block Club Chicago.* Accessed August 28, 2020. https://blockclubchicago.org/2020/05/26/chicago-police-only-arrested-people-for-social-distancing-on-the-south-and-west-sides-data-shows/.

Finn, B. M., and L. C. Kobayashi. 2020. "Structural Inequality in the Time of COVID-19: Urbanization, Segregation, and Pandemic Control in sub-Saharan Africa." *Dialogues in Human Geography* 10 (2): 217–220.

Fryer, R. G. 2016. An empirical analysis of racial differences in the use of force. National Bureau of Economic Research Working Paper 22399 at http://www.nber.org/papers/w22399.

Goff, P. A., T. Lloyd, A. Geller, S. Raphael, and J. Glaser. 2016. *Science of Justice: Race, Arrests, and Police use of Force.* Los Angeles, CA: Center for Policing Equity, University of California.

Heitzeg, N. A. 2015. "'Whiteness,' Criminality, and the Double Standards of Deviance/Social Control." *Contemporary Justice Review* 18 (2): 197–214. doi:10.1080/10282580.2015.1025630.

Jee-Lyn García, J., and M. Z. Sharif. 2015. "Black Lives Matter: A Commentary on Racism and Public Health." *American Journal of Public Health* 105 (8): e27–e30.

Kahn, K. B., P. A. Goff, J. K. Lee, and D. Motamed. 2016. "Protecting Whiteness: White Phenotypic Racial Stereotypically Reduces Police use of Force." *Social Psychological and Personality Science* 7 (5): 403–411. doi:10.1177/1948550616633505.

Kaplan, J., and B. Hardy. 2020, May 8th. Early Data Shows Black People Are Being Disproportionally Arrested for Social Distancing Violations. *ProPublica*. Accessed May 28th, 2020. https://www.propublica.org/article/in-some-of-ohios-most-populous areas-black-people-were-at-least-4-times-as-likely-to-be-charged-with-stay-at-homeviolations-as-whites.

Katznelson, I. 2005. *When Affirmative Action was White: An Untold History of Racial Inequality in Twentieth-Century America*. New York: WW Norton & Company.

Levinson, J. D., H. Cai, and D. Young. 2010. "Guilty By Implicit Racial Bias: The Guilty/not Guilty Implicit Association Test." *Ohio State Journal of Criminal Law* 8: 187–208.

Levinson, J. D., and D. Young. 2009. "Different Shades of Bias: Skin Tone, Implicit Racial Bias, and Judgments of Ambiguous Evidence." *West Virginia Law Review* 112: 307–338.

Lynch, M., and C. Haney. 2011. Mapping the Racial Bias of the White Male Capital Juror: Jury Composition and the "Empathic Divide." *Law & Society Review* 45 (1): 69–102.

Natividad, I. 2020, April 27th. Police Violence Makes Covid-19 Worse for Black Americans. *Futurity*. Accessed May 25th, 2020. https://www.futurity.org/police-violence-covid-19-2348242/.

Nix, J., B. A. Campbell, E. H. Byers, and G. P. Alpert. 2017. "A Bird's eye View of Civilians Killed by Police in 2015: Further Evidence of Implicit Bias." *Criminology & Public Policy* 16 (1): 309–340. doi:10.1111/1745-9133.12269.

Olivarius, K. 2019. "Immunity, Capital, and Power in Antebellum New Orleans." *The American Historical Review* 124 (2): 425–455.

Olivarius, K. 2020, April 12th. The Dangerous History of Immunoprivilege. *New York Times*. Accessed August 16th, 2020. https://www.nytimes.com/2020/04/12/opinion/coronavirus-immunity-passports.html.

Payne, B. K. 2001. "Prejudice and Perception: the Role of Automatic and Controlled Processes in Misperceiving a Weapon." *Journal of Personality and Social Psychology* 81 (2): 181–192. doi:10.1037/0022-3514.81.2.181.

Pizzi, W. T., I. V. Blair, and C. M. Judd. 2004. "Discrimination in Sentencing on the Basis of Afrocentric Features." *Michigan Journal of Race & Law* 10: 327–354.

Ruiz, N. G., J. M. Horowitz, and C. Tamir. 2020, July 1st. Many Black and Asian Americans Say They Have Experienced Discrimination Amid the COVID-19 Outbreak. *Pew Research Center*. Accessed October 11, 2020. https://www.pewsocialtrends.org/2020/07/01/many-black-and-asian-americans-say-they-have-experienced-discrimination-amid-the-covid-19-outbreak/.

Smith, R. J., J. D. Levinson, and Z. Robinson. 2014. "Implicit White Favoritism in the Criminal Justice System." *Alabama Law Review* 66: 871–925.

Smith, J., and T. Linnemann. 2015. "Whiteness and Critical White Studies in Crime and Justice." *Contemporary Justice Review* 18 (2): 101–104. doi:10.1080/10282580.2015.1023045.

Southall, A. 2020, May 29th. Scrutiny of Social-Distance Policing as 35 of 40 Arrested Are Black. *The New York Times*. Accessed June 2, 2020. https://www.nytimes.com/2020/05/07/nyregion/nypd-social-distancing-race-coronavirus.html.

Spohn, C. 2017. "Race and Sentencing Disparity." *Reforming Criminal Justice: A Report of the Academy for Justice on Bridging the Gap Between Scholarship and Reform* 4: 169–186.

Steffensmeier, D., J. Ulmer, and J. Kramer. 1998. "The Interaction of Race, Gender, and age in Criminal Sentencing: The Punishment Cost of Being Young, Black, and Male." *Criminology; An interdisciplinary Journal* 36 (4): 763–798. doi:10.1111/j.1745-9125.1998.tb01265.x.

Tessler, H., M. Choi, and G. Kao. 2020. "The Anxiety of Being Asian American: Hate Crimes and Negative Biases During the COVID-19 Pandemic." *American Journal of Criminal Justice* 45: 1–11.

Tolbert, J., J. Kates, and L. Levitt. 2020, May 4th. Lifting Social Distancing Measures in America: State Actions & Metrics. *Kaiser Family Foundation*. Accessed October 11, 2020. https://www.kff.org/policy-watch/lifting-social-distancing-measures-in-america-state-actions-metrics/.

U.S. Bureau of Labor Statistics. 2019. Labor force characteristics by race and ethnicity, 2018. Accessed August 24th 2020. https://www.bls.gov/opub/reports/race-and ethnicity/2018/home.htm.

U.S. Census Bureau. 2019. Population Estimates, July 1, 2019 (V2019) – New York City, NY [data table]. https://www.census.gov/quickfacts/newyorkcitynewyork?

Walker, S. 2020, May 11th. Europe's marginalised Roma people hit hard by coronavirus. *The Guardian*. Accessed October 11, 2020. https://www.theguardian.com/world/2020/may/11/europes-marginalised-roma-people-hit-hard-by-coronavirus.

Wood, S. D., J. T. Jakubek Jr, and K. Kelly. 2015. "You've Got to Fight to be White: The Rural Foundation of the new Militia for Race Control." *Contemporary Justice Review* 18 (2): 215–230. doi:10.1080/10282580.2015.1025633.

Zuberi, T., and E. Bonilla-Silva, eds. 2008. *White Logic, White Methods: Racism and Methodology*. Lanham: Rowman & Littlefield Publishers.

Racism and nationalism during and beyond the COVID-19 pandemic

Amanuel Elias ⓘ, Jehonathan Ben, Fethi Mansouri and Yin Paradies

ABSTRACT

Racism and xenophobia associated with the coronavirus (COVID-19) pandemic disproportionately affect migrants and minority groups worldwide. They exacerbate existing patterns of discrimination and inequity, impacting especially those already facing intersecting social, economic and health vulnerabilities. In this article, we explore the nature and extent of racism sparked by COVID-19. We briefly introduce the relationship between historical pandemics and racist sentiments and discuss ethnic and racial disparities in relation to COVID-19. We contextualize racism under COVID-19, and argue that an environment of populism, resurgent exclusionary ethno-nationalism, and retreating internationalism has been a key contributor to the flare-up in racism during the COVID-19. We then discuss links between racism, nationalism and capitalism, and consider what intercultural relations may look like in a post-outbreak world. We conclude by highlighting the potential effects of COVID-racism on intercultural relations, and the national and global implications for social policy.

Introduction

Emerging research indicates that racism and xenophobia have increased during the outbreak of the coronavirus (COVID-19) pandemic (Clissold et al. 2020; McCoy 2020). This has happened against a backdrop of rising nationalism and populism that have been spreading worldwide over the last two decades. Scholars contend that nationalism thrives during times of crisis (Bieber 2020; Clarke 2010; Rantanen 2012). Clissold et al. (2020, p. 421) argue that, under COVID-19, "rising levels of nationalism in many affected countries" have compounded "a sense of xenophobia pervading into the political and social responses". According to Su and Shen (2020), COVID-19 has led to a heightened ideological divide in the United States, with more nationalist sentiments particularly among conservative groups, while in many national contexts, the outbreak and its progression are driving the increasing prominence of far-right political parties. As a result, minority groups across European countries as well as the United States have experienced racism, discrimination and hate crimes under the heightened COVID-19 context (Croucher, Nguyen, and Rahmani 2020; Devakumar et al. 2020).

The pandemic has also signalled the re-emergence of a form of politicized ethno-cultural racism aimed specifically at people from Asian backgrounds (Mansouri 2020). Anti-Asian (particularly anti-Chinese) racism saw a rapid rise, for example, in North America (Gover, Harper, and Langton 2020), in the UK (Bhala et al. 2020), Australia (Priest et al. 2020) and India (Haokip 2020). This manifested in a plethora of incidents including racial slurs, graffiti, hate speech and physical attacks (Russell 2020), and has been amplified by political propaganda characterizing the COVID-19 virus as a "Chinese virus" and hashtags such as "Kung-flu" (Barreneche 2020). COVID-19 era racism against other groups has also been evident, for example, in reports of racial discrimination against African migrants in China and Muslims in various countries.

And yet, racism during global emergencies is not altogether new, as previous pandemics have shown throughout history. Certain pandemics have indeed been associated with hate and violence against minority groups (e.g. based on ethnicity, religion, migration, and sexuality; Cohn 2018). For example, the 1900 plague epidemic, thought to have originated in San Francisco's Chinatown, was labelled an "Oriental disease, peculiar to rice eaters" by the then United States' Surgeon General.[1] The response was widespread racism and the arbitrary detention, for months, of almost a quarter of a million Asian immigrants (Gorelick 2020; Risse 2012). McCoy (2020) also draws a parallel between the 1918 Spanish Flu and the COVID-19 outbreak: both events occurred in an environment of similar racial prejudice and systemic racism.

In addition to rising xenophobic sentiments, minority groups are disproportionately affected by racial disparities in the prevalence of COVID-19. Often, pandemics "follow the fault lines of society – exposing and often magnifying power inequities" (Gravlee 2020, 1). As such, COVID-19 has exposed and exacerbated systematic discrimination and social inequities across the globe (McCoy 2020; Gravlee 2020). The people most negatively impacted by COVID-19 are those who already face numerous social, economic and health vulnerabilities, and who are now encountering intensified exclusion and marginalization. The direct and indirect, systematic effects of COVID-racism represent novel examples of the multidimensional nature of racism.

In this article, we argue that an environment of populism, resurgent ethno-nationalism, and retreating internationalism has been a key contributor to the flare-up in racism during the COVID-19 pandemic. We explore the nature and extent of racism kindled by COVID-19 in this context. In the next section, we contextualize racism, xenophobia and race relations in the wake of COVID-19. We then consider what racism, xenophobia, and nationalism may look like in a post-outbreak world. Finally, we conclude with suggestions for tackling COVID-19-racism at the national level and consider implications for social policy affecting intercultural relations and social justice.

Racism and nationalism during COVID-19

The COVID-19 outbreak is related to racism and xenophobia in two fundamental ways: first, it has contributed to heightened levels of racist sentiments towards minority groups; second, the pandemic has occurred in an environment of exclusionary nationalism, which exacerbated xenophobic racism.

The first relationship depicts an indirect social ramification of a national and indeed global emergency. Pandemics are among the deadliest natural disasters and global health emergencies, with far-reaching effects on human societies (Bavel et al. 2020). In addition to their heightened risks to lives, pandemics can cause significant economic shocks that also affect a significant proportion of the world's population. Depressive socio-economic environments often lead to scapegoating, heightened levels of racism, and currents of xenophobia in a context of rising levels of exclusionary nationalism (Bieber 2020), a pattern evident during the current COVID-19 pandemic (Gover, Harper, and Langton 2020).

The COVID-19 pandemic broke out in Wuhan, China in December 2019 (Johns Hopkins University 2020). In a few months, anti-Asian racism rose sharply internationally as the virus began to spread across countries, with Chinese and Asian people becoming a feared, blamed and harassed group (Gover, Harper, and Langton 2020). By the time the World Health Organization declared it a global emergency, allegations of cover-up by the Chinese government fanned widespread anti-Chinese sentiments and inflammatory reactions by global politicians, stirring racist and xenophobic sentiments, and exacerbating an already tense intercultural environment (Barreneche 2020; Gover, Harper, and Langton 2020).

Racism and xenophobia during a global pandemic like COVID-19 are not entirely new phenomena. The spread of infectious disease can be strongly associated with heightened levels of prejudice, racial intolerance and xenophobia (Schaller and Neuberg 2012; Kim, Sherman, and Updegraff 2016). Historical pandemic outbreaks show the occurrence of similar racial prejudices targeting ethnic and racial minorities (McCoy 2020). This is often associated with fear, one of the main behavioural responses triggered during pandemics (Bavel et al. 2020). Fear affects how people think, feel and react towards perceived out-groups. Sometimes, fear associated with the spread of infectious disease can trigger attitudes and behaviours including prejudice, racial intolerance and xenophobia (Schaller and Neuberg 2012; Kim, Sherman, and Updegraff 2016). For example, this has occurred during the bubonic plague (Black Death), syphilis, cholera, smallpox, typhus, the 1918 influenza ("Spanish Flu"), and HIV/AIDS pandemics (Cohn 2018; Echenberg 2002). Emotional reaction to the threat of infection can diminish empathy, leading to scapegoating, stigmatization and dehumanization of minority groups (Navarrete and Fessler 2006). Given that pandemics can give rise to hate and violent responses as well as to acts of compassion (Cohn 2018; Hoppe 2018), it seems the "outsider" status of minorities within societies is a key factor in their persectuion during disease outbreaks (Echenberg 2002).

The second relationship between COVID-19 and racism arises via the effect on rising nationalism and populism, and their effects on race relations during a pandemic outbreak. Exclusionary nationalism and racism are often inter-related (Mosse 1995; Balibar 1991). Historically, the first half of the twentieth century was a period of rising nationalism around the world. When the bubonic plague broke out, anti-immigrant sentiments intensified in many countries such as the US, South Africa, Argentina, and Australia (Echenberg 2002). In the US, this was a period when anti-black racism was peaked with Jim Crow segregation, and widespread lynching and racial violence. Similarly, the outbreak of the Spanish Flu of 1918 resulted in hate and violence against African Americans who were scapegoated in its midst (McDonald 2020). In Europe, the outbreak of typhus, which caused significant deaths in the con-tinent, was used to justify persecution and killings, and has been implicated in the genocides, of Jews during the Holocaust, and in the Armenian Massacre (Cohn 2012; Weindling 2000).

While the examples discussed above indicate events that sparked racism and xenophobic violence, Cohn (2012) has argued that pandemics did not always lead to racial violence. We contend that pre-pandemic state of inten-sified nationalist sentiments along with intercultural/ethnic polarization offer possible channels by which a pandemic exacerbates racism and xenophobia. An environment of social polarization created by widespread socio-economic oppression and trust deficit under global capitalism (Paul 2020) severely undermines social cohesion and intercultural relations (Elias & Mansouri 2020). When a pandemic occurs in such conditions, it can aggravate already tense intercultural relations, and trigger racial conflict and violence.

COVID-19 worsened existing social polarization and reinforced ideological entrenchment towards exclusionary nationalism (Su and Shen 2020). It fos-tered exclusionary nationalism and weakened global coordination and col-laboration (Bieber 2020). While the pandemic has forced countries to close their borders, putting them in *de facto* localization and isolation, it has also led to increased forms of authoritarianism. For example, in the Philippines, Brazil, India, South Africa, Hungary and Hong Kong, emergency laws and other measures have been invoked and used for greater political control in response to both the direct public health crisis and growing popular dissatisfaction with its handling by national governments. Another key indicator of countries' reactions to the pandemic relates to the conduct of national elections. Since the pandemic was announced, 17 countries have conducted national and sub-national elections while 66 have postponed them (IDEA 2020).

So far, the societal ramifications of COVID-19 have been significant, and have varied across countries (Delvin and Connaughton 2020). According to Fukuyama (2020, 26), "the factors responsible for successful pandemic responses have been state capacity, social trust, and leadership". By comparison, countries experiencing social polarization have done worse, and this can have an adverse effect on intercultural relations (Fukuyama 2020). The effect is evident in the intercultural tension, with racism, xenophobic nationalism and discrimination against minorities expected to rise for years to come (Bavel et al. 2020; Nicola et al. 2020). The recent anti-Asian xenophobic sentiment is a typical example, whereby COVID-19-related racism and discrimination have not been limited to people of Asian descent but cut across various minoritized groups. Examples of other minorities subjected to racism include Muslim minority groups who were attacked in India, Sri Lanka and Myanmar (Human Rights Watch 2020). Moreover, a sharp increase in anti-African discrimination in the Chinese city of Guangzhou has been reported, where African residents have faced evictions and refusal of services, and have been targeted by a racialized campaign to have them compulsorily tested for COVID-19, self-isolated or quarantined (Human Rights Watch 2020).

Furthermore, COVID-19 has led to a global increase in discrimination against migrant workers, refugees and asylum seekers. For example, in Singapore, Malaysia and some Middle Eastern countries, strict COVID-19 related sanctions, as well as raids, detentions and blame have affected foreign workers disproportionately (Human Rights Watch 2020). For refugees and asylum seekers in particular, the pandemic presents additional threats to their already vulnerable lives, particularly while awaiting status determination and settlement decisions (WHO 2020). Indeed, given the inadequacy of available health care, particularly for those in crowded refugee camps in war-torn countries such as Syria and Yemen, the risks posed to these individuals and groups are catastrophic. As with the differential impact of work and housing situations on racial and ethnic groups during the pandemic, this illustrates how discrimination is compounded in ways that disproportionately affect already vulnerable groups.

At a time when the pandemic continues to impact racial minorities across many countries around the world, resistance against xenophobic nationalism and racism is also intensifying. COVID-19 has highlighted the social determinants of health and the consequent ethnic disparity in health outcomes. The widespread public reaction against systemic racism, as exemplified by the

Black Lives Matter (BLM) movement, indicates a growing solidarity in anti-racism struggles tackling ongoing racial oppression. The recent outburst against police violence in the US is a clear indicator that this sentiment is widely shared by people of colour and many others (Jee-Lyn García and & Sharif 2015).

Against the backdrop of COVID-19's disproportionate death toll for people of colour, and galvanized by the George Floyd incident – Mr Floyd died of racism while being infected by COVID-19 – the BLM movement has shored up worldwide support, with global condemnation of racism and xenophobic nationalism generating global solidarity, leading to assertive global anti-racism across North America, Europe, Africa, Asia, and Oceania (Krieger 2020). Founded in 2013, the BLM movement has networks around the world with a mission "to eradicate white supremacy and build local power to inter-vene in violence inflicted on Black communities by the state and vigilantes" (Black Lives Matter Global Network 2020). The BLM movement has stimulated important anti-racism debates, particularly in the context of COVID-19, which has exposed the structural injustice that perpetuates economic deprivation and systemic racism (Krieger 2020). Indeed, these profound disparities thrown into stark relief by COVID-19 have affected policy debates that under-line the need for tackling institutional racism not only in policing and mass incarceration but also in education, healthcare, and community services.

A post-outbreak world: re-thinking the relationship between nationalism, capitalism and racism under COVID-19

To better understand the current moment in race relations, we need to grapple with emerging intersections between racism, capitalism and nation-alism (Paul 2020). Racism may be defined as thoughts, attitudes and practices that create hierarchies of superiority and inferiority based on characteristics such as "race", ethnicity, and nation (e.g. Banton [1969] 2018; Garner 2010). It circulates across many levels of social life and may be expressed through stereotypes, prejudice or discrimination that serve to maintain or exacerbate unfair and avoidable inequalities (Berman and Paradies 2010). Nationalism, when narrowly defined, often refers to an ideology that privileges nations as "imagined communities" and/or "natural" units of socio-political organiz-ation and favours membership in the nation or national movements (Ander-son 2006; Gellner 2008) while capitalism is a system that is fundamentally based on hierarchical exploitation of economic output and alienation from the fruits of labour.[2] Nationalism and racism may pertain to many – and quite different – things, yet they also contain obviously pertinent overlaps and intersections, from their historical embeddedness in colonialism, to the convergence of negative social attitudes towards immigrants and the poor. Some of their fundamental concepts and ideas are closely connected too;

indeed, "the discourses of race and nation are never very far apart" (Balibar 1991, 37), while the transformation of nations into plutocracies is virtually ubiquitous.

Some of the early scholarly observations about how these relationships have unfolded under COVID-19 may help explain the current moment of race relations and the varied forms racism presently takes. For example, Bieber (2020) depicts the increasing biases against certain groups during the COVID-19 pandemic as one of the handful of important features of exclusionary nationalism that often manifest during crises. We may thus see racism both as a constituent element within versions of nationalism emerging periodically and an enduring feature of the oppression intrinsic to capitalist (de)valuing of human life. Observations about how quickly, long-rehearsed anti-Asian tropes have resurfaced and surged, are typical examples of the relationship between plague and otherness (Echenberg 2002; Hoppe 2018). They suggest that seemingly diminishing racist sentiments may remain close to the surface, ready to be reinvigorated and acted upon with a contemporary twist – this time with China at its epicentre – and flavoured by the intractable combination of pandemic, global recession and nationalist fervour (Hartman, forthcoming; Woods et al. 2020).

Finally, we want to consider some new directions in thinking about the possible futures of race relations in a post-outbreak world. Over the past several months, we have witnessed an emergent sliding back into a primal, survivalist mode of approaching our own existence vis-à-vis racialized and feared Others. Yet, similar patterns of nationalism and nationalist racism that thrive on heightened xenophobia have spread far and wide. The "sharing" of nationalism, capitalism and racism is also telling given changes and contestation to mobilities, globalization, and movement of a tremendous amount of human and economic activity, online. This will stimulate rapid expansion and transformations of racism in online platforms, thereby challenging social science research both in theoretical framing and in methodological design (Krieger 2020). COVID-related racism predominantly takes place in virtual environments, driven by individuals and groups that are spatially and temporally beyond the traditional milieus of intercultural encounters and race relations. Such racism of the moment also strives on misinformation and conspiracy thinking, on misconstruing norms, values, practices, and moralities of different groups, and on issues that encompass, for example, hygiene, care, proximity, and "good" citizenship. It is a racism contingent on tropes of intimidation, often nationally instigated, on "blame games", a general evasion of responsibility and leadership and expanding scapegoating practices. Likewise, state-inflicted racism and socio-economic neglect, blatant and unashamed, through discriminatory policies against minority groups and discursive violence, will likely remain a force to reckon with and contest.

Conclusion

In the wake of the COVID-19 pandemic, a surge of racism has impacted minority groups within countries across the world. Emerging research has particularly documented the link between the pandemic and heightened anti-Asian racism. This renewed form of ethno-cultural racism can be contextualized in relation to rising hate speech, cultural prejudice, and racial attacks that have occurred during historical pandemics. In this article, we have argued that an environment of rampant exclusionary nationalism and unprecedented economic inequalities created conditions for the resurgence of xenophobia and racism following the outbreak and progression of COVID-19. In a context of exclusionary nationalism and global recession, fear plays an adverse role, triggering attitudes and behaviours that foment hate and xenophobic sentiments. Such sentiments, crystallized by exclusionary ideologies, threaten the future of social reform and racial justice, both due to potential for intercultural and resource conflict as well as the reinforcement of ideological divides, and intensified polarization.

We argued that COVID-racism should not be viewed from an interpersonal ethno-cultural relations perspective alone. Equally, and perhaps more consequential is the systemic discrimination and socio-economic injustice that is exacerbating the disproportionate adverse outcomes for racialized ethnic minority groups. While the rise in racism and xenophobia have affected these groups, racism at policy, institutional and societal levels have also been exposed during the progression of the pandemic. This has implications for public policy, adding pressure on national and international governments to pursue policies that address growing exclusionary social attitudes, yawning economic chasms and burgeoning racism, while paradoxically, these factors constitute a "major process in the construction and existence of nation-states" themselves (Paul 2020, 27). Callous consumer greed facilitated abused animal life leading to infected bats birthing COVID-19, which then flowed freely along neo-liberal gouges in societal bodies thereby intensifying reliance on the very capitalist technologies of self, surveillance and supervision that instigated the initial predicament (Braidotti 2020). Extricating ourselves from such a paradox will require no less than a questioning of modernity itself, in order to genuinely challenge the triumvirate of racism, capitalism and nationalism (Paradies 2020).

Notes

1. Todd, F. M. (1909). *Eradicating plague from San Francisco*. Cited in Trauner (1978).
2. Anderson (2006, 5) argues that nationalism belongs to the socio-cultural notions of kinship and religion [more] than with ideological notions of "liberalism" and "fascism".

Disclosure statement

No potential conflict of interest was reported by the author(s).

ORCID

Amanuel Elias ⓘ http://orcid.org/0000-0001-8871-5956

References

Anderson, B. 2006. *Imagined Communities: Reflections on the Origin and Spread of Nationalism*. London: Verso Books.
Balibar, E. (1991) 2005. "Racism and Nationalism." In *Nations and Nationalism: A Reader*, edited by P. Spencer, and H. Wollman, 163–174. Edinburgh: Edinburgh University Press. DOI:10.3366/j.ctvxcrmwf.15.
Balibar, E. 1991. "Racism and Nationalism." In *Race, Nation, Class: Ambiguous Identities*, edited by E. Balibar, and I. Wallerstein, 37–68. London: Verso.
Banton, M. (1969) 2018. "The Concept of Racism." In *Race and Racialism*, edited by S. Zubida, 17–34. London: Routledge.
Barreneche, S. M. 2020. "Somebody to Blame: on the Construction of the Other in the Context of the Covid-19 Outbreak." *Society Register* 4 (2): 19–32.
Bavel, J. J., K. Baicker, P. S. Boggio, V. Capraro, A. Cichocka, M. Cikara, and M. E. Crockett. 2020. "Using Social and Behavioural Science to Support COVID-19 Pandemic Response." *Nature Human Behavior* 4: 460–471.
Berman, G., and Y. Paradies. 2010. "Racism, Disadvantage and Multiculturalism: Towards Effective Anti-Racist Praxis." *Ethnic and Racial Studies* 33 (2): 214–232.
Bhala, N., G. Curry, A. R. Martineau, C. Agyemang, and R. Bhopal. 2020. "Sharpening the Global Focus on Ethnicity and Race in the Time of COVID-19." *Lancet* 395 (10238): 1673–1676. DOI:10.1016/S0140-6736(20)31102-8.
Bieber, F. 2020. "Global Nationalism in Times of the COVID Pandemic." *Nationalities Papers*, 1–19. DOI:10.1017/nps.2020.35.
Black Lives Matter Global Network. 2020. "Black Lives Matter." Accessed October 20, 2020, https://blacklivesmatter.com/about/.
Braidotti, R. 2020. "'We' Are in This Together, But We Are Not One and the Same." *Bioethical Inquiry*, DOI:10.1007/s11673-020-10017-8.
Clarke, J. 2010. "After Neo-Liberalism? Markets, States and the Reinvention of Public Welfare." *Cultural Studies* 24 (3): 375–394.
Clissold, E., D. Nylander, C. Watson, and A. Ventriglio. 2020. "Pandemics and Prejudice." *International Journal of Social Psychiatry* 66 (5): 421–423.
Cohn, S. K. 2012. "Pandemics: Waves of Disease, Waves of Hate from the Plague of Athens to AIDS." *Historical Research* 85: 535–555.
Cohn, S. K. 2018. *Epidemics: Hate and Compassion from the Plague of Athens to AIDS*. Oxford: Oxford University Press.
Croucher, S. M., T. Nguyen, and D. Rahmani. 2020. "Prejudice Toward Asian Americans in the Covid-19 Pandemic: The Effects of Social Media use in the United States." *Frontiers in Communication* 5 (39): 1–12. DOI:10.3389/fcomm.2020.00039.
Delvin, K., and A. Connaughton. 2020. "Most Approve of National Response to COVID-19 in 14 Advanced Economies." *Pew Research*. August 27. https://www.

pewresearch.org/global/2020/08/27/most-approve-of-national-response-to-covid-19-in-14-advanced-economies/.

Devakumar, D., G. Shannon, S. S. Bhopal, and I. Abubakar. 2020. "Racism and Discrimination in COVID-19 Responses." *Lancet* 395 (10231): 1194–1194. DOI:10.1016/S0140-6736(20)30792-3.

Echenberg, M. 2002. "Pestis Redux: The Initial Years of the Third Bubonic Plague Pandemic, 1894-1901." *Journal of World History* 13 (2): 429–449.

Elias, A., and F. Mansouri. 2020. "A Systematic Review of Studies on Interculturalism and Intercultural Dialogue." *Journal of Intercultural Studies* 41 (4): 490–523.

Fukuyama, F. 2020. "The Pandemic and Political Order." *Foreign Affairs* 99: 26.

Garner, S. 2010. *Racisms: An Introduction*. Thousand Oaks, CA: Sage Publications.

Gellner, E. 2008. *Nations and Nationalism*. New York: Cornell University Press.

Gorelick, S. M. 2020. "On Resisting our Need for Certainty in a Global Catastrophe." *Violence & Gender* 7 (2): 38–39. DOI: 10.1089/vio.2020.0014.

Gover, A. R., S. B. Harper, and L. Langton. 2020. "Anti-Asian Hate Crime During the COVID-19 Pandemic: Exploring the Reproduction of Inequality." *American Journal of Criminal Justice* 45: 647–667. DOI:10.1007/s12103-020-09545-1.

Gravlee, C. C. 2020. "Systemic Racism, Chronic Health Inequities, and COVID-19: A Syndemic in the Making?" *American Journal of Human Biology* 32 (5): 1–8. DOI:10.1002/ajhb.23482.

Haokip, T. 2020. "From 'Chinky' to 'Coronavirus': Racism Against Northeast Indians During the Covid-19 Pandemic." *Asian Ethnicity*, DOI:10.1080/14631369.2020.1763161.

Hartman, T. K., T. V. Stocks, R. McKay, J. G. Miller, L. Levita, A. P. Martinez, L. Mason, et al. Forthcoming. The Authoritarian Dynamic During the COVID-19 Pandemic: Effects on Nationalism and Anti-Immigrant Sentiment.

Hoppe, T. 2018. ""Spanish Flu": When Infectious Disease Names Blur Origins and Stigmatize Those Infected." *American Journal of Public Health* 108 (11): 1462–1464.

Human Rights Watch. 2020. "China: COVID-19 Discrimination Against Africans." Accessed June 13, 2020, from https://www.hrw.org/news/2020/05/05/china-covid-19-discrimination-against-africans.

IDEA. 2020. *Global Overview of COVID-19: Impact on Elections*. International Institute for Democracy and Electoral Assistance. Accessed June 13, 2020. https://www.idea.int/news-media/multimedia-reports/global-overview-covid-19-impact-elections.

Jee-Lyn García, J., and M. Z. & Sharif. 2015. "Black Lives Matter: a Commentary on Racism and Public Health." *American Journal of Public Health* 105 (8): e27–e30. DOI: 10.2105/AJPH.2015.302706.

Johns Hopkins University. 2020. "Coronavirus Resource Center." *Maps & Trends*. Accessed July 2, 2020: https://coronavirus.jhu.edu/data/hubei-timeline.

Kim, H. S., D. K. Sherman, and J. A. Updegraff. 2016. "Fear of Ebola: The Influence of Collectivism on Xenophobic Threat Responses." *Psychological Science* 27 (7): 935–944.

Krieger, N. 2020. "Enough: COVID-19, Structural Racism, Police Brutality, Plutocracy, Climate Change – and Time for Health Justice, Democratic Governance, and an Equitable, Sustainable Future." *American Journal of Public Health* 110 (11): 1620–1623. DOI: 10.2105/AJPH.2020.305886.

Mansouri, F. 2020. "The Socio-Cultural Impact of COVID-19: Exploring the Role of Intercultural Dialogue in Emerging Responses." UNESCO Briefing Papers, Paris.

McCoy, H. 2020. "Black Lives Matter, and Yes, You Are Racist: The Parallelism of the Twentieth and Twenty-First Centuries." *Child and Adolescent Social Work Journal* 37: 463–475. DOI: 10.1007/s10560-020-00690-4.

McDonald, S. D. 2020. *In 1918 and 2020, Race Colors America's Response to Epidemics*. The Undefeated. Accessed June 9, 2020. https://theundefeated.com/features/in-1918-and-2020-race-colors-americas-response-to-epidemics/

Mosse, G. L. 1995. "Racism and Nationalism." *Nations and Nationalism* 1 (2): 163–173.

Navarrete, C. D., and D. M. Fessler. 2006. "Disease Avoidance and Ethnocentrism: The Effects of Disease Vulnerability and Disgust Sensitivity on Intergroup Attitudes." *Evolution and Human Behavior* 27 (4): 270–282.

Nicola, M., Z. Alsafi, C. Sohrabi, A. Kerwan, A. Al-Jabir, C. Iosifidis, M. Agha, and R. Agha. 2020. "The Socio-Economic Implications of the Coronavirus Pandemic (COVID-19): A Review." *International Journal of Surgery* 78: 185–193.

Paradies, Y. 2020. "Unsettling Truths: Modernity, (de-)Coloniality and Indigenous Futures." *Postcolonial Studies* 23 (4): 1–19.

Paul, E. 2020. "Racism as Nationalism and Capitalism." In *Australia in the Expanding Global Crisis*, edited by E. Paul, 27–81. Singapore: Palgrave Macmillan.

Priest, N., K. Thurber, R. Maddox, R. Jones, and M. Truong. 2020. COVID-19 Racism is Making Kids Sick. *InSight*. Accessed June 25, 2020. https://insightplus.mja.com.au/2020/18/covid-19-racism-is-making-kids-sick/.

Rantanen, T. 2012. "In Nationalism we Trust?" In *Aftermath: The Cultures of the Economic Crisis*, edited by M. Castells, J. Caraça, and G. Cardoso, 132–153. Oxford: Oxford University Press.

Risse, G. B. 2012. *Plague, Fear, and Politics in San Francisco's Chinatown*. Baltimore, MD: Johns Hopkins University Press.

Russell, A. 2020. "The Rise of Coronavirus Hate Crimes." *New Yorker*, March 17. Accessed June 20, 2020. https://www.newyorker.com/news/letter-from-the-uk/the-rise-of-coronavirus-hate-crimes.

Schaller, M., and S. L. Neuberg. 2012. "Danger, Disease, and the Nature of Prejudice(s)." *Advances in Experimental Social Psychology* 46: 1–54. DOI: 10.1016/B978-0-12-394281-4.00001-5.

Su, R., and W. Shen. 2020. "Is Nationalism Rising in Times of the COVID-19 Pandemic? Individual-Level Evidence from the United States." *Journal of Chinese Political Science*, DOI: 10.1007/s11366-020-09696-2.

Trauner, J. B. 1978. "The Chinese as Medical Scapegoats in San Francisco, 1870-1905." *California History* 57 (1): 70–87.

Weindling, P. J. 2000. *Epidemics and Genocide in Eastern Europe 1890–1945*. Oxford: Oxford University Press. https://doi.org/10.1093/acprof:oso/9780198206910.001.0001

WHO. 2020. Preparedness, Prevention and Control of Coronavirus Disease (COVID-19) for Refugees and Migrants in non-Camp Settings." *World Health Organization*. Accessed June 26, 2020. https://apps.who.int/iris/bitstream/handle/10665/331777/WHO-2019-nCoV-Refugees_Migrants-2020.1-eng.pdf.

Woods, E. T., R. Schertzer, L. Greenfeld, C. Hughes, and C. Miller-Idriss. 2020. "COVID-19, Nationalism, and the Politics of Crisis: A Scholarly Exchange." *Nations and Nationalism*, DOI: 10.1111/nana.12644.

Compounded inequality: how the U.S. Paycheck Protection Program is failing Los Angeles Latino small businesses

Karina Santellano

ABSTRACT
The CARES Act, passed in March 2020, included the Paycheck Protection Program (PPP) which designated $350-billion for small businesses in the United States. Data shows that small businesses, particularly those owned by Latinos and African Americans, have confronted challenges in accessing PPP funds. At the same time, high profile companies like the LA Lakers have admitted to have received and repaid millions of dollars from the PPP. These large companies' disclosures signal that the PPP is favouring highly resourced and well-connected businesses while failing to help small businesses owned by people of colour. Drawing on interview data from my dissertation on Latino-owned coffee shops in Los Angeles during Covid-19, I use Feagin's conceptualization of institutional racism to contend that the way PPP has played out is not out of the ordinary but rather part of an exclusionary history in entrepreneurship.

Introduction

> This country's major institutions have long involved social arrangements that are racially exploitative, hierarchical, and white supremacist in rationale, and undemocratic in operation. (Feagin 2006, 262)

In April 2020, the Los Angeles Lakers announced they had repaid the $4.6 million coronavirus relief loan they received from the federal government's Paycheck Protection Program (PPP). A Lakers spokesperson announced that the multi-million-dollar loan was returned after the PPP announced that their funds had been depleted (Wallace 2020). This announcement was shocking given that PPP was meant specifically for small businesses and not large companies like the Lakers, a NBA team worth $4.4 billion. The popular basketball team was not the only high profile large company that made news regarding their PPP loan. Shake Shack and Ruth's Hospitality also announced they would return their loans to the federal government (Wallace 2020). At the same time, small business owners of colour reported that they were having difficulty accessing PPP funds (Gamboa 2020; Los Angeles Commerce 2020; Stanford Latino Entrepreneurship Initiative 2020). According to a nation-wide survey published by advocacy organizations Unidos US and Colour of Change, only 12 per cent of Black and Latino small business owners who have applied for funds through the Small Business Administration (SBA), mostly the PPP, reported receiving the amount they asked for while 26 per cent reported only receiving a fraction of the amount they applied for (Unidos US 2020). Almost half of the owners who participated in this survey anticipated closing permanently within six months (Unidos US 2020; Flitter 2020a). Indeed, a new report finds that between February and April 2020, Black owned small businesses have declined by 41 per cent and Latino owned small businesses have declined by 32 per cent (Fairlie 2020). This is in contrast to white owned small businesses that have declined by only 17 per cent, which is below the national average and below every other racial and ethnic group (Fairlie 2020).

The revelation that the PPP funds were not being distributed to small businesses owners in need suggests that the programme has not met its mission to aid small businesses. In addition, these disclosures suggest that future iterations of this programme require critical racial justice-conscious fund distribution that prioritize small business owners of colour, particularly African Americans and Latinos. The Trump administration has not addressed racial disparities in the PPP programme. With President Trump's recurrent conjecture that COVID-19 will soon disappear, his ties to corporate entities and interests, and his focus on the 2020 Presidential election, such improved iterations of the programme are uncertain at best.

This article specifically focuses on Latinos as they are the second fastest-growing ethnic group and the largest racial/ethnic minority in the U.S (Orozco et al. 2020). In the past ten years, Latinos have started more small businesses than any other racial/ethnic demographic (Orozco et al. 2020). These businesses contribute nearly $500 billion in annual sales to the national economy (Stanford Latino Entrepreneurship Initiative 2019). Moreover, Latinos represent 18 per cent of the nation's workforce but they are overrepresented in industries, like accommodation and food services, that have been hit hard by the pandemic induced economic crisis (Parra 2020).

In this article, I provide background information on the PPP and share preliminary data on my research on Latino coffee shop owners in Los Angeles. In addition, I give important business context that helps to explain how the PPP is failing business owners that navigate an already challenging start-up and operation terrain. While the data presented here are based on a specific industry, it highlights how Latino entrepreneurs do not have the same in-house business and legal resources, strong pre-existing bank relationships, and wealth accumulation as large companies like the Lakers do. In accordance with Feagin's quote above, I discuss how Latino business owners have historically faced barriers in accessing resources from United States' major institutions like those of education, banks, and bodies of government. In this respect, the PPP, yet another example of institutional racism, has been an insult to a long term and deep rooted injury.

COVID-19 and the Paycheck Protection Program

The Coronavirus has affected every realm of life, including small businesses. Small business owners have had to think creatively given that most of their clientele are working from home and are no longer committed to their daily routines that take place outside of the home.

The Coronavirus Aid, Relief, and Economic Security (CARES) Act, passed on 27 March 2020, included loan support for small businesses in the United States through the Paycheck Protection Program (PPP). This programme was set to be a $350-billion programme that would provide American small businesses with eight weeks of cash-flow assistance through federally guaranteed loans. In April 2020, the Paycheck Protection Program and Health Care Enhancement Act added an additional $320 billion funding (U.S. Small Business Administration 2020a). The Paycheck Protection Program Flexibility Act provided more time for businesses to use the funds, making them eligible for a fully forgiven loan. PPP loans required business owners to use at least 60 per cent on payroll and employee benefit costs and 40 per cent on mortgage interest payments, rent and lease payments, and utilities. To apply to PPP, small business owners had to go through a SBA 7(a) lender or through a federally insured repository institution, federally insured credit union, or participating Farm Credit system institution (U.S. Small Business Administration 2020b).

Initial reports on small business owners of colour suggest that the PPP compounded on the historically weak relationships between banks and Latino and Black entrepreneurs. Many banks only accepted applications from existing customers (Flitter 2020a). Bank of America was reported to have turned away potential applicants who had credit card accounts at other banks (Flitter 2020b). For many Latino small business owners, language has proven to be a barrier to applying to PPP. These business owners have found it difficult to understand what PPP and other assistance programmes are and what the application process entails (Garnham 2020; Gomez 2020). Therefore, institutional racism in the form of weak relationships with banks and a cumbersome application process resulted in many Latinos missing out in PPP loan access in the first round of the programme (Garnham 2020).

Since news broke about the first round of the PPP application, there have been updates to the programme. In June, the U.S. Small Business Administration and the Department of Treasury created a "borrower-friendly" application that "requires fewer calculation and less documentation for eligible borrowers" (U.S. Small Business Administration 2020b). The EZ application also gives borrowers the opportunity to choose a 24-week extension to allow for businesses to obtain full forgiveness of their PPP loan. On 6 July 2020, the President signed the programme's extension, making 8 August 2020 the deadline to apply for a PPP loan. As of mid-October 2020, President Trump and Congress have not passed additional federal small business relief nor have they addressed the racial inequity embedded in the PPP.

Indeed, the exclusionary and unequal nature in which the PPP has played out is not random or out of the ordinary. To argue that the PPP has been a practice of institutionalized racism, I draw from Feagin's conceptualization of institutional racism (2006; Feagin and Elias 2013). Institutional racism acknowledges that racism goes beyond individual attitudes and behaviours by becoming institutionalized "within and across all important institutional areas" (Benokraitis and Feagin 1977, 136). In order to perpetuate systemic racism, major organizational structures and institutions must be created, re-created, and protected by institutionalization via different yet interrelated ways like taken-for-granted bureaucratic procedures, policy, and social networks. Social institutions have the power to continue the highly racialized dominance of white controlled structures and social networks while exploiting and excluding people of colour generation after generation (Feagin 2006). Race scholars note that institutionalized racism is one way how systemic racism is perpetuated in the U.S. (Benokraitis and Feagin 1977; Bonilla-Silva 1997; Feagin 2006; Feagin and Elias 2013). PPP is not aiding small business owners of colour but rather, reinforcing income and wealth racial disparities during a time of social and economic crisis.

Deepening inequality for Latino small business entrepreneurship

Entrepreneurship offers a pathway for economically disadvantaged groups to reduce income inequality, build wealth, and improve living conditions for families and communities (Verdaguer 2009; Orozco et al. 2020). However, Latino entrepreneurs experience challenges in accessing start-up capital. Social scientists find that Latinos experience challenges and racial discrimination in accessing bank loans. Latinos report not knowing how to access this type of funding, not having a contact that can help them, and not feeling qualified (Orozco and Perez 2020). As a result, Latinos have to rely on personal savings, credit cards, home equity lines of credit, or rely on family and friends for financial assistance (Fairlie and Woodruff 2008;

Valdez 2011; Orozco and Perez 2020). Lower levels of formal educational attainment and personal wealth are also critical factors that contribute to low rates of Latino rates of business ownership (Fairlie, Valdez, and Vallejo 2020). In addition, according to an analysis of data from American Community Survey 2011–2015, scholars found that Latinos have lower average business owner income across industries than non-Latino Whites (Fairlie, Valdez, and Vallejo 2020). This means that after the start-up process, there continues to be disparities in operation processes.

PPP presents yet another way in which Latino entrepreneurs experience institutional racism and exclusion. Given the uncertainty of the current moment, there is a likely chance that deepening inequality is happening and will continue to happen. This is an issue as Latinos already face insurmountable economic inequality. The average Latino household has less than one-fifth the wealth of a typical American household (Orozco et al. 2020). For this reason, it is key that small business programmes and fund distribution processes do not favour the wealthy and well-connected. Instead, they need be aptly designed to go to entrepreneurs of colour who have limited financial safety nets for business survival. Examining Latino small businesses in this context is necessary in order to advocate for racially and economically equitable policies that ensure that Latinos and other entrepreneurs of colour have access to financial relief assistance during and beyond our current global pandemic.

Insight on PPP: Latino-owned coffee shops in Los Angeles

The new generation of Latino millennial entrepreneurs, many of whom are women, and their middle-class businesses, such as coffee shops, have yet to be examined (Orozco and Perez 2020). The rise of this industry reflects the growing Latino middle-class and millennial consumer base in Los Angeles and in the broader United States. I examine how race/ethnicity, specifically Latinidad, is commodified and sold for largely later-generation Latino communities. Like other researchers, I have incorporated Covid-19 into my dissertation work to see how shelter-in-place orders exacerbate entrepreneurial challenges for Latinos. In the following section, I present interview data from five Latino coffee shop business owners on their experiences of applying to PPP. While this data is limited in the number of interviews I had as of July 2020, it is important to understand how pandemic-specific policy is affecting Latino small business owners on the ground. Three of the five interviewees identified as Mexican Americans. The other two identified as Venezuelan and Guatemalan American, respectively. The average age of the interviewees was 32 years old with a range of 26–41. The average number of years in the coffee shop business is 2.8 years with a range of two to five years. Two out of the five held a bachelor's degree. The quotes presented here come from all five interviewees in the sample. I use pseudonyms for the business owners and their coffee shops.

Cynthia and Diana are co-owners of Chingona Café which is located in a predominately Latino neighbourhood in East Los Angeles. Cynthia spends the most time at the coffee shop since Diana is also an owner of a major auto insurance office in the neighbourhood. In fact, it was Diana that covered the start-up costs of Chingona Café. Without her cousin, Cynthia would not have been able to trade in her clerical job for her current role as a business owner. When asked about applying to the PPP, she mentioned that Chingona Café did not receive a loan from the first round of the PPP. She felt that the bank gave her and Diana the "runaround". She stated:

> But when we applied for Chingona Café, because we're a small company, we're not a big chain, you know, we're a mom and pop location, it was the runaround. It was like, "Oh, well, we need this from you. Oh, we need that from you. Oh, actually, whoops, there's no more funds." And we were like, "What the fuck." You know and we weren't the only ones. We talked to the owners of Theresa's which is the bar two doors down and they had the same experience. They were like, "Oh, yeah, they kept giving us the runaround. It was a headache." It was like just impossible. Once we submitted everything, then, they were like, "Oh, whoops, yeah, there's no more funds." So, it was like, it was meant to keep the small companies down and to – it just went – all the money went towards like big companies, big brand name companies.

Cynthia's interview was particularly insightful because she witnessed how differently she and her cousin were treated as small business owners compared to how her cousin was treated as an owner of a major auto insurance office which did benefit from a strong bank relationship as a nationally established auto insurance company branch. Cynthia's statement demonstrates how larger companies with strong bank relations experience a smoother process than that of a small business owned by two Latinas like Chingona Café. Given the barriers in developing strong relationships with banks, we see that institutionalized racism via the bank made it difficult for Cynthia to apply to the first round of the PPP.

In a related vein, Latino small business owners discussed how difficult it was to apply given their busy schedules and limited staff members available to help with the PPP. For example, Cassandra and her mother Leti are co-owners of Juanita's Café in Huntington Park. Cassandra shared she had to sell her car, crowdsource funds from family and community members, and use her and her mother's personal savings to start Juanita's. Besides herself and her mother, Cassandra only has one other full time employee. She and others I have interviewed shared how they have struggled to find the time and the energy to fill out small loan applications written exclusionary language. Cassandra shared the following about the PPP process:

It's very laborious. Especially food businesses. You have to be fully present, mind, body, soul, everything. You can't half-ass it. And having that mental space to come home after a long day to apply to that, it can be hard, especially if you don't have the help.

A prominent theme in my data is that Latino business owners need expert guidance and time to navigate the complicated PPP process. As indicated by her start-up story, Cassandra and her mother struggled to get Juanita's up and running. Operating the business has been laborious and time-consuming with limited financial opportunity to hire extra help that Cassandra could lean on for business matters. Hence, the effects of institutional racism had manifested long before the PPP and such effects surfaced during the pandemic. She now had to deal with figuring out the PPP and other small business relief loan programmes on top of shifting her sale strategies due to LA city-wide orders that only allowed for take-out or delivery. Cassandra's experience with applying to PPP suggests that the PPP was not designed to be accessible to small business owners of colour like her and her mother.

A few miles south of Cassandra's coffee shop, in Southgate, was Francisco's coffee shop. Francisco started his business with personal savings and a loan from his father and grandmother. The loan had been his family's life savings. When the pandemic hit, Francisco decided to take the lead on any pandemic-related small loan relief application labour for his father who owned a mechanic shop and himself. However, when he began to prepare to submit a city-specific loan relief application, he had trouble understanding what the application was asking of him. Since Francisco did not pursue college studies after high school, he asked a friend who was majoring in accounting at a local university for help. After the friend took a look at the loan application, he told Francisco that he would reach out to his college professor for help because he, too, did not understand the application. With the help of his friend's college professor, Francisco was able to figure out the small business loan application. Unfortunately, he was only able to apply for his father's mechanic shop because as soon as he refreshed the website to begin the application for his coffee shop, the city website had closed due to depleted funds. After Francisco recounted this upsetting story, I asked him if he was planning to apply to the PPP. He answered:

Yeah, it's depressing seeing that, oh the Lakers got $4.6 million? It's like, okay, I guess they really don't really care about the smaller businesses. It's so weird seeing it too, because I think 40% or something like that of Americans work for a small business, so it's kind of like, you know? And then another thing too is also like these guys, again, like Lakers and Shake Shack, I'm sure they had lawyers ready to break down the terminology and sort everything out. Again, it was the resources. I lucked out [in relation to the city small business loan] and I was able to know someone who was able to break it down, but again, like what if someone didn't have those resources? Or someone who doesn't understand all this crazy stuff?

Francisco's quote points to the exclusionary nature of dense language on small business relief loan forms that negatively impact people with less formal education. It also points to the uneven amount and quality of social, human, and economic resources that large companies have compared to small businesses like his and his father's. Small businesses may not have the in-house business and legal assistance or strong pre-existing bank relationships that could facilitate relief loan applications. As Francisco detailed in his interview, he had to spend additional time and energy finding people, including a college professor, who could help him understand the "crazy stuff" on the small business loan application. Knowing that the PPP application process would be challenging and that large companies were being favoured over small businesses was very frustrating for Francisco and other interviewees who had heard the news about the Lakers. Thus, the application process itself, which favoured highly resourced and well-connected companies, was a discouraging deterrent for the Latino coffee shop owners in this study.

Cassandra and others discussed how they were not under any illusion that the federal government would be of any assistance. Rather, they were interested in improving the customer experience. For example, most were learning how to use food delivery systems for the first time and relying on Instagram to share their updated hours of operation. Cassandra said:

> I'm definitely not holding my breath for those loan opportunities. And we're kind of used to working with the little that we do have and the resources. We're trying to focus on what we can do as a business.

Others were looking to introduce new menu items that could bring in more clientele from the community. For example, Ignacio, an owner of coffee shop in Compton, was working to create a healthy version of a frappe. He wanted to introduce frappes as they are popular among young people but he did not want them to be sugary unhealthy concoctions. Rather, he wanted to attract the clientele without foregoing his ethics on community health during a time when the future of his business was constantly on his mind. Ignacio shared:

> It's a fine line between possibilities and caring for our communities. I am not going to sell out the health of the people. We are working on a frappe that is not powder based because that has all kinds of chemicals.

Ignacio's focus was on introducing his healthy frappe because like other Latino coffee shop owners I interviewed, he felt that his neighbourhood community, not the government or the PPP programme, would be the ones to sustain his business during this time. Ignacio had also crowd-sourced funds from friends and community members to start up his coffee shop. He believed they could come through for him again.

Therefore, his strategy was to stay true to his beliefs about the type of business owner he wanted to be and what menu items he thought customers would like to purchase.

The PPP is not fit to best aid small businesses owners of colour. Cynthia shared that even if she had received PPP funds, she would have struggled to meet the loan requirements that would have helped her turn the loan into a grant. She believed that, given the very strict rules of the programme, she most likely would have had to pay back the loan to the federal government. Since the first round of the PPP required business owners to use the funds within two months, business owners were not allowed to stretch out the funds across more time. Cynthia voiced her frustration with "the rules" of the PPP.

> You have to prove that you used it within two months, otherwise, you have to pay it back. But if you used it for payroll and rent and you used it in like two months, then, you don't have to pay it back. But they're not – it means like you can't stretch that money out, you know? Like, you have to use it up and if you don't use it up, then, you have to pay it – you have to give it back. Who makes up these rules? You know, why can't you just let me have it? Why can't I just spend it how I wanna spend it? How I need to? You know, like right now, other bills, other expenses. But these restrictions are ridiculous.

Through Cynthia's quote, we understand that while access to PPP funding is one problem, the PPP legal stipulations are another. Small business owners are not able to use the funds for necessary expenses besides payroll and rent. These rules are limiting to small business owners of colour because they are not able to use the funds in ways beneficial to their business according to their specific needs. Rather, the PPP instructs business owners that the loan must be used in a specific time frame or it must be paid back in full. In this way, the PPP is not attentive to issues that matter to business owners of colour. For Latino business owners who may not have much accumulated wealth, the economic crises brought on by the pandemic may mean a large number of permanently closed businesses.

In East Hollywood, Juan Luis shared that he had to lay off his employees, leaving him to manage the coffee shop by himself. Juan Luis shared, "My employees will get more from unemployment than from me right now. I hope to get them back when things get better."

Given his exhausting schedule, Juan Luis' girlfriend helped to gather the necessary documents and fill out the PPP business owner application form. Fortunately, Juan Luis received PPP funds. However, he was disappointed to only receive $2,500 from the PPP, a much smaller amount than what he expected and needed to hire back his employees. For now, he is working six days a week at the shop in order to keep it open. His experience highlights the reality that even those that do receive PPP funds may not be getting enough to make a difference in their everyday managing of their business.

This finding suggests that some Latino business owners will have to rely on a limited or even nonexistent safety net to outlast COVID-19.

As data demonstrates there are several issues about PPP. Large corporations with considerable of resources and funds are being advantaged in PPP fund access. Latino small business owners are given the "runaround" and experiencing language barriers. Latino small business owners who already experience challenges accessing bank loans are experiencing a disadvantage in small business loans during a context of economic precarity, making them more likely to close than businesses with financial and legal resources. In other words, a major shift is required in the PPP to ensure loans and loan forgiveness reach small business of owners of colour.

Discussion and conclusion

In Los Angeles, Latino small business owners wish they had the same resources in the form of social and economic capital and as the Lakers. The institutional racism that saturates the PPP application and distribution process is negatively affecting small businesses owned by Latinos. Businesses owned by Latinos, African Americans, and other people of colour are closing at an alarming rate compared to their white counterparts. Scholars will need to pay close attention to how inequality manifested via the PPP and compounded entrepreneurship barriers affects not just small businesses owned by people of colour but also neighbourhoods in which these businesses are located and the communities to which these businesses are important to. Even if PPP is re-designed in an equitable manner to aid small business owners of colour during or after the pandemic, the problem of entrepreneurship inequity remains. PPP is a one-time loan programme that does not erase decades of institutional inequality that has led to widening racial income and wealth inequality in the U.S.

While small business owners of colour hope to stay up and running to see the end of Covid-19, their communities are being ravaged by the pandemic and police brutality. Our current moment has offered us yet another opportunity to acknowledge and challenge undemocratic, and hierarchal systems of inequality in hopes of moving closer to a more just society. We must take it.

Disclosure statement

No potential conflict of interest was reported by the author(s).

Funding

This work was supported by ASA Section on Sociology of Culture [Small Crisis Grant]; USC Center for the Changing Family [Covid-19 Small Grant]; Society for the Study of

Social Problems [Racial/Ethnic Minority Fellowship]; USC Graduate School [Summer Research and Writing Fellowship].

References

Benokraitis, Nicole, and Joe Feagin. 1977. "Institutional Racism: A Perspective in Search of Clarity and Research." In *Black/Brown/White Relations: Race Relations in the 1970s*, edited by C. V. Willie, 121–146. New Brunswick, NJ: Routledge.

Bonilla-Silva, Eduardo. 1997. "Rethinking Racism: Toward a Structural Interpretation." *American Sociological Review* 62 (3): 465.

Fairlie, Robert W. 2020. *The Impact of Covid-19 on Small Business Owners: Evidence of Early-Stage Losses from the April 2020 Current Population Survey.* Working Paper. The National Bureau of Economic Research. https://www.nber.org/papers/w27309.

Fairlie, Robert W., Zulema Valdez, and Jody Agius Vallejo. 2020. "The Economic Contributions of Latino Entrepreneurs." In *Advancing U.S. Latino Entrepreneurship*, edited by J. I. Porras, M. J. Pisani, Alfonso Morales, and M. Orozco, 59–76. West Lafayette, IN: Purdue University Press.

Fairlie, Robert W., and Christopher Woodruff. 2008. *Mexican-American Entrepreneurship.* IZA Working Paper No. 3488. https://ssrn.com/abstract=1136289.

Feagin, Joe. 2006. *Systemic Racism: A Theory of Oppression.* London: Routledge.

Feagin, Joe, and Sean Elias. 2013. "Rethinking Racial Formation Theory: A Systemic Racism Critique." *Ethnic and Racial Studies* 36 (6): 931–960.

Flitter, Emily. 2020a. "Few Minority-Owned Businesses Got Relief Loans They Asked For." *Nytimes.com.* https://www.nytimes.com/2020/05/18/business/minority-businesses-coronavirus-loans.html?smtyp=cur&smid=tw-nytimes.

Flitter, Emily. 2020b. "Black-Owned Businesses Could Face Hurdles in Federal Aid Program." *Nytimes.com.* https://www.nytimes.com/2020/04/10/business/minority-business-coronavirus-loans.html.

Gamboa, Suzanne. 2020. "Few Hispanic Business Owners Got Coronavirus Relief Loans, Latino Survey Finds." *NBC News.* https://www.nbcnews.com/news/latino/few-hispanic-business-owners-got-coronavirus-relief-loans-latino-groups-n1192086.

Garnham, Juan Pablo. 2020. "Language Barriers, Absence of Bank Loans Leave Latino Small-Business Owners Struggling – Latino USA." *Latino USA.* https://www.latinousa.org/2020/05/12/language-barriers/.

Gomez, Brandon. 2020. "How Latino Small Business Owners Are Keeping Their Businesses Running During Coronavirus." *CNBC.* https://www.cnbc.com/2020/05/03/how-latino-entrepreneurs-are-adapting-businesses-during-coronavirus.html.

Los Angeles Commerce. 2020. "The Los Angeles Latino Chamber of Commerce is Appalled at Findings that the CARE Act's Small Business Relief Program – the SBA's Paycheck Protection Program is Excluding the Vast Majority of Businesses Owned by People of Color." *Prnewswire.com.* https://www.prnewswire.com/news-releases/the-los-angeles-latino-chamber-of-commerce-is-appalled-at-findings-that-the-care-acts-small-business-relief-programthe-sbas-paycheck-protection-program-is-excluding-the-vast-majority-of-businesses-owned-by-people-of-color-301054374.html.

Orozco, Marlene, Alfonso Morales, Michael J. Pisani, and Jerry I. Porras. 2020. *Advancing U.S. Latino Entrepreneurship: A New National Economic Imperative.* West Lafayette, IN: Purdue University Press.

Orozco, Marlene, and Iliana Perez. 2020. "The State of Latino Entrepreneurship: SLEI Research and Findings." In *Advancing U.S. Latino Entrepreneurship*, edited by J. I. Porras, M. J. Pisani, Alfonso Morales, and M. Orozco, 77–98. West Lafayette, IN: Purdue University Press.

Parra, Daniel. 2020. "Amid Unemployment and Restrictions, Latino Businesses Struggle." *City Limits*. https://citylimits.org/2020/09/17/amid-unemployment-and-restrictions-latino-businesses-struggle/.

Stanford Latino Entrepreneurship Initiative. 2019. *State of Latino Entrepreneurship: 2019 Research Report*. https://www.gsb.stanford.edu/sites/gsb/files/publication-pdf/report-slei-state-latino-entrepreneurship-2019.pdf.

Stanford Latino Entrepreneurship Initiative. 2020. *The Impact of COVID-19 on Latino-Owned Businesses*. https://www.gsb.stanford.edu/sites/gsb/files/2020_slei_first_covid_survey_results.pdf.

U.S. Small Business Administration. 2020a. "Paycheck Protection Program." *Paycheck Protection Program*. https://www.sba.gov/funding-programs/loans/coronavirus-relief-options/paycheck-protection-program#section-header-0.

U.S. Small Business Administration. 2020b. "SBA and Treasury Announce New EZ and Revised Full Forgiveness Applications for the Paycheck Protection Program | The U.S. Small Business Administration | SBA.Gov." *Sba.gov*. Accessed July 16, 2020. https://www.sba.gov/about-sba/sba-newsroom/press-releases-media-advisories/sba-and-treasury-announce-new-ez-and-revised-full-forgiveness-applications-paycheck-protection.

Unidos US. 2020. *Federal Stimulus Survey Findings*. https://theblackresponse.org/wp-content/uploads/2020/05/COC-UnidosUS-Abbreviated-Deck-F05.13.20.pdf.

Valdez, Zulema. 2011. *The New Entrepreneurs: How Race, Class, and Gender Shape American Enterprise*. Stanford, CA: Stanford University Press.

Verdaguer, Maria Eugenia. 2009. *Class, Ethnicity, Gender and Latino Entrepreneurship*. New York: Routledge.

Wallace, Alicia. 2020. "Lakers Return $4.6 Million Coronavirus Relief Loan." *CNN*. CNN Business. https://www.cnn.com/2020/04/27/business/los-angeles-lakers-return-ppp-loan-trnd/index.html.

Perceived COVID-19 health threat increases psychological distress among Black Americans

Ryon J. Cobb ⑩ , Christy L. Erving ⑩ and W. Carson Byrd ⑩

ABSTRACT

The present study used data from the American Trends Panel to examine the interplay between the perceived COVID-19 health threat, discriminatory beliefs in medical settings, and psychological distress among Black Americans. We measured psychological distress as an average of five items modified from two established scales and used self-reports of perceived COVID-19 health threat and beliefs about discrimination in medical settings as focal predictors. Ordinary least squares regression was used to examine these relationships. Holding all else constant, we found that perceived COVID-19 health threat and the belief that Black Americans face racial discrimination in medical settings were both positively and significantly associated with higher levels of psychological distress. We also found a significant perceived COVID-19 health threat by belief about discrimination in medical settings interaction in the full model. Future studies should assess how these relationships vary across age groups and over time.

The coronavirus outbreak represents a significant social problem in the United States (U.S.). Data from the Centers for Disease Control and Prevention indicate that the coronavirus outbreak is responsible for more than nineteen million infections and over 330,000 deaths in the U.S. (CDC COVID Data Tracker n.d.) Research also suggests that the burden of the coronavirus outbreak is unequally distributed across society, as Black Americans face a higher risk of contracting and dying from coronavirus, and are at greater risk of knowing someone who has been hospitalized or died from the coronavirus than non-Black Americans (Kramer and Kramer 2020; Yancy 2020). Not surprisingly, several scholars have argued that the coronavirus outbreak represents a stressful event for Black Americans, leading to mental health problems (Novacek et al. 2020). Given that psychological distress is also a risk factor for increased morbidity and mortality, issues related to the coronavirus outbreak are likely to remain a visible public health concern among Black Americans well into the future.

Scholars of ethnoracial health disparities devote considerable attention to theorizing the mental health implications of the coronavirus outbreak among Black Americans. For example, drawing from critical race theory (CRT) and the stress process model, Laster Pirtle (2020) contends that Black Americans reside in a racist and capitalist society that creates and sustains within-group health disparities through the unequal distribution of perceived threats and social resources. Over time, repeated exposure to racism and other perceived threats overwhelm one's personal resources, which in turn leads to poorer health. A long tradition of research has examined ethnoracial disparities in perceived threats and shown that Black Americans face greater exposure to interpersonal racism, discrimination, and other perceived threats than their White counterparts (Pratt 2009). Not surprisingly, scholars in this area have both developed measures of stress exposure related to the coronavirus outbreak (Conway, Woodard, and Zubrod 2020) and also find that a greater proportion of Black Americans believe the coronavirus outbreak to be a "major threat" to one's health relative to non-Black Americans (Pew Research Center 2020). Though important, we are not aware of any published study that examines how a perceived COVID-19 health threat influences mental health among Black Americans. This absence is curious, given the importance of perceived threats in shaping Black Americans' mental health inequalities (Jackson et al. 2011). This neglect also occurs despite recent evidence that Black Americans are disproportionally affected by the coronavirus outbreak (Egede and Walker 2020).

There are grounds for contending that beliefs regarding racial discrimination are associated with psychological distress among Black Americans and may moderate the possible relationship between perceived COVID-19 health threat and psychological distress. First, CRT scholars have long claimed that racial bias in the healthcare system manifests in clinicians' opinions, beliefs, behaviours, and attitudes, significantly and disproportionately disadvantage Black Americans (Feagin and Bennefield 2014; Gengler and Jarrell 2015). For instance, research demonstrates that White clinicians hold negative implicit biases towards Black patients (Stepanikova 2012), which "can influence providers' beliefs about and expectations of patients, independent of other factors" (van Ryn et al. 2006, 497). At the same time, nearly three-quarters of Black Americans believe they encounter racial bias in clinical encounters to an extent or very often (Malat and Hamilton 2006). Second, a growing body of research examines how Black American's beliefs about racial bias when seeking medical treatment influences their mental health (Chae et al. 2011). Given the high "prevalence" of discrimination in medical settings among Black Americans, anticipatory stress may emerge in the coronavirus pandemic context. As some Black Americans and their family members contract coronavirus, interactions with healthcare providers and the healthcare system become inevitable. Consequentially, when Black Americans enter these medical settings, the stress of potential unfair treatment may induce psychological distress. Moreover, for Black Americans who perceive coronavirus as a threat to their health, discriminatory treatment could exacerbate distress levels.

The current study responds to ongoing calls to integrate CRT into mental health (Brown 2003; Assari and Habibzadeh 2020) by examining the interplay between perceived COVID-19 health threat, beliefs about racial discrimination in medical settings, and psychological distress among Black Americans. Though we are not the first to examine the interrelationships between stress exposure, beliefs about discrimination in medical settings, and mental health, there are critical differences between the present study and prior studies on this topic. First, this study relies on a within-group approach (e.g. differences in mental health among Black Americans based on psychosocial, demographic, and other factors) to illuminate the interplay between the perceived health threat of coronavirus outbreak, beliefs about discrimination in medical settings, and mental health among self-identified Black Americans (Whitfield et al. 2008). Second, we draw on a subsample of Black Americans from a nationally representative sample of adults, who were administered the survey shortly before and after the coronavirus occurred in the U.S. to examine these claims.

Based on prior research, we hypothesize that perceiving the COVID-19 outbreak as a threat to one's health and believing Black Americans receive inferior treatment in medical settings can be independently associated with higher psychological distress levels. Considering prior research, we tested whether there would be a significant interaction between the perceived COVID-19 health threat and beliefs about racial discrimination in medical settings. We also hypothesized that Black Americans who report that the coronavirus outbreak represented a threat to their health *and* who believe that Black Americans face worse treatment in medical settings than White Americans would be associated with higher psychological distress levels than Black Americans who do not.

Data

The data examined was derived from the Pew Research Center (PRC)'s American Trends Panel (ATP), a probability-based online survey panel of non-institutionalized adults above the age of 17 in the U.S. Internet users participated in the panel via monthly self-administered web surveys. PRC provided a tablet and internet access to respondents who lacked internet access [for more information regarding ATP, see Additional information on ATP's construction can be found here: https://www.pewresearch.org/methods/u-s-survey-research/

american-trends-panel/]. Though ATP is primarily a public opinion survey, recent innovations render this an ideal dataset to address the current research questions. First, in Wave 43 (January 22–February 5, 2019), the PRC asked panelists to provide detailed answers regarding their views of race relations in the U.S. Second, the ATP included a battery of questions regarding the coronavirus outbreak in Wave 64. The PRC fielded this wave of the ATP shortly after the nation shut down in response to the coronavirus outbreak (March 19–24, 2020). To our knowledge, this is the only nationally representative dataset that covers responses regarding a perceived COVID-19 health threat, beliefs about racial discrimination in medical settings, and mental health among Black Americans. The current study drew on responses from a subsample of self-identified Black Americans from the Wave 43 who also participated in Wave 64 (n = 747) and had no missing values of interest (n = 652).

Dependent variable

Psychological distress

Our outcome, psychological distress, is a summary score based on five questionnaire items in Wave 64 that the ATP adapted from the Center for Epidemiologic Studies Depression and the Generalized Anxiety Disorder scales. Specifically, the PRC asked ATP panelists how often, in the past seven days, they (1) felt nervous, anxious, or on edge; (2) felt depressed; (3) felt lonely; (4) had trouble sleeping; and (5) felt hopeful about the future. Original response items were placed on a scale that ranged from one ("rarely or none of the time") to five ("most of the time"). The positive valanced item "felt hopeful about the future") was reverse-coded and rescaled such that the responses ranged from zero ("rarely or none of the time") to four ("most of the time"). Following this, we summed the items to produce a psychological distress score reflecting increasing levels of psychological distress within the past seven days (possible range: 0–20; Cronbach's $a = 0.69$).

Independent variables

Perceived COVID-19 health threat

One of our focal predictors, perceived COVID-19 health threat, was derived from respondents' answer to the following question during Wave 64: "How much of a threat, if any, is the coronavirus outbreak for your personal health?" Responses included "a major threat" (1), "minor threat" (2), and "not a threat" (3).

Beliefs about discrimination in medical settings

Beliefs about racial discrimination in medical settings were assessed in Wave 43 by asking respondents: "In general, in our country these days, would you say that Black people are treated less fairly than [W]hite people, [W]hite people are treated less fairly than Black people, or both are treated about equally when seeking medical treatment." Given sample size issues, we created a dichotomous measure for this measure (1 = believe Black Americans are treated less fairly than Whites in medical settings, 0 = believe Black Americans are not treated less fairly than Whites in medical settings).

Control variables

Our study controlled for several factors included in Wave 43 that may influence the interplay between perceived COVID-19 health threat, beliefs about racial discrimination in medical settings, and psychological distress. Demographic factors include gender (1 = females, 0 = males), age (18–29 [base category], 30–49, 50–64, and 65 and above), and region of residence (Northeast, Midwest, South [reference group], and West). Economic indicators include degree attainment (high school graduate or less [reference group], some college, and college graduate), and household income ($75,000 and above, $30,000–$74,999, and less than $30,000 [reference group]). Our measure of politics includes party affiliation and political ideology. Party identification is a categorical variable that divides respondents into four groups (Democrat, Republican [reference group], Independent, and Something Else). At the same time, political ideology is an ordinal variable that ranges from "very conservative" (1) to "very liberal" (5).

Statistical analysis

Descriptive characteristics were summarized for the entire sample in Table 1. Given that our dependent variable is continuous, we used ordinary least squares regression. We presented the unstandardized beta coefficients, standard errors, and p-values obtained from these models in Table 2. To examine whether the possible relationship between perceived COVID-19 health threat and psychological distress varies according to beliefs about racial discrimination in medical settings, we also tested an interaction between perceived COVID-19 health threat and beliefs about racial discrimination in medical settings. Sampling weights and design factors were used to account for the survey's complex study design, and we conducted all analyses in STATA 16.

Findings

Table 1 provides summary statistics for respondents in our study. The mean psychological distress score, measured in Wave 64, was 5.04 (standard deviation = 3.39). Nearly half of respondents (48%) viewed the coronavirus outbreak as a "major threat" to their health. In comparison, 42% viewed the

Table 1. Sample characteristics, American trends panel ($N = 652$).

	M/%	S.D.	Min	Max
Psychological Distress[a]	5.05	3.39	0	15
Perceived COVID-19 health threat[b]				
A major threat	48%		0	1
A minor threat	42%		0	1
No threat at all	10%		0	1
Beliefs about Discrimination in Medical Settings [b]				
Black Americans face worse treatment in medical settings than White Americans	62%		0	1
Black Americans face the same or better treatment in medical settings than White Americans	38%		0	1
Controls				
Age Groupings [b]				
18–29	15%		0	1
30–49	40%		0	1
50–64	34%		0	1
65+	12%		0	1
Female [b]	62%		0	1
Region [b]				
Northeast	14%		0	1
Midwest	16%		0	1
South	61%		0	1
West	9%		0	1
Degree Attainment [b]				
College graduate+	29%		0	1
Some College	37%		0	1
H.S. graduate or less	34%		0	1
Annual Household Income [b]				
$75,000 or more	19%		0	1
$30,000–$74,999	36%		0	1
Less than $30,000	45%		0	1
Politics [b]				
Republican	5%		0	1
Democrat	67%		0	1
Independent	22%		0	1
Something Else	6%		0	1
Political Ideology	3.11	.86	1	5

[a]Measured in Wave 64.
[b]Measured in Wave 43.

coronavirus outbreak as "a minor threat," and the remaining 10% regarded the coronavirus outbreak as "no threat at all" when asked in Wave 64. Sixty-two percent of respondents believe Black Americans face worse treatment in medical settings than Whites. Fifteen percent of our sample were between the ages of 18–29, while 40% were between 30 and 49, 34% between 50 and 64, and the remaining 12% were aged 65 and above. Sixty-two percent of our respondents are women, and 38% of our sample are men. Sixty-one percent of our responded resided in the South during Wave 43 of the ATP. Twenty-nine percent of respondents reported having at least a college degree in Wave 43. In comparison, 37% of respondents had some college education level, and 34% of respondents reported having a high-school degree or less in Wave 43. Nearly half of our respondents (45%) had an annual household income of less than $30,000 when

Table 2. Unstandardized beta coefficients from linear regression models predicting psychological distress among Black Americans, American Trends Panel (N = 652).

	Model 1	Model 2
Perceived COVID-19 health threat (Ref: Not a threat)		
A major threat	1.61***	.24
	(.42)	(.68)
A minor threat	.37	−1.17
	(.40)	(.63)
Beliefs about Discrimination in Medical Settings (Ref: White Americans face equal or worse treatment)		
Black Americans face worse treatment in medical settings than Whites	.64*	−1.47*
	(.27)	(.72)
Age Groupings (Ref: Age 18-29)		
30–49	-.32	-.38
	(.40)	(.40)
50–64	-.79	-.89*
	(.41)	(.41)
65 and above	−1.83***	−2.01***
	(.48)	(.48)
Female	.34	.32
	(.28)	(.27)
Region (Ref: South)		
Northeast	.68	.69
	(.40)	(.39)
Midwest	.10	.06
	(.34)	(.34)
West	-.04	.02
	(.46)	(.47)
Degree Attainment (Ref: High School or less)		
College Graduate	−1.11**	−1.11**
	(.38)	(.37)
Some College	-.70	-.70
	(.38)	(.38)
Annual Household Income (Ref: $0-$29,999)		
$75,000 or more	-.94**	-.90*
	(.36)	(.36)
$30,000–$74,999	-.48	-.44
	(.32)	(.32)
Politics (Ref: Republican)		
Democrat	.58	.70
	(.59)	(.57)
Independent	.23	.29
	(.63)	(.61)
Something Else	.82	.94
	(.81)	(.79)
Political Ideology	-.23	-.22
	(.15)	(.15)
Interactions		
Major threat x Black Americans face worse treatment in medical settings than Whites		2.29**
		(.83)
Minor threat x Black Americans face the same or worse treatment in medical settings than Whites		2.51**
		(.79)
Constant	5.34***	6.52***
	(1.10)	(1.16)
R-squared	.14	.15

Standard errors in parentheses, *** $p < .001$, ** $p < .01$, * $p < .05$.

asked in Wave 43. Most respondents were Democrats, and the mean political ideology score was 2.90 (standard deviation: .86) when asked in Wave 43.

The association between our focal predictors and the dependent variable is shown in Table 2, and findings from the survey-weighted multivariate linear regression models indicated that perceived COVID-19 health threat and beliefs about racial discrimination in medical settings were significantly associated with psychological distress scores. Specifically, holding all else constant, results from Model 1 suggest that respondents who perceived COVID-19 as a major threat to their health (unstandardized beta = 1.61, p < .001) reported higher psychological distress levels relative respondents who did not perceive COVID-19 as not a threat to their personal health. Interestingly, individuals who perceived coronavirus as a minor threat did not differ from those who perceived no threat. Believing Black Americans face worse treatment when seeking medical treatment than Whites (unstandardized beta = .64, p < .05) was significantly associated with higher psychological distress levels.

In Model 2, we used interaction terms to test whether beliefs about racial discrimination in medical settings moderated the association between perceived COVID-19 health threat and psychological distress. Results from these interaction terms revealed a significant conditional relationship between perceived COVID-19 health threat, beliefs about racial discrimination in medical settings, and psychological distress. Specifically, psychological distress levels were higher for respondents who reported that the COVID-19 outbreak represented a major (unstandardized beta = 2.29, p < .01) or minor threat (unstandardized beta = 2.51, p < .001) to their health *and* believed that Black Americans were treated poorly than Whites when seeking medical treatment relative to those who did not.

Figure 1 provides a visual depiction of the statistical interactions. Respondents who reported coronavirus as a major threat and believed in

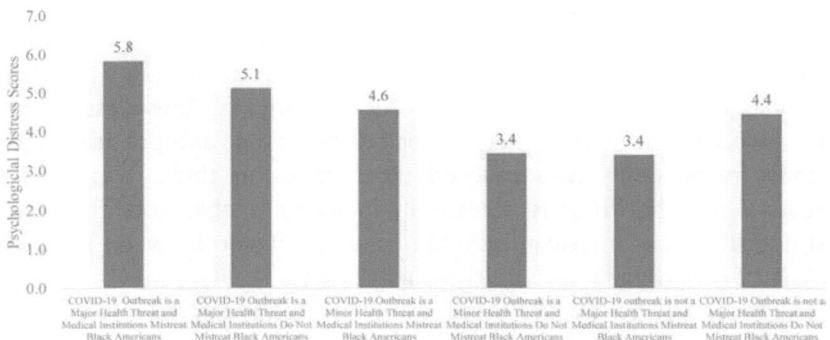

Figure 1. Psychological distress by perceived COVID-19 health threat and beliefs about discrimination in medical settings.

discrimination against Black Americans in medical settings experienced the highest distress (Mean: 5.8) followed by the major threat and no discrimination in medical settings respondents (Mean: 5.1). Furthermore, 30% of respondents perceived both a major coronavirus threat and discrimination against Black Americans in medical settings. Therefore, it is clear that a substantial proportion of Black Americans are distressed by the ongoing coronavirus threat combined with anticipatory stress of unfair treatment in the healthcare system.

Discussion

A long tradition of research has shown that perceived threats and beliefs about discrimination in medical settings are risk factors for poorer mental health among Black Americans (Pearlin 1999). Though important, we are unaware of previous research examining the interplay between perceived COVID-19 health threat, discrimination in medical settings, and psychological distress among Black Americans (Chowkwanyun and Reed 2020). This empirical void is curious, given the disproportionate impact of the coronavirus outbreak on Black Americans (Yancy 2020). Moreover, this absence in the literature persists despite ongoing evidence that issues related to the coronavirus outbreak will remain a critical social problem among Black Americans for some time to come (Webb Hooper et al. 2020). To address this gap, we drew on a subsample of Black Americans from a probability-based online survey panel representative of the U.S. adult population to assess the interplay between perceived COVID-19 health threat, beliefs about discrimination in medical settings, and psychological distress. Our findings suggest that perceiving the coronavirus outbreak as a major threat to one's health and beliefs about racial bias in medical settings are associated with increased psychological distress among Black Americans.

Our primary goal was to shed light on the mental health-related consequences of perceived COVID-19 health threat among Black Americans. Consistent with prior research, we observed that perceiving the coronavirus as a major (but not minor) threat to one's health was associated with higher psychological distress levels among Black Americans. These associations were independent of differences in sociodemographic and political factors. Because respondents who believed the coronavirus threat was a minor threat to their health were statistically indistinguishable from those who did not, there was a clear threshold in the association between perceived COVID-19 health threat and psychological distress.

Our secondary goal was to examine how beliefs about racial discrimination in medical settings relate to psychological distress among Black Americans and assess whether these beliefs about discrimination exacerbated the relationship between perceived COVID-19 health threat and psychological distress. Findings revealed that Black Americans who perceived the corona-virus outbreak as a significant threat to their health *and* believed in discrimi-nation in medical settings are especially at risk for elevated distress levels. Furthermore, even respondents who only perceived the coronavirus out-break as a minor threat experienced heightened distress if they also believed that Black Americans receive poorer service in medical settings. The aware-ness of discrimination in medical settings, combined with perceived COVID-19 health threat, are sources of compounded distress. Though our measures are perceptual, they are rooted in empirical realities; perhaps, more importantly, these beliefs have psychological ramifications.(Egede and Walker 2020) Black Americans must navigate the contemporary sociopo-litical context marked by a pandemic, racial unrest, and ongoing racial dispar-ities in health and healthcare. These compounded co-occurring stressors, in turn, appear to impose a greater psychological tax on Black Americans than if only one of these stressors were operant.

Scholars of racial health disparities have not systematically examined the interplay between perceived COVID-19 health threat, beliefs about discrimi-nation in medical settings, and mental health among Black Americans.(Khazan-chi, Evans, and Marcelin 2020) Thus, knowledge on the mechanisms that might explain our observed interrelationships examined in this study is lacking. Laster Pirtle (2020) argues that neighbourhood conditions (e.g. census-based or self-assessed measures of neighbourhood characteristics) play an essential role in shaping health disparities during the coronavirus outbreak. Prior research has uncovered links between poorer neighbourhood contexts and perceived threats, beliefs about discrimination, and mental health among Blacks Ameri-cans. Therefore, neighbourhood contexts may be a potential mechanism through which perceived COVID-19 health threat and beliefs about racial dis-crimination in medical settings might have influenced psychological distress levels among Black Americans. Research also suggests that older Black Ameri-cans are disproportionally are most affected by COVID-19 stressors, morbidity, and mortality (Chatters, Taylor, and Taylor 2020). Therefore, future work should examine how the interplay between perceived COVID-19 health threat, beliefs about discrimination, and health among older Blacks.

We acknowledge there are dimensions of the current study that warrant comment. Given that the PRC has not consistently included psychological dis-tress measures in panel data, we cannot make inferences about causality between our variables of interest or assess whether these relationships vary over time. Our measures of psychological distress are derived from estab-lished, well-validated measures. However, the PRC adjusted the response options in these measures to the past week, which limited our ability to capture the highly dynamic course of the coronavirus outbreak. Nevertheless, this study has some important strengths. We rely on data from a nationally representative sample of adults that contains both a measure of perceived

COVID-19 health threat, beliefs about racial discrimination in medical settings, and psychological distress. Though limited, the measure of psychological distress used in this study suggests it has sufficient internal reliability. To
date, we are not aware of any nationally representative dataset with a
sufficient number of Black Americans, nor a rich set of psychosocial and attitudinal measurements that were also administered before and shortly after
the coronavirus outbreak.

The coronavirus outbreak represents a significant social problem in the
United States and will usher in many health challenges facing Black Americans. This examination spotlighted the importance of the perceived threats
and beliefs about discrimination in shaping Black Americans' psychological
distress levels.(Novacek et al. 2020; Poteat et al. 2020) Moreover, our
findings highlight the need to create policy-based interventions that offset
this outbreak's health-related consequences and severely affect Black Americans' quality of life.

Disclosure statement

No potential conflict of interest was reported by the author(s).

ORCID

Ryon J. Cobb ⓘ http://orcid.org/0000-0002-1775-4621
Christy L. Erving ⓘ http://orcid.org/0000-0001-5619-5482
W. Carson Byrd ⓘ http://orcid.org/0000-0003-0769-0983

References

Assari, S., and P. Habibzadeh. 2020. "The COVID-19 Emergency Response Should
    Include a Mental Health Component." *Archives of Iranian Medicine* 23 (4): 281–
    282. doi:10.34172/aim.2020.12.
Brown, T. N. 2003. "Critical Race Theory Speaks to the Sociology of Mental Health:
    Mental Health Problems Produced by Racial Stratification." *Journal of Health and
    Social Behavior* 44 (3): 292. doi:10.2307/1519780.
CDC COVID Data Tracker. n.d. Retrieved December 12, 2020, from https://covid.cdc.
    gov/covid-data-tracker/#cases_casesper100klast7days.
Chae, D. H., A. M. Nuru-Jeter, K. D. Lincoln, and D. D. Francis. 2011. "Conceptualizing
    Racial Disparities in Health: Advancement of a Socio-Psychobiological Approach."
    Du Bois Review: Social Science Research on Race 8 (1): 63–77. doi:10.1017/
    S1742058X11000166.
Chatters, L. M., H. O. Taylor, and R. J. Taylor. 2020. "Older Black Americans During
    COVID-19: Race and Age Double Jeopardy." *Health Education & Behavior* 47 (6):
    855–860. doi:10.1177/1090198120965513.
Chowkwanyun, M., and A. L. Reed. 2020. "Racial Health Disparities and Covid-19:
    Caution and Context." *New England Journal of Medicine* 383 (3): 201–203. doi:10.
    1056/NEJMp2012910.

Conway, L. G., S. R. Woodard, and A. Zubrod. 2020. *Social Psychological Measurements of COVID-19: Coronavirus Perceived Threat, Government Response, Impacts, and Experiences Questionnaires* [Preprint]. PsyArXiv. doi:10.31234/osf.io/z2x9a.

Egede, L. E., and R. J. Walker. 2020. "Structural Racism, Social Risk Factors, and Covid-19: A Dangerous Convergence for Black Americans." *New England Journal of Medicine* 383 (12): e77. doi:10.1056/NEJMp2023616.

Feagin, J., and Z. Bennefield. 2014. "Systemic Racism and U.S. Health Care." *Social Science & Medicine* 103: 7–14. doi:10.1016/j.socscimed.2013.09.006.

Gengler, A. M., and M. V. Jarrell. 2015. "What Difference Does Difference Make? The Persistence of Inequalities in Healthcare Delivery: The Persistence of Inequalities in Healthcare Delivery." *Sociology Compass* 9 (8): 718–730. doi:10.1111/soc4.12286.

Jackson, J. S., D. Hudson, K. Kershaw, B. Mezuk, J. Rafferty, and K. K. Tuttle. 2011. "Discrimination, Chronic Stress, and Mortality Among Black Americans: A Life Course Framework." In *International Handbook of Adult Mortality*, 311–328. Dordrecht: Springer. doi:10.1007/978-90-481-9996-9_15

Khazanchi, R., C. T. Evans, and J. R. Marcelin. 2020. "Racism, Not Race, Drives Inequity Across the COVID-19 Continuum." *JAMA Network Open* 3 (9): e2019933. doi:10.1001/jamanetworkopen.2020.19933.

Kramer, A., and K. Z. Kramer. 2020. "The Potential Impact of the COVID-19 Pandemic on Occupational Status, Work from Home, and Occupational Mobility." *Journal of Vocational Behavior* 119. doi:10.1016/j.jvb.2020.103442.

Laster Pirtle, W. N. 2020. "Racial Capitalism: A Fundamental Cause of Novel Coronavirus (COVID-19) Pandemic Inequities in the United States." *Health Education & Behavior* 47 (4): 504–508. doi:10.1177/1090198120922942.

Malat, J., and M. A. Hamilton. 2006. "Preference for Same-Race Health Care Providers and Perceptions of Interpersonal Discrimination in Health Care." *Journal of Health and Social Behavior* 47 (2): 173–187. doi:10.1177/002214650604700206.

Novacek, D. M., J. N. Hampton-Anderson, M. T. Ebor, T. B. Loeb, and G. E. Wyatt. 2020. "Mental Health Ramifications of the COVID-19 Pandemic for Black Americans: Clinical and Research Recommendations." *Psychological Trauma: Theory, Research, Practice, and Policy* 12 (5): 449–451. doi:10.1037/tra0000796.

Pearlin, L. I. 1999. "The Stress Process Revisited." In *Handbook of the Sociology of Mental Health*, edited by C. S. Aneshensel, J. C. Phelan, and A. Bierman, 395–415. Dordrecht, Netherlands: Springer.

Pew Research Center. 2020. *U.S. Public Sees Multiple Threats From the Coronavirus - and Concerns are Growing.* Washington, D.C: Pew Research Center.

Poteat, T., G. A. Millett, L. E. Nelson, and C. Beyrer. 2020. "Understanding COVID-19 Risks and Vulnerabilities among Black Communities in America: The Lethal Force of Syndemics." *Annals of Epidemiology* 47: 1–3. doi:10.1016/j.annepidem.2020.05.004.

Stepanikova, I. 2012. "Racial-Ethnic Biases, Time Pressure, and Medical Decisions." *Journal of Health and Social Behavior* 53 (3): 329–343. doi:10.1177/0022146512445807.

van Ryn, M., D. Burgess, J. Malat, and J. Griffin. 2006. "Physicians' Perceptions of Patients' Social and Behavioral Characteristics and Race Disparities in Treatment Recommendations for Men With Coronary Artery Disease." *American Journal of Public Health* 96 (2): 351–357. doi:10.2105/AJPH.2004.041806.

Whitfield, K. E., J. C. Allaire, R. Belue, and C. L. Edwards. 2008. "Are Comparisons the Answer to Understanding Behavioral Aspects of Aging in Racial and Ethnic

Groups?" *The Journals of Gerontology Series B: Psychological Sciences and Social Sciences* 63 (5): P301–P308. doi:10.1093/geronb/63.5.P301.

Webb Hooper, M., A. M. Napoles, & E. J. Perez-Stable. 2020. "COVID-19 and Racial/Ethnic Disparities." *JAMA* 323 (24): 2466–2467. doi: 10.1001/jama.2020.8598.

Yancy, C. W. 2020. "COVID-19 and African Americans." *JAMA* 323 (19): 1891. doi:10.1001/jama.2020.6548.

Anti-Asian discrimination and the Asian-white mental health gap during COVID-19

Cary Wu ⓘ, Yue Qian ⓘ and Rima Wilkes ⓘ

ABSTRACT
In this article, we consider how, due to a spike in anti-Asian hate crimes, Asians might face a disproportionate mental health impact of the COVID-19 pandemic. Analyzing data from the University of Southern California's Center for Economic and Social Research Understanding Coronavirus in America survey, we report several findings. First, since the onset of the pandemic, Asians (Asian Americans in particular) have experienced higher levels of mental disorders than whites. Second, Asian Americans and Asian immigrants are about twice as likely as whites to report having encountered instances of COVID-19-related acute discrimination. Third, experiences of COVID-19-related discrimination increase mental disorders for all Americans. Finally, COVID-19-related discrimination partially explains the disproportionate mental health impact of the pandemic on Asians. In conclusion, we highlight the importance of tackling hate, violence, and discrimination so as to address the disproportionate mental health impacts of COVID-19 on minority populations.

Introduction

On 19 March 2020, Asian American and Pacific Islander (AAPI) Civil Rights Organizations launched the STOP AAPI HATE project to track incidents of anti-Asian violence and discrimination during COVID-19. Since its inception, the STOP AAPI HATE reporting centre has received over 2,500 reports of coronavirus hate events from Asian Americans across the United States. A majority of respondents believed that they were targeted because of their race.[1] This race-based targeting has occurred despite the fact that, prior to the pandemic, Asians reported low levels of harassment, threats, and insults.[2]

Asian Americans also reported fewer mental health conditions than their white American counterparts prior to the pandemic (Asnaani et al. 2010).

Encountering instances of acute discrimination may well impact Asians' mental health (Lee and Ahn 2011). Indeed, racism is a central societal force that adversely affects the health of racial and ethnic minority populations (Williams and Mohammed 2013). In particular, a large body of research has shown that experiences and perceptions of racial discrimination have deleterious mental health consequences (Noh et al. 1999; Harrell 2000; Meyer 2003; Carter 2007; Gee et al. 2007; Beiser and Hou 2016; Ong et al. 2017). For example, focusing on Asian American and Latino college students, Hwang and Goto (2008) find that perceived racial discrimination is associated with higher psychological distress, suicidal ideation, anxiety, and depression (see also Gee et al. 2007). Gee et al. (2009) review a total of 62 empirical studies that consider the relationship between discrimination and health among Asian Americans. Most studies in their review show that discrimination is associated with poorer health, and that there is a significant impact of discrimination on mental health problems.

Recently, we have conducted a nationally representative survey studying the social impacts of the COVID-19 pandemic on Canadians (Kennedy et al. 2020). Analyzing the data, we find that higher incidences of acute discrimination encountered by East Asian Canadians during the COVID-19 pandemic explain their higher levels of mental health symptoms as compared to white Canadians (Wu et al. 2020). In this study, we investigate whether Asians in the United States have experienced more mental health symptoms than whites during the COVID-19 pandemic and if so, whether the instances of acute discrimination they have encountered help to explain this disproportionate mental health impact of the COVID-19 pandemic. We focus on Asians because research suggests that the rise in the animosity is directed at Asians rather than other minority groups (Lu and Sheng 2020) and that Asians are more likely than other racial or ethnic groups to perceive COVID-19-related discrimination (Liu et al. 2020). While several studies have already considered the effect of anti-Asian racism on mental health among the targeted populations (e.g. Cheah et al. 2020; Liu et al. 2020; Ma and Zhan 2020; Zhai and Du 2020; Wu et al. 2020), we seek to advance the current knowledge in two major ways.

First, we pay particular attention to the difference between US-born Asians (i.e. Asian Americans) and foreign-born Asians (i.e. Asian immigrants). There are a number of reasons to expect that immigrants might have better health including selection effects, previous experience with managing challenges, and a lack of socialization into a context of racialization (Güngör and Perdu 2017; Feliciano 2020). Thus, during the COVID-19 pandemic, Asian Americans and Asian immigrants may have fared differently in the face of rising racist attacks. In doing so, this study will provide evidence for the need of group-specific mental health interventions and support in response to the COVID-19 pandemic (Wu et al. 2020; Xiang et al. 2020).

Second, we use temporal analysis and panel data analysis to better establish causality between COVID-19-related discrimination and mental health. We use data from the ongoing *Understanding Coronavirus in America* survey conducted by the University of Southern California's Center for Economic and Social Research. Not only is the dataset large, it is also a longitudinal panel in structure. The sample we analyze includes 68,218 data points that track 7,778 individuals over 13 survey waves from March to September (including 5,958 whites, 244 US-born Asians, and 300 foreign-born Asians). Given that temporality is central to causal inference (Grzymala-Busse 2011), the dataset allows to consider how acute discrimination interacts with time to shape mental health among Asian Americans, Asian immigrants, and whites. This temporal analysis allows us to assess whether changes in COVID-19-related discrimination are associated with changes in mental health among Asians and whites. Because of the panel design of the data, we are also able to use fixed and random effects models to estimate both within- and between-individual changes. Therefore, this study provides a strong causal test of whether COVID-19-related discrimination leads to poorer mental health.

Background

The rise of Anti-Asian hate in the Wake of COVID-19

Asians have increasingly been discriminated against and become the targets of racism attacks since the onset of the COVID-19 pandemic. In March, a national online survey of 1,141 US residents showed that more than 40% of Americans reported that they had engaged in at least one discriminatory behaviour toward people of Asian descent (Dhanani and Franz 2020). Based on a survey of Chinese American parents and their children conducted between March 2020 and May 2020, Cheah et al. (2020) found that nearly half of the parents and youth reported being directly targeted by COVID-19-related racial discrimination online. In June, the Pew Research Center (2020) surveyed 9,654 US adults and found that, since the start of the coronavirus outbreak, 31% of Asians had been subject to slurs or jokes because of their race/ethnicity, compared to 21% for Blacks, 15% for Hispanics, and 8% for whites. In addition, 26% of Asian Americans said that they feared someone might threaten or physically attack them. Moreover, the survey found that more than 40% of US adults agreed that "it has become more common for people to express racist views toward Asians".

Factors that lead to the rise of anti-Asian racism include not only fear and uncertainty inherent to novel infectious disease (Noel 2020), the presumptive origin of COVID-19 (Cheng 2020), and misleading media coverage (Darling-Hammond et al. 2020; Wen et al. 2020) but also, more importantly, the historical antecedents that link Asian Americans to infectious diseases and the long-standing stereotype that characterizes Asian Americans as "perpetual foreigners" (Cheah et al. 2020; Litam 2020; Man 2020; Mamuji et al. 2020; Tessler, Choi, and Kao 2020). Indeed, people of Asian descent have experienced both verbal and physical violence motivated by racism and xenophobia from the time they arrived in America in the late 1700s up until the present day (Gover et al. 2020). Therefore, as Chen, Trinh, and Yang (2020, 556) put it, "In the midst of the COVID-19 pandemic we see not only a rise in anti-Asian sentiment, but also a recapitulation of history".

Minority stress theory

To explain how racism and discrimination adversely affect the mental health of those who have this experience, scholars draw on minority stress theory (Harrell 2000; Meyer 2003; Carter 2007). Minority stress theory was first developed and mainly used to understand mental health conditions of sexual minorities such as lesbians and gays (e.g. Meyer 1995; Szymanski and Sung 2010). This theory posits that stigma, prejudice, and discrimination often create "a hostile and stressful social environment" and that excess in social stressors explains the higher prevalence of mental disorders among minority populations (Meyer 2003, 674; Harrell 2000).

Minority stress theory is increasingly applied in studies of how racism and discrimination affect mental health of ethnic and racial minorities (e.g. Wei et al. 2008). In this line of research, Carter (2007) has used a new term, race-based traumatic stress, to specifically explain how targets of racism can be harmed psychologically by stress and trauma. At length, Carter (2007) explains that acute stress disorder and post-traumatic stress disorder can arise from the events or danger related to real or perceived racial discrimination, including threats of harm and injury, humiliating and shameful events, and witnessing harm to other minorities or people of colour. Furthermore, everyday experiences of racial discrimination often lead to a chronic state of "racial battle fatigue" that taxes the mental and emotional resources of targeted populations (Smith et al. 201: 64). Consistent with this body of theoretical work, empirical studies that focus on Asians in North America have demonstrated that both real and perceived discrimination are a unique source of stress that leads to mental disorders above and beyond general stress (e.g. Dion, Dion, and Pak 1992; Wei et al. 2010).

Anti-Asian racism and mental health among Asians

Several studies have specifically looked into the rise of anti-Asian racism and how it might affect mental health among the targeted populations. For example, drawing on a survey conducted between March and May, Cheah et al. (2020) found that being the direct target of racial discrimination, both in-person and online, and perceptions of Sinophobia were associated with poorer psychological well-being for Chinese American parents and their children. Through increased stress, parents' own racial victimization experiences also impacted their children's mental health (Cheah et al. 2020). In addition, using data from the first few waves of the *Understanding Coronavirus in America* survey, scholars show that the increased perception of COVID-19-associated discrimination has led to increased mental distress among Asians (Liu et al. 2020).

Other studies have considered more specific groups such as Chinese overseas students (Ma 2020; Ma and Miller 2020) and ethnic Chinese travellers (Zheng, Goh, and Wen 2020). These studies largely conclude that experiencing or witnessing anti-Asian racism has deleterious mental health impacts. For example, Zhai and Du (2020) point out that, since the pandemic began, not only have international Chinese students been living with the fear that their families in China are at risk of contracting COVID-19, they also have to face discrimination, endure isolation, and experience or witness hate crimes. Fear and negative experiences likely cause mental health problems for Chinese international students (Zhai and Du 2020; see also Ma and Miller 2020).

When explaining the association between COVID-19-associated discrimination and mental health, scholars have also drawn on minority stress theory or race-based traumatic stress theory. Litam (2020) points out that Asians' ongoing experiences of microaggressions and racial discrimination during the pandemic contribute to not only the presence of race-related stress but also race-based trauma. Additionally, experiences of racial discrimination can threaten individuals' identity and sense of control, thereby leading to hopelessness and the internalization of negative attitudes (Cheah et al. 2020). Race-based stress and racial trauma in turn have deleterious effects on mental health (Cheah et al. 2020; Cheng 2020; Hu, Wang, and Lu 2020).

Data and methods

The data come from the University of Southern California's Center for Economic and Social Research *"Understanding Coronavirus in America"* tracking survey. Survey respondents are members of their Understanding America Study (UAS), which is a nationally representative Internet panel of American households that includes approximately 8,500 individuals aged 18 and older. Specifics about the survey design and methodology are available online (https://covid19pulse.usc.edu/). Note that data collection through the UAS Internet surveys matches that in high-quality traditional surveys (Angrisani, Finley, and Kapteyn 2019).

The ongoing *Understanding Coronavirus in America* survey tracks both attitudes and behaviours related to the COVID-19 pandemic. On 10 March 2020, all UAS panel members were invited to participate in the first wave of the

Understanding Coronavirus in America survey. The first wave of the survey stayed in the field through March 31 (Wave 1, 10 March to 31 March 2020). Starting from April 1, a new survey has been fielded every two weeks where one fourteenth of the panel members are invited to take the survey on a pre-assigned day of the two weeks. The total field period is four weeks because respondents have two weeks to answer the survey. By the end of September 2020, thirteen waves of data have been collected. We use data from all 13 waves collected from 10 March to 30 September 2020. The final sample we analyze includes 68,218 data points, tracking 7,778 individuals over 13 survey waves from March to September.

In this research, we focus on three groups: whites, Asian Americans (US-born), and Asian immigrants (foreign-born). We define whites as respondents who self-identified as white only. Among those who self-identified as Asian, we make the distinction between those who were born in the US, and those who were born outside the US. Of the 7,778 respondents in our analysis, 5,958 were non-Hispanic whites, 244 were US-born Asians, and 300 were foreign-born Asians. Because we find no significant gap in mental health between US-born and foreign-born whites, we combine them as one single group in the analysis.

The survey includes the four-item Patient Health Questionnaire (PHQ-4), a widely-used measure of anxiety and depression (Löwe et al. 2004). The PHQ-4 index ranges from 0 to 12 representing the combined responses to four questions: *"over the last two weeks, how often the respondent had been bothered by (1) feeling nervous, anxious or on edge, (2) not being able to stop or control worrying, (3) feeling down, depressed or hopeless, and (4) little interest or pleasure in doing things"* (see also Riehm et al. 2020, 631). The responses range from *0 = not at all, 1 = several days, 2 = more than half the days,* to *3 = nearly every day.* Higher scores indicate a greater prevalence of mental health issues.

The survey also asks whether, during the past two weeks, the respondent was treated with less courtesy and respect due to others thinking they had COVID-19, received poorer service due to others thinking they had COVID-19, was threatened or harassed due to others thinking they had COVID-19, and was the subject of other people's fear due to others thinking they had COVID-19. All four items were answered on a 3-point scale (0 = no, 1 = unsure, 2 = yes). We combine these items to create an acute discrimination scale ranging from 0 to 8, with higher scores indicating more encounters of acute discrimination (Williams et al. 1997; Wu et al. 2020). As all the items are specifically related to COVID-19, we use the combined scale to indicate COVID-19-associated discrimination. We also note here that these items were not asked in Waves 7 and 9; therefore, data from these two waves were not included in some of our analyses.

Our analysis also includes controls such as a continuous measure of educational level (1-16), a continuous measure of household income level (1-16), gender (0 = male, 1 = female), age, and dummies indicating the month when the wave of survey was carried out. Table 1 provides the descriptive statistics of key variables in our analysis.

Our estimation takes two steps. First, taking advantage of the panel structure of the survey, we use a fixed-effects model to estimate how experiencing COVID-19-related discrimination affects mental health. Fixed-effects models remove the effect of time-invariant characteristics (e.g. race, gender, place of birth) and thus, estimate the effect of acute discrimination on mental health that is unbiased by person-level unobserved heterogeneity (Torres-Reyna 2007). The use of a fixed-effects model is further supported by the Hausman test (Chi^2 = 461.95, $p < 0.000$). The fixed-effects model helps establish whether experiencing COVID-19-related discrimination *causally* affects mental health.

Second, we use random-effects models to investigate to what extent differences in encounters of COVID-19-related discrimination explain the mental health gap between Asians and whites. We use the random-effects models for this purpose for two reasons. First, Asian-white categories are time-invariant. Second, we believe that differences in socioeconomic status, cultural backgrounds, and life experiences across Asian Americans, Asian immigrants, and whites may also have a major influence on the mental health gaps between these groups.

Findings

To begin with, Figure 1(A) compares the mental disorders across whites, Asian Americans (US-born), and Asian immigrants (foreign-born). Overall, whites had a depression and anxiety score of 1.98 [95% CI, 1.95–2.00], Asian Americans had a score of 2.96 [95% CI, 2.82–3.11], and Asian immigrants had a score of 2.16 [95% CI, 2.05–2.28]. These numbers show that the mental health gap between Asian Americans and whites (gap = 0.98, $p < 0.000$) is greater than the gap between Asian immigrants and whites (gap = 0.18, $p < 0.000$). When we compare people who reported no mental health symptoms at all (PHQ-4 score = 0), we find that 47% of whites had no mental

Table 1. Descriptive statistics of key variables in the analysis, calculated at the person-wave level.

Variable	Whites (n = 53,051)		Asian Americans (n = 2,006)		Asian immigrants (n = 2,534)	
	Mean	Std. Dev.	Mean	Std. Dev.	Mean	Std. Dev.
Mental disorders (PHQ-4, 0-12)	1.98	2.80	2.96	3.36	2.16	2.92
Acute discrimination (0-8)	0.31	1.04	0.75	1.69	0.68	1.57
Household income (level, 1-16)	11.70	3.87	11.83	4.35	11.42	4.53
Education (level, 1-16)	11.38	2.25	12.36	1.99	12.52	2.36
Female (0 = male, 1 = female)	0.57	0.49	0.54	0.50	0.58	0.49
Age (in years, 18-110)	52.27	16.00	40.42	14.77	45.87	15.46

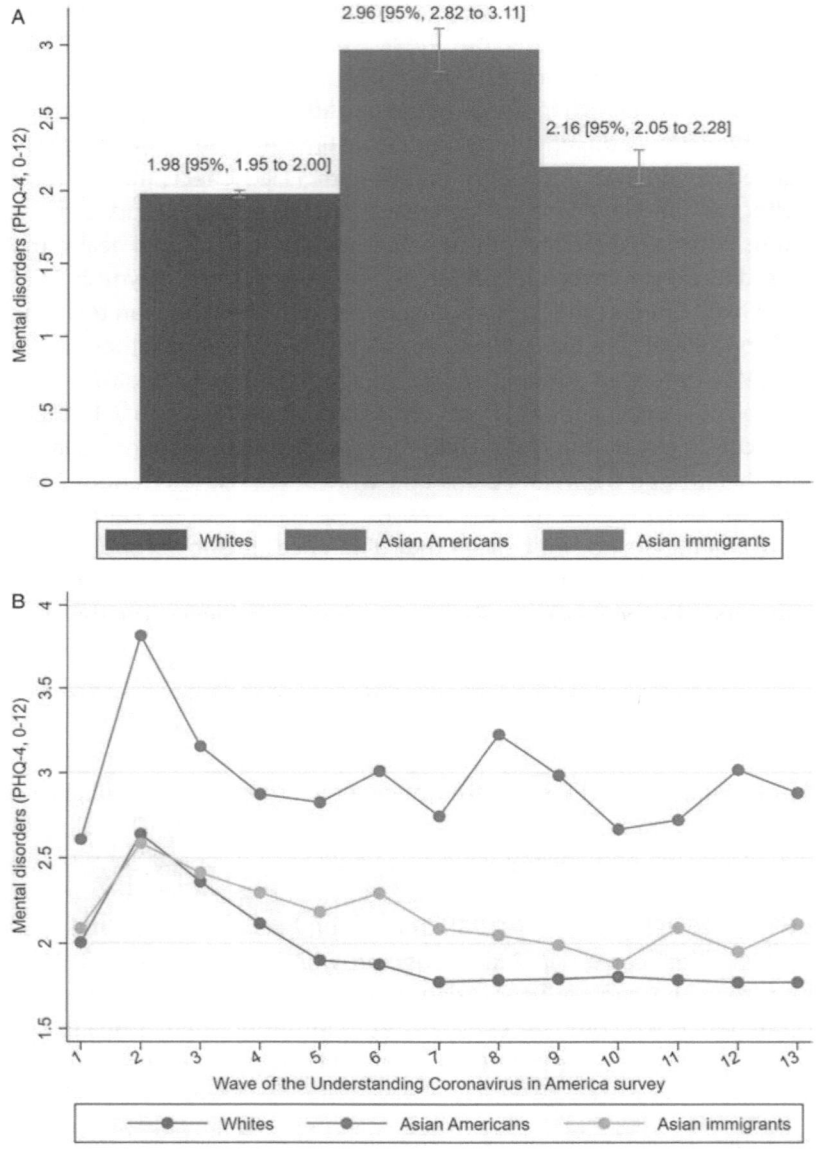

Figure 1. (A) Comparing mental disorders across whites, Asian Americans, and Asian immigrants; (B) Temporal changes in mental disorders across whites, Asian Americans, and Asian immigrants.

health symptoms, whereas the respective figures were 33% for Asian Americans and 46% for Asian immigrants. Taken together, the results show that while the mental health gap between Asian Americans and whites is substantial, the gap between Asian immigrants and whites is small.

Figure 1(B) shows the temporal changes in mental disorders across the three groups from March to September (Waves 1-13; Wave 1 in March and thereafter, two waves in each month). It reveals several findings. First, the level of mental disorders is highest in April (Wave 2) for all three groups, suggesting that the COVID-19 pandemic has affected the mental health of all Americans. Indeed, across all three groups, we see an "n"-shaped pattern in changes of their mental disorders before, during, and after April. Second, Asian Americans were hit harder than both whites and Asian immigrants. We see a significant gap in mental health between Asian Americans and whites regardless of months or waves of the data. In terms of the mental health gap between Asian immigrants and whites, it was small in the early stages of the pandemic (Waves 1-3) but became greater after April (Waves 4-13).

Next, we consider whether experiences of acute discrimination differed between whites, Asian Americans, and Asian immigrants. Figure 2(A) shows that, overall, whites had a mean discrimination score of 0.31 [95% CI, 0.30–0.32], Asian Americans had a mean score of 0.75 [95% CI, 0.68–0.82], and Asian immigrants had a mean score of 0.68 [95% CI, 0.62–0.74]. When we recode acute discrimination into a binary measure, we find that 11% of whites, 22% of Asian Americans, and 21% of Asian immigrants reported having encountered instances of COVID-19-related acute discrimination.

Figure 2(B) shows the temporal changes in experiences of acute discrimination across whites, Asian Americans, and Asian immigrants. Both Asian Americans and Asian immigrants reported significantly more instances of acute discrimination than whites, regardless of survey waves. Overall, Asian immigrants and Asian Americans reported a similar level of discrimination. Still, we see that the relative gap between these two groups has been inconsistent. For example, while Asian immigrants reported a slightly higher level of discrimination than Asian Americans in March (Wave 1, the gap is not significant), this changed in April and early May (Waves 2-4), with Asian Americans reporting significantly higher levels of discrimination than Asian immigrants.

These temporal analyses suggest that Asians face a disproportionate mental health impact of the COVID-19 pandemic (Figure 1(B), see also Figure A1 in Appendix), and the higher instances of COVID-19-related acute discrimination Asians expereinced especially during April might explain the disproportionate mental health impact on them (Figure 2(B), see also Figure A2 in Appendix). To test these arguments, we consider the extent to which experiences of acute discrimination during the pandemic explain the mental health gaps between whites and Asian Americans/immigrants.

To do so, we first consider whether COVID-19-associated discrimination contributes to mental disorders. Table 2 presents the results of our fixed-

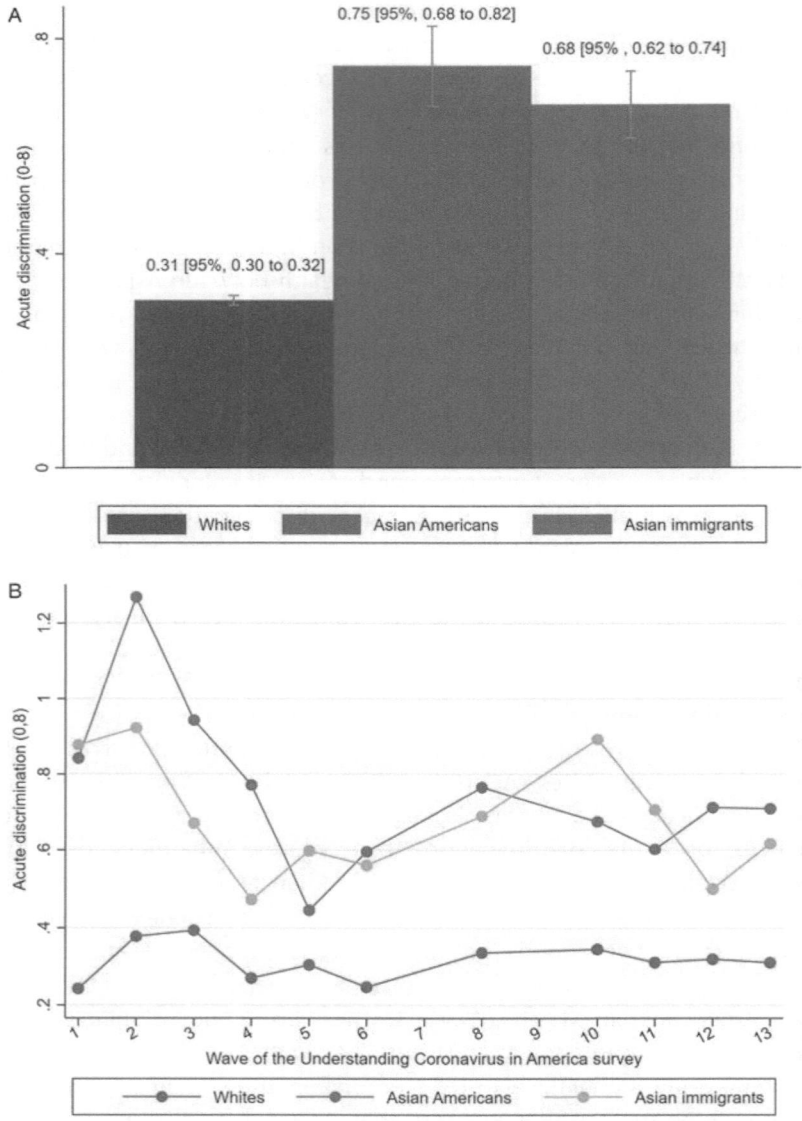

Figure 2. (A) Comparing acute discrimination across whites, Asian Americans, and Asian immigrants; (B) Temporal changes in acute discrimination across whites, Asian Americans, and Asian immigrants.

effects model (Model 1). It shows that a one-unit within-person increase in acute discrimination leads to a within-person increase in mental disorders by 0.066 units ($p < 0.001$). The significant effect demonstrates that experiencing acute discrimination causally leads to increased mental disorders among all Americans.

Table 2. Fixed-effects model estimating the effect of COVID-19-related discrimination on mental disorders.

	Model (1) Mental disorders (PHQ-4)
Acute discrimination	0.066***
	[0.052, 0.08]
Constant	1.975***
	[1.96, 1.99]
Residuals	
sigma_u	2.447
sigma_e	1.595
Rho	0.701
N (persons)	7,778
N (person_wave observations)	68,218
95% confidence intervals in brackets	

* $p < 0.05$, ** $p < 0.01$, *** $p < 0.001$.

Next, we examine mental health gaps between whites and Asians and consider to what extent COVID-19-related discrimination accounts for these gaps. Table 3 reports the results from random-effects models. Model (2) shows that, after controlling for demographics including age, gender, education, and household income as well as the survey month, Asian Americans experienced 0.569-unit [95% CI, 0.267–0.872] higher anxiety and depression than whites, whereas Asian immigrants experienced 0.012-unit [95% CI, −0.284–0.259] lower anxiety and depression than whites despite the gap not being statistically significant.

Model (3) shows that acute discrimination has a strong and significant impact on mental health: every one-unit increase in acute discrimination is associated with a 0.09-unit [95% CI, 0.075–0.105] increase in anxiety and depression. Model (3) also shows that, after taking acute discrimination into account, the mental health gap between Asian Americans and whites decreases from 0.569 to 0.538, suggesting that acute discrimination explains about 5% of the mental health gap between whites and Asian Americans. Furthermore, Model (3) shows that the magnitude of the mental health gap between whites and Asian immigrants increases from 0.012 to 0.044 after controlling for acute discrimination. This is to suggest that, in the absence of the higher instances of acute discrimination encountered by Asian immigrants as compared to whites (0.68 vs. 0.31), Asian immigrants would have had even lower relative levels of depression and anxiety than whites. Nevertheless, we interpret findings regarding the mental health gap between Asian immigrants and whites with caution, as neither coefficients (−0.012 in Model 2; −0.044 in Model 3) were significant.

Conclusion

Fear, stress, and depression are common experiences during public health crises. While the COVID-19 pandemic has led to widespread mental health

Table 3. Random-effects models estimating Asian-white mental health gaps and the explanatory effect of acute discrimination encountered during the COVID-19 pandemic.

	Model (2) Mental disorders (PHQ-4)	Model (3) Mental disorders (PHQ-4)
Asian-white mental health gaps (ref. whites)		
Asian Americans	0.569***	0.538***
	[0.27, 0.87]	[0.24, 0.84]
Asian immigrants	−0.012	−0.044
	[−0.28, 0.26]	[−0.31, 0.23]
Acute discrimination		0.090***
		[0.08, 0.11]
Controls		
Household income	−0.073***	−0.071***
	[−0.09, −0.06]	[−0.08, −0.06]
Female	0.645***	0.655***
	[0.53, 0.76]	[0.54, 0.77]
Age	−0.031***	−0.030***
	[−0.03, −0.03]	[−0.03, −0.03]
Education	0.005	0.007
	[−0.02, 0.03]	[−0.02, 0.03]
Month of survey (ref. March)		
April	0.508***	0.495***
	[0.46, 0.56]	[0.44, 0.55]
May	0.038	0.035
	[−0.01, 0.09]	[−0.02, 0.09]
June	−0.066*	−0.066*
	[−0.13, −0.01]	[−0.13, −0.01]
July	−0.145***	−0.154***
	[−0.20, −0.09]	[−0.21, −0.10]
August	−0.156***	−0.163***
	[−0.21, −0.11]	[−0.21, −0.11]
September	−0.174***	−0.180***
	[−0.23, −0.17]	[−0.24, −0.12]
Constant	4.01***	3.89***
	[3.66, 4.36]	[3.55, 4.24]
Random-effects Parameters		
sigma_u	0.802***	0.796***
	[0.78, 0.82]	[0.78, 0.81]
sigma_e	0.448***	0.447***
	[0.44, 0.46]	[0.44, 0.45]
N (persons)	6,487	6,487
N (person_wave observations)	57,591	57,591
95% confidence intervals in brackets		

* $p < 0.05$, ** $p < 0.01$, *** $p < 0.001$.

issues, this has been unevenly borne (Pfefferbaum and North 2020). In this study, we find that Asian Americans and Asian immigrants reported having encountered more instances of COVID-19-related acute discrimination than whites. Asian immigrants and Asian Americans also experienced higher levels of mental disorders during the pandemic. Furthermore, we demonstrate that COVID-19-related acute discrimination partially explained mental health gaps between Asians and Whites. Our findings suggest that Asians worldwide may have to deal with not only the COVID-19 crisis but also the associated stigmatization, violence, and discrimination. Therefore, they are particularly vulnerable during the crisis. Notably, all types of acute discrimination examined in our study are directly related to COVID-19. As we are still in the pandemic, our consideration of COVID-19-associated discrimination and how it affects mental health of different population groups is unique and urgently needed.

It is essential to develop and implement group-specific mental health assessment and support (see also Xiang et al. 2020). For example, considering that Asians often have the lowest utilization of mental health services, coordinating response to anti-Asian racism such as investment in mental health services and community-based efforts is much needed (Misra et al. 2020). Because health professionals play a key role in countering racism and its consequences, it is also important to ensure that medicine as a field continues to care for all minority communities (Li and Galea 2020; Hu, Wang, and Lu 2020). At the policy level, public policies that aim to alleviate mental health issues in times of crisis must tackle the hate, violence, and discrimination experienced by members of targeted groups.

Notes

1. http://www.asianpacificpolicyandplanningcouncil.org/wp-content/uploads/STOP_AAPI_Hate_National_Report_3.19-8.5.2020.pdf
2. https://naasurvey.com/wp-content/uploads/2017/05/NAAS16-post-election-report.pdf

Disclosure statement

No potential conflict of interest was reported by the author(s).

Funding

Funding provided by the Canadian Institutes of Health Research (CIHR, FRN-170368 & OV7-170372).

ORCID

Cary Wu ⓘ http://orcid.org/0000-0003-2652-5684
Yue Qian ⓘ http://orcid.org/0000-0003-2120-5403
Rima Wilkes ⓘ http://orcid.org/0000-0003-2078-3308

References

Angrisani, M., B. Finley, and A. Kapteyn. 2019. Can Internet Match High-quality Traditional Surveys? Comparing the Health and Retirement Study and its Online Version', The Econometrics of Complex Survey Data (Advances in Econometrics, Volume 39).

Asnaani, A., J. A. Richey, R. Dimaite, D. E. Hinton, and S. G. Hofmann. 2010. "A Cross-Ethnic Comparison of Lifetime Prevalence Rates of Anxiety Disorders." *The Journal of Nervous and Mental Disease* 198 (8): 551.

Beiser, M., and F. Hou. 2016. "Mental Health Effects of Premigration Trauma and Postmigration Discrimination on Refugee Youth in Canada." *The Journal of Nervous and Mental Disease* 204 (6): 464–470.

Carter, R. T. 2007. "Racism and Psychological and Emotional Injury: Recognizing and Assessing Race-Based Traumatic Stress." *The Counseling Psychologist* 35 (1): 13–105.

Cheah, C. S., C. Wang, H. Ren, X. Zong, H. S. Cho, and X. Xue. 2020. "COVID-19 Racism and Mental Health in Chinese American Families." *Pediatrics* 146, (5): e2020021816. https://doi.org/10.1542/peds.2020-021816.

Chen, H. A., J. Trinh, and G. P. Yang. 2020. "Anti-Asian Sentiment in the United States–COVID-19 and History." *American Journal of Surgery* 220 (3): 556–557.

Cheng, H. L. 2020. "Xenophobia and Racism Against Asian Americans During the COVID-19 Pandemic: Mental Health Implications." *Journal of Interdisciplinary Perspectives and Scholarship* 3 (1): 3.

Darling-Hammond, S., E. K. Michaels, A. M. Allen, D. H. Chae, M. D. Thomas, T. T. Nguyen, M. M. Mujahid, and R. C. Johnson. 2020. "After "The China Virus" Went Viral: Racially Charged Coronavirus Coverage and Trends in Bias Against Asian Americans." *Health Education & Behavior,* https://doi.org/10.1177/1090198120957949.

Dhanani, L. Y., and B. Franz. 2020. "Unexpected Public Health Consequences of the COVID-19 Pandemic: a National Survey Examining Anti-Asian Attitudes in the USA." *International Journal of Public Health* 65 (6): 747–754.

Dion, K. L., K. K. Dion, and A. W. Pak. 1992. "Personality-based Hardiness as a Buffer for Discrimination-Related Stress in Members of Toronto's Chinese Community." *Canadian Journal of Behavioural Science/Revue Canadienne des Sciences du Comportement* 24 (4): 517–536.

Feliciano, C. 2020. "Immigrant Selectivity Effects on Health, Labor Market, and Educational Outcomes." *Annual Review of Sociology* 46: 315–334.

Gee, G. C., A. Ro, S. Shariff-Marco, and D. Chae. 2009. "Racial Discrimination and Health among Asian Americans: Evidence, Assessment, and Directions for Future Research." *Epidemiologic Reviews* 31 (1): 130–151.

Gee, G. C., M. Spencer, J. Chen, T. Yip, and D. T. Takeuchi. 2007. "The Association Between Self-Reported Racial Discrimination and 12-Month DSM-IV Mental Disorders among Asian Americans Nationwide." *Social Science & Medicine* 64 (10): 1984–1996.

Gover, A. R., S. B. Harper, and L. Langton. 2020. "Anti-Asian Hate Crime during the COVID-19 Pandemic: Exploring the Reproduction of Inequality." *American Journal of Criminal Justice* 45 (4): 647–667.

Grzymala-Busse, A. 2011. "Time Will Tell? Temporality and the Analysis of Causal Mechanisms and Processes." *Comparative Political Studies* 44 (9): 1267–1297.

Güngör, D., and N. Perdu. 2017. "Resilience and Acculturative Pathways Underlying Psychological Well-Being of Immigrant Youth." *International Journal of Intercultural Relations* 56: 1–12.

Harrell, S. P. 2000. "A Multidimensional Conceptualization of Racism-Related Stress: Implications for the Well-Being of People of Color." *American Journal of Orthopsychiatry* 70 (1): 42–57.

Hu, J. R., M. Wang, and F. Lu. 2020. "COVID-19 and Asian American Pacific Islanders." *Journal of General Internal Medicine* 35, 2763–2764. https://doi.org/10.1007/s11606-020-05953-5.

Hwang, W. C., and S. Goto. 2008. "The Impact of Perceived Racial Discrimination on the Mental Health of Asian American and Latino College Students." *Cultural Diversity and Ethnic Minority Psychology* 14 (4): 326–335.

Kennedy, E. B., J. Vikse, C. Chaufan, K. O'Doherty, C. Wu, Y. Qian, and P. Fafard. 2020. *Canadian COVID-19 Social Impacts Survey. Rapid Summary of Results #1: Risk Perceptions, Trust, Impacts, and Responses* (York University Disaster and Emergency Management Technical Report #004). http://dx.doi.org/10.6084/m9.figshare.12121905.

Lee, D. L., and S. Ahn. 2011. "Racial Discrimination and Asian Mental Health: A Meta-Analysis." *The Counseling Psychologist* 39 (3): 463–489.

Li, Y., and S. Galea. 2020. "Racism and the COVID-19 Epidemic: Recommendations for Health Care Workers." *American Journal of Public Health* 110 (7): 956–957.

Litam, S. D. A. 2020. "'Take Your Kung-Flu Back to Wuhan': Counseling Asians, Asian Americans, and Pacific Islanders With Race-Based Trauma Related to COVID-19." *Professional Counselor* 10 (2): 144–156.

Liu, Y., B. K. Finch, S. G. Brenneke, K. Thomas, and P. D. Le. 2020. "Perceived Discrimination and Mental Distress amid the COVID-19 pandemic: Evidence from the understanding America study." *American Journal of Preventive Medicine* 59 (4): 481–492.

Löwe, B., J. Unützer, C. M. Callahan, A. J. Perkins, and K. Kroenke. 2004. "Monitoring Depression Treatment Outcomes with the Patient Health Questionnaire-9." *Medical Care* 42 (12): 1194–1201.

Lu, R., and Y. Sheng. 2020. "From Fear to Hate: How the Covid-19 Pandemic Sparks Racial Animus in the United States." Available at SSRN 3646880. https://papers.ssrn.com/sol3/papers.cfm?abstract_id=3646880.

Ma, Y., and N. Zhan. 2020. "To Mask or Not to Mask amid the COVID-19 Pandemic: How Chinese Students in America Experience and Cope with Stigma." *Chinese Sociological Review* 1–26.

Mamuji, A., J. Rozdilsky, C. Lee, N. Mwarumba, M. Tubula, and T. Chu. 2020. *Expanding the Narrative on Anti-Chinese Stigma During COVID-19: Lessons on Complexity & Capacity in Toronto and Nairobi.* (York University Disaster and Emergency Management Technical Report #005). http://dx.doi.org/10.6084/m9.figshare.12759512.

Man, S. 2020. "Anti-Asian Violence and US Imperialism." *Race & Class* 62 (2): 24–33.

Meyer, I. H. 1995. "Minority Stress and Mental Health in Gay Men." *Journal of Health and Social Behavior* 36 (1) 38–56.

Meyer, I. H. 2003. "Prejudice, Social Stress, and Mental Health in Lesbian, Gay, and Bisexual Populations: Conceptual Issues and Research Evidence." *Psychological Bulletin* 129 (5): 674.

Misra, S., P. D. Le, E. Goldmann, and L. H. Yang. 2020. "Psychological Impact of Anti-Asian Stigma Due to the COVID-19 Pandemic: A Call for Research, Practice, and Policy Responses." *Psychological Trauma: Theory, Research, Practice, and Policy* 12 (5): 461–464.

Noel, T. K., 2020. "Conflating Culture with COVID-19: Xenophobic Repercussions of a Global Pandemic." *Social Sciences & Humanities Open* 2 (1): 100044.

Noh, S., M. Beiser, V. Kaspar, F. Hou, and J. Rummens. 1999. "Perceived Racial Discrimination, Depression, and Coping: A Study of Southeast Asian refugees in Canada." *Journal of Health and Social Behavior* 9 (1): 193–207.

Ong, A. D., C. Cerrada, R. A. Lee, and D. R. Williams. 2017. "Stigma Consciousness, Racial Microaggressions, and Sleep Disturbance among Asian Americans." *Asian American Journal of Psychology* 8 (1): 72–81.

Pew Research Center. 2020. "Many Black and Asian Americans Say They Have Experienced Discrimination Amid the COVID-19 Outbreak." Available: https://www.pewsocialtrends.org/2020/07/01/many-black-and-asian-americans-say-they-have-experienced-discrimination-amid-the-covid-19-outbreak/.

Pfefferbaum, B., and C. S. North. 2020. "Mental Health and the COVID-19 Pandemic." *New England Journal of Medicine* 383: 510–512. http://dx.doi.org/10.1056/NEJMp2008017.

Riehm, K. E., C. Holingue, L. G. Kalb, D. Bennett, A. Kapteyn, Q. Jiang, and C. B Veldhuis, et al. 2020. "Associations between Media Exposure and Mental Distress among US Adults at the Beginning of the COVID-19 Pandemic." *American Journal of Preventive Medicine* 59 (5): 630–638.

Szymanski, D. M., and M. R. Sung. 2010. "Minority Stress and Psychological Distress among Asian American Sexual Minority Persons 1Ψ7." *The Counseling Psychologist* 38 (6): 848–872.

Tessler, H., M. Choi, and G. Kao. 2020. "The Anxiety of Being Asian American: Hate Crimes and Negative Biases During the COVID-19 Pandemic." *American Journal of Criminal Justice* 45: 636–646.

Torres-Reyna, O. (2007). Panel Data Analysis. Fixed & Random Effects [online]. http://dss.princeton.edu/training/Panel101.pdf.

Wei, M., P. P. Heppner, T. Y. Ku, and K. Y. H. Liao. 2010. "Racial Discrimination Stress, Coping, and Depressive Symptoms among Asian Americans: A Moderation Analysis." *Asian American Journal of Psychology* 1 (2): 136.

Wei, M., T. Y. Ku, D. W. Russell, B. Mallinckrodt, and K. Y. H. Liao. 2008. "Moderating Effects of Three Coping Strategies and Self-Esteem on Perceived Discrimination and Depressive Symptoms: A Minority Stress Model for Asian International Students." *Journal of Counseling Psychology* 55 (4): 451–462.

Wen, J., J. Aston, X. Liu, and T. Ying. 2020. "Effects of Misleading Media Coverage on Public Health Crisis: A Case of the 2019 Novel Coronavirus Outbreak in China." *Anatolia* 31 (2): 331–336.

Williams, D. R., and S. A. Mohammed. 2013. "Racism and Health I: Pathways and Scientific Evidence." *American Behavioral Scientist* 57 (8): 1152–1173.

Williams, D. R., Y. Yu, J. S. Jackson, and N. B. Anderson. 1997. "Racial Differences in Physical and Mental Health: Socio-Economic Status, Stress and Discrimination." *Journal of Health Psychology* 2 (3): 335–351.

Wu, C., R. Wilkes, Y. Qian, and E. B. Kennedy. 2020. "Acute Discrimination and East Asian-White Mental Health gap During COVID-19 in Canada." *Canadian Diversity* 17 (3): 62–66. *Available at SSRN 3626460.*

Xiang, Y. T., Y. Yang, W. Li, L. Zhang, Q. Zhang, T. Cheung, and C. H. Ng. 2020. "Timely Mental Health Care for the 2019 Novel Coronavirus Outbreak is Urgently Needed." *The Lancet Psychiatry* 7 (3): 228–229.

Zhai, Y., and X. Du. 2020. "Mental Health Care for International Chinese Students Affected by the COVID-19 Outbreak." *The Lancet Psychiatry* 7 (4): e22.

Zheng, Y., E. Goh, and J. Wen. 2020. "The Effects of Misleading Media Reports About COVID-19 on Chinese Tourists' Mental Health: A Perspective Article." *Anatolia* 31 (2): 337–340.

Appendix

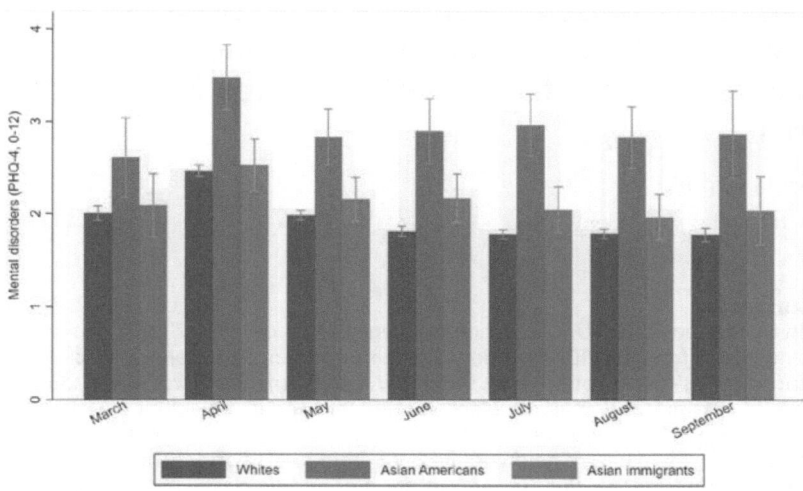

Figure A1. Temporal changes in mental disorders across whites, Asian Americans, and Asian immigrants

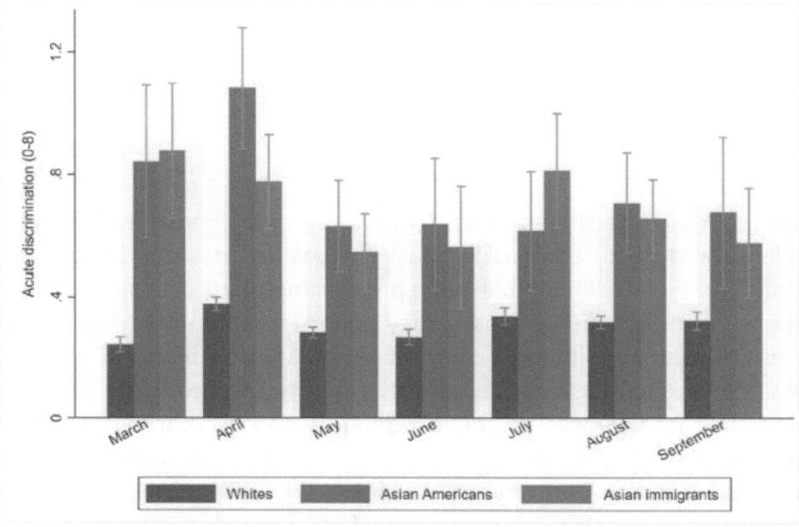

Figure A2. Temporal changes in acute discrimination across whites, Asian Americans, and Asian immigrants

COVID-19, Black jurisdictions, and budget constraints: how fiscal footing shapes fighting the virus

Angela Simms

ABSTRACT

In the United States (U.S.), most reports regarding racial disparities in incidence and death from COVID-19 understate the importance of majority-Black local jurisdictions' fiscal capacity in shaping African Americans' resilience during the pandemic and majority-Black locales' economic trajectories afterward. Black households and jurisdictions manage legacy and ongoing racialized capitalism. My data are fieldwork findings from a 2017 and 2018 study of the U.S. county with the highest concentration of middle-class African Americans, Prince George's County (PGC), Maryland, a suburb of Washington, D.C., alongside government reports on how D.C.-area counties experience COVID-19 fallout. I find PGC's fragile fiscal state prior to the coronavirus means it weathers harsher consequences from COVID-19 than two neighbouring counties with significantly smaller Black populations. My analysis explicates how layers of racial disadvantage compound across time, region, and level of social organization.

News reports in the United States (U.S.) about racial inequality in COVID-19 incidence and death emphasizes Blacks' exposure rates due to their occupations and their likelihood of having pre-existing physical health conditions. While these are proximate causes, they understate the underlying pre-existing *fiscal* health conditions in counties where African Americans live, which leads to Black jurisdictions having less capacity to absorb the health and economic consequences of the pandemic without compromising public service quality. Public services – from clean water, to public schools, to parks and recreation – are critical for a high quality of life. Strained public services in majority-Black communities have been pervasive since the post-Civil War Reconstruction period (Du Bois 2007 [1935]; Drake and Cayton 1993

[1945]; Massey and Denton 1993). Governments' retreat from robust invest-ment in public services in all communities, irrespective of racial composition, from the 1970s forward has resulted in many local governments struggling to maintain budgets sufficient for maintaining service quality and meeting resi-dent service demand (Harvey 2007; Logan and Molotch 2007).

However, majority-Black locales are generally more burdened than juris-dictions with larger White populations because African Americans and their communities pursue fiscal resilience in the face of racialized capitalism and policies. As a result, in many metropolitan areas Whites are more likely to corral a disproportionate share of economic benefits while not shouldering their proportionate share of responsibilities, such as providing services to low- and moderate-income households (Lung-Amam 2017). The weight of what Black jurisdictions bear is cumulative over time. Prior harm creates vul-nerability to future adverse circumstances. When COVID-19 struck in February 2020, most majority-Black jurisdictions were still recovering from the Great Recession of 2009–11 (Burd-Sharps and Rasch 2015), while most majority-White jurisdictions had largely rebounded.

Prince George's County (PGC) Maryland's experience, relative to that of neighbouring jurisdictions, demonstrates how long-standing racial inequality shapes local jurisdictions' ability to withstand the health and economic chal-lenges stemming from COVID-19 without compromising public service budgets. PGC has the largest concentration of middle-class African Americans in the country and is the only majority-Black county in the Washington, D.C. region. But even with relative class advantage, PGC is caught in vicious fiscal cycles, while nearby counties with larger White populations are not. I show how uneven local jurisdiction fiscal capacity reinforces racial inequity in access to public services by combining fieldwork I conducted in PGC prior to the coronavirus pandemic with current government data regarding how PGC and two counties it borders are experiencing COVID-19 prevalence and economic harm.

Theory: covid-19 meets racialized capitalism and decades of government retreat

Since the 1980s, all levels of government – federal, state, and local – have retrenched significantly, guided by an ethos President Ronald Reagan cap-tured as "starving the beast" when he signed major tax cuts into law in 1981 (Harvey 2007). Governments nationwide have adapted to increasing fiscal austerity, but local jurisdictions with majority-African American popu-lations do so while bearing the consequences of legacy and ongoing anti-Black discrimination across opportunity structures, among them education, job, and housing markets (Du Bois 2007[1935]; Pager and Shepherd 2008; Taylor 2019).

The White–Black wealth gap is among the most apt measures of the cumulative effects of anti-Black racism since the founding of the United States
(Darity and Mullen 2019). Today, White Americans have about ten times
the wealth of their Black counterparts. Since the Civil War Reconstruction
period when African Americans gained citizenship, after the majority had
been enslaved, their incorporation into United States society on equitable
terms with European Americans has evinced both "racial progress" and the
"progression of racism" (Kendi 2016). After Reconstruction, "separate, but
equal" Jim Crow policies burgeoned throughout the United States. Many
African Americans pursued economic opportunity through geographic mobility. During the Black Great Migration from the late-1800s to mid-1900s, about
six million Black Americans moved from the South to northern and western
cities, leaving behind agricultural labour for jobs in factories (Foner 1998).
Blacks realized notable class advancement outside of the South (Drake and
Cayton 1993 [1945]). Yet they also contended with White vigilante violence
in northern and western cities, which led to, among other things, Blacks' rele-
gation to increasingly overcrowded neighbourhoods where they experienced
lower quality public services than Whites (Foner 1998). In addition, union
leaders' refusal to admit Blacks tempered African Americans' economic
advancement trajectories (Foner 1998). Landmark laws enacted in the wake
of the Great Depression investing in Americans' economic stability and
quality of life during their working years and retirement, such as the Social
Security Act of 1935, did not extend to Blacks to the same degree as
Whites (Foner 1998).

Though pre-World War II policies discriminated against Black Americans,
laws promulgated after the war most concertedly created a more expansive
middle class that could attain and retain wealth. Key among these policies
were: (1) federally-sponsored mortgage insurance, which enabled more
Americans to buy homes using a 20–30 year fixed-rate, fully amortized
loan; (2) the development of the interstate highway system, which spurred
suburban growth; and (3) The Servicemen's Readjustment Act of 1944, a
$95 billion investment in housing, education, and job benefits for veterans
(Katznelson 2005, 113). Together, these policies not only disproportionately
benefited White Americans, they reinforced racial residential segregation
and thus the geography of opportunity in metropolitan areas.

In most cities today, African Americans live in roughly the same neighbourhoods their families have resided in for decades. Still, as of 2010, Blacks, like all
racial and ethnic groups, are majority-suburban (Frey 2014). But African
Americans' neighbourhoods, regardless of location, generally experience
more poverty and/or are adjacent to high-poverty areas, when compared
to those of European Americans (Pattillo 2013). They are also more likely to
offer inadequate public services (Pattillo 2013). Furthermore, assets in Black
neighbourhoods, including homes, are undervalued by about 23 per cent

because Whites stigmatize majority-Black spaces (Perry, Rothwell, and Harsh-barger 2018).

Legislation passed in the wake of the Modern Civil Rights Movement – notably, the Civil Rights Act of 1964, the Voting Rights Act of 1965, and Fair Housing Act of 1968 – and court decisions in that period attenuated explicitly racist practices. Current racial inequity is embedded in routine market and government policies, disadvantaging Blacks through supposedly "color blind" policies – laws not overtly racist, but that have disparate impact on racial groups because of their differing histories of access to material and social resources. Therefore, local government decisionmakers' capacity to respond to COVID-19 is a function of long-standing racialized government and market practices.

Methods and socio-geographic context

Prince George's County (PGC), Maryland, a suburb of Washington, D.C., offers an exceptional window into the extent of fiscal challenge majority-Black local jurisdictions face. PGC has the largest concentration of middle class Blacks of any local jurisdiction in the U.S., and is embedded in an economically thriving metropolitan region, creating development and demographic dynamics similar to other regions with growing populations (U.S. Census Bureau 2018a; U.S. Census Bureau 2018b). Assessing how this county experiences COVID-19 demonstrates how both race and class composition of jurisdictions determine counties' fiscal fate. My analysis also suggests PGC's experience is a best-case scenario for Black jurisdictions, given it has more class advantage than most majority-Black locales.

The D.C. region is majority-minority. Whites account for 47 per cent of the population. But racial and ethnic groups and household socio-economic status are not evenly distributed across jurisdictions (Lung-Amam 2017). PGC is home to about 909,000 people, about 65 per cent of whom are Black; and the majority of residents are middle class, with middle class here defined as earning the U.S. median income or more (U.S. Census Bureau 2019b). Latinos of any race, at about 19 per cent of the population, are the second largest ethno-racial group in PGC, most of whom are foreign born (Stepler and Lopez 2016, U.S. Census Bureau 2019a).

In Figure 1 below, I compare PGC to two counties that occupy similar geographic positions as suburban jurisdictions contiguous with the District of Columbia and that have similar-size populations at about one million residents: Montgomery County, Maryland; and Fairfax County, Virginia. This figure displays four dimensions influencing fiscal health because they shape the amount of revenue jurisdictions garner and demand for public services from residents: (1) the percentage of the population non-Hispanic Black, (2) the percentage with a college degree, (3) the percentage of households

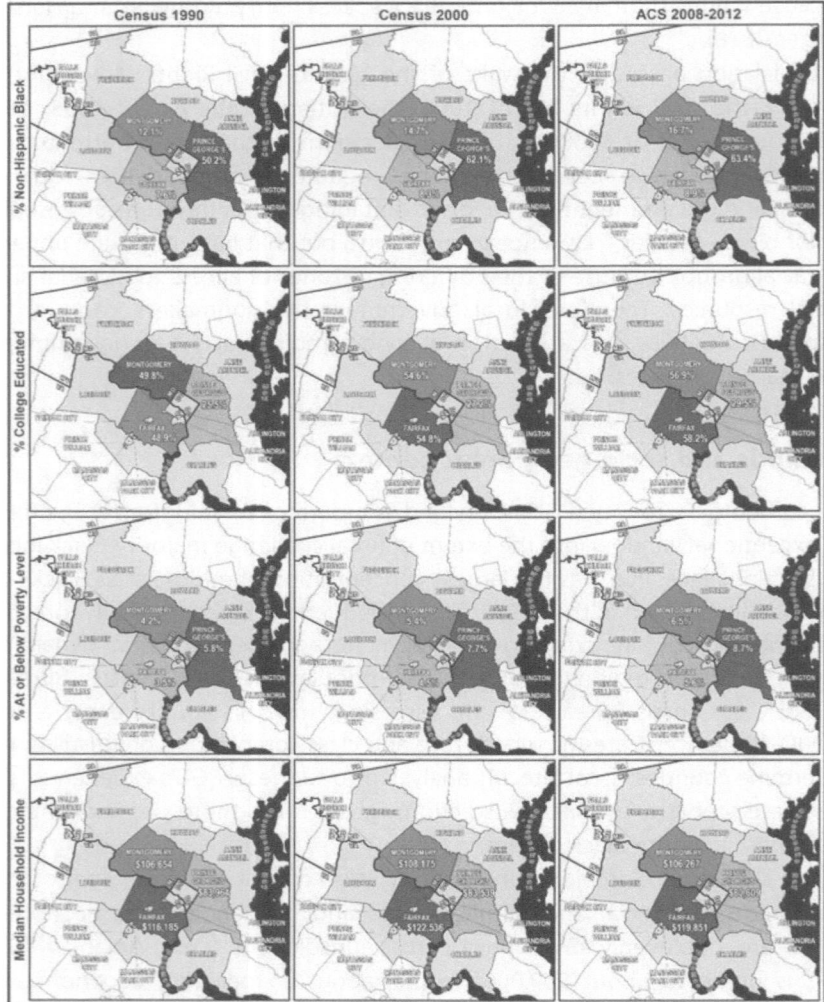

Figure 1. Washington, D.C. Region.

with incomes at or below the poverty level, and (4) median household income. I show this data in 10-year intervals – 1990, 2000, and 2008–12. Maps for 1990 and 2000 use decennial census data and 2010 is estimated by providing the average of 2008–12 American Community Survey data.

There is an upward trend over time in all categories measured. Among the three counties, PGC has the largest Black population, the greatest proportion of people in poverty, as well as a lower median income and lower percentage of the population with a college degree. PGC's position, relative to its neigh-bours, highlights social processes underpinning the county's more fragile fiscal condition. Yet when PGC is compared to the U.S. as a whole, it is decidedly affluent. In 2018, the U.S. median household income was $60,293, while PGC's was $81,969 (U.S. Census Bureau 2018a; U.S. Census Bureau 2018b). PGC's college attainment rate nearly matches the U.S. average of about 30 per cent (U.S. Census Bureau 2018a; U.S. Census Bureau 2018b).

In 2017 and 2018, I conducted a two-year ethnography of PGC government institutions, attending council and committee hearings focused on policy and budget development. I also interviewed thirty county decisionmakers and other leaders, and an additional twenty eight residents. All residents I spoke to are Black non-Hispanic, and most are middle class. I recruited respondents at community events and through snowball sampling. My ethnographic work is combined with data available on how Prince George's, Montgomery, and Fairfax Counties have weathered COVID-19 in terms of health and economic outcomes.

Findings

PGC's fiscal health before COVID-19

Before the coronavirus, PGC was still overcoming the last national economic contraction that particularly harmed majority-Black jurisdictions: The Great Recession of 2009–11. The recession technically ended in 2011, but Black communities continued to reel long after 2011, in part because lenders targeted Black neighbourhoods for toxic mortgage and refinancing schemes (Burd-Sharps and Rasch 2015; Lacy 2012). Prince George's County was no exception (Fletcher 2015). As the recession deepened, thousands of Prince Georgians experienced home foreclosure. As shown in Figure 2 below, PGC's foreclosure rate of about 4.75 per cent was more than two percent greater than the D.C. region's and those of Montgomery and Fairfax Counties, which were about 2.5, 1.8, and 1.6 per cent, respectively.

A county council member described her district's Great Recession experience this way, words akin to what I heard from other council members:

> We still have a lot of foreclosures in Prince George's County. There was a moment in time when I came into office [in 2016] where every neighborhood that I door knocked as I was running for elected office there was hands down a vacant house in every one of them and you could obviously detect it. The grass was growing high. Maybe it was boarded up. It was clearly poorly maintained. Nowadays, we still have vacant homes in our neighborhoods.

Due to the Great Recession, PGC decisionmakers fought to provide core government services in a context where demand for service was increasing while tax revenue was decreasing. In 2017 and 2018, more than six years after the Great Recession, PGC was still making budget decisions indicating economic recovery was on going. For example, union contracts with teachers and police

Percent of First-lien Mortgages in the Foreclosure Inventory, December 2010
Source: Washington, DC Metropolitan Area Foreclosure Monitor

Figure 2. 2010 D.C. metropolitan area foreclosure rates by County.

officers for fiscal year 2019 included pay raises to account for recession-era losses. When I interviewed county leaders, officials framed their assessments of PGC's fiscal strength in terms of how well the county was "digging out" of revenue shortfalls. This council member's comments encapsulate those I heard from her colleagues:

> It took us longer than anyone in the region to dig out ... We're still digging out and it affected our African American middle class in the worst way. People lost their homes and that's how you build wealth in this country, is by home ownership and it hit us hard. There's a consequence to that that I think we're still trying to figure out.

The tax base, the sum total of all properties and transactions eligible for tax or fee assessment, is local jurisdictions' life blood – without sufficient revenue, jurisdictions cannot fund services. As shown in Figure 3 below, in 2018, PGC

	County		
	Prince George's	**Montgomery**	**Fairfax**
Spending Per Capita[1]	$3,574	$4,541	$3,580
Spending Per Pupil[2]	$14,774	$15,623	$14,747
Percent Low-income Students	61	33	31

Footnote 1: Calculated by dividing FY 2018 general fund appropriation by total population
Footnote 2: Calculated by dividing FY 2018 school system operating budget by student population
Sources: Prince George's County, MD, Montgomery County, MD, and Fairfax County, VA budget offices

Figure 3. Counties' fiscal year 2018 spending and student poverty.

spent $996 less than Montgomery County per resident and $2,328 less than Fairfax County. Regarding per pupil spending, PGC spent $1,151 less than Montgomery and $343 less than Fairfax. K-12 schools are usually locales' largest budget expenditure, at about half of their budgets. Moreover, funding for schools is both a proxy for fiscal health and a harbinger of housing demand in an area, as high-performing schools are the sin quo non criterion of most prospective homebuyers (Rhodes and Warkentien 2017). Figure 3 also reveals that 61 per cent of PGC students qualified for reduced price meals in 2018, whereas Montgomery and Fairfax serve half as many students from low-income households, thus highlighting the disproportionate service demand in PGC schools before the coronavirus pandemic.

PGC became one of the premier majority-Black counties in the United States in the mid-1990s when it transitioned from being majority White to majority Black. In 1994, it elected its first Black county executive, Wayne Curry (Johnson 2002). Curry called PGC the "land of milk and honey" for well-to-do African Americans. He assiduously pursued development opportunities to bolster the tax base, including courting developers for high-end housing and retail. As more middle-class Blacks moved in, Whites, most of them working class, left the county.

However, PGC's status as class advantaged, compared to other majority-Black jurisdictions does not insulate it from its relative economic position in the D.C. region, nor the long-term effects of legacy and ongoing racialized capitalism and policies. Indeed, because PGC is the most affordable county in the region contiguous with D.C., it attracts and retains a greater share of the region's low-income households, most of whom are Black or Latinx. As PGC stretches an already tight budget, overall service quality diminishes, making it less likely the county will attract upper middle-class households who can afford to live elsewhere in the region and attain higher quality services.

A middle-class Black resident when I asked him to describe his neighbourhood and what, if anything, stood out as significant changes over the past few years remarked:

> With the new influx of the Hispanic population and that continuing to grow, and then a new influx of persons of lesser income who are coming from the Washington, D.C.'s or other places where gentrification is running rampant, the county is having to reconfigure the way that it implements policy and programs to be able to meet the needs of new folks who are coming into the county.

A former Maryland appointed official, education activist, and retired professor frames PGC's position in the DC region in a similar way:

> ... Even though we call ourselves living in Prince George's we really [aren't] ... we're living in an economic commercial racial circle. A circumference. And it's

called D.C., and it's called Virginia, and it's called Prince George's, but when you look at the dynamics of resources and housing structures and banking and finance it's where you live in that circle [that matters].

Notwithstanding Prince George's unique constraints, PGC leaders, from Curry forward, play by the rules of racialized capitalism. Among the fiercest headwinds officials encounter are investors reluctant to inject new capital into the county and developers disproportionately placing less-than-ideal investments in PGC neighbourhoods, such as gas stations, fast food restaurants, and liquor stores. Encapsulating this point, A PGC agency director who recruits investors to the county stated:

> Many people still think it's crime ridden ... difficult to do business with ... undereducated work force. You don't really have the talent to be able to satisfy their needs. I really have to sell hard to show them [developers and other private investors] the facts on it because I think some of that is just ... the 65 per cent African-American.

Despite the aforementioned challenges, PGC leaders have accrued major development "wins" in the past fifteen years. For instance, the entertainment and residential complex National Harbor and MGM casino opened in 2008 and 2017, respectively (Simms 2019). In 2018, the casino generated $23 million in new tax revenue (Simms 2019). Still, recent development has led to tens of millions of additional tax dollars, while the scale of need is hundreds of millions.

PGC's fight for fiscal strength during COVID-19

PGC officials must balance the county budget each year. As decisionmakers appropriate funds, they consider the county's short and long-term financial needs. Short-term interests largely revolve around how much money programmes will receive that year. Among county leaders' primary long-term considerations is garnering a favourable bond rating. Adhering to financial industry guidelines for a AAA rating, the highest rating possible, means the county can finance infrastructure projects, such as building schools and roads, at the lowest interest rate. A key factor in achieving AAA is the amount in local jurisdictions' reserve fund (Prince George's Council 2017). Therefore, while PGC officials might want to use this fund to forestall cuts to core services, they cannot do so without penalty from lenders. The County Executive effectively noted this when she made the following statement during a June 2020 teleconference in which she explained how COVID-19 has affected PGC's financial status: "despite economic impact from COVID-19, we maintain our AAA bond rating ... we have over $130 million in lost revenue due to COVID-19 ... but we have sound financial policies".

	County		
	Prince George's	**Montgomery**	**Fairfax**
Case Rate	3,356	2,211	1,869
Death Rate	91	81	52

Note: Cases and Deaths recorded per 100,000 people
Source: The New Times, "COVID in the U.S.: Latest Map and Case Count"

Figure 4. COVID-19 case and death rates by County.

PGC's experience with COVID-19, including health consequences for residents and household and county-level financial outcomes, indicate the county's heightened vulnerability when compared to neighbouring counties with smaller Black populations. Figure 4 below shows PGC's case and death rates from the coronavirus are noticeably higher than those of Montgomery and Fairfax Counties.

Regarding economic consequences, in May 2020, PGC's unemployment rate of 10.8 per cent was about two percentage points higher than the rates in Montgomery and Fairfax Counties (Maryland Department of Labor 2020; Virginia Department of Labor 2020). PGC businesses also likely struggle more than those in nearby counties because PGC has a greater share of Black-owned businesses (Minority Business Development Agency 2016). Blacks' businesses tend to be more vulnerable than those of Whites, even during robust economic seasons due to their size, access to capital in a financial system that discriminates against Black people, and their reliance on Black clientele whose earnings are tempered by racism (Pager and Shepherd 2008).

In June 2021, PGC officials cut about $134 million from county services to account for tax revenue losses since the COVID-19 quarantine began in March 2020 (Maryland Association of Counties 2020b). By contrast, Montgomery and Fairfax Counties have held spending flat between fiscal years 2020 and 2021 (Fairfax County Office of the Executive 2020; Maryland Association of Counties 2020a). PGC's County Executive explained in her letter to the PGC Council her rationale for reducing 2021 spending:

> When the FY 2021 Proposed Budget was presented on March 11, 2020, it was unknown at that time the COVID-19 pandemic could so quickly and significantly change the economic outlook of the world, country and Prince George's County. The pandemic has permanently altered the lives of our citizens, residents, businesses and employees.

Great Recession-era policy decisions portend harsh budget tradeoffs under COVID-19

A protracted budget discussion regarding increasing funding for developmentally disabled adults (DDA) agencies during my fieldwork likely foretells the kinds of tough budget decisions PGC will make as the county manages increasingly constrained finances. In 2013, Prince George's and Montgomery County decisionmakers started a process of phased increases in their jurisdictions' minimum wage. This policy had the unintended consequence of creating a deficit for entities serving the DDA community because their employees are paid Maryland's minimum wage. PGC policymakers held several hearings to discuss whether to allocate $3.5 million in funding to cover the wage gap. In the end, PGC decisionmakers provided the funding by transferring money from another programme. Montgomery County, in contrast, offered gap funding when passing its fiscal year 2018 budget without significant discussion, nor by taking money from another programme (Montgomery County 2017).

The first round of budget cuts the PGC County Executive announced is probably not the last, as the pandemic's effects are likely to continue for several years, given a vaccine will likely not be widely publicly available until 2021. Federal relief, most notably through the CARES Act, provides some help to local governments (U.S. Department of Treasury 2020). But given CARES Act allotments do not account for racial disparities in how COVID-19 has burdened communities and the greater precarity Black communities endured prior to the virus, federal aid to local jurisdictions will likely be a fraction of what is needed in majority-African American locales.

Discussion and conclusion

The confluence of social and viral catastrophes – racism and COVID-19

Prince George's County plays by the rules of racialized capitalism from a disadvantaged position, relative to counties with smaller Black populations. PGC residents, neighbourhoods, and the local government manage inter-connected layers of economic distress. Distress in majority-Black locales is compounded across: (1) time, (2) metropolitan jurisdictions, and (3) levels of government and scales of social organization more broadly. Regarding time, Black residents and jurisdictions contend with cumulative, intergenerational effects of slavery, Jim Crow, and present-day "color blind" racism. Regarding political geography, local decisionmakers manage their weaker economic position, relative to neighbouring counties with smaller Black populations, often leading to majority-Black locales absorbing a disproportionate share of regional flows of people with low incomes – thus increasing pressure on their budgets. The share of PGC's student population qualifying for free- and reduced-price meals demonstrates this additional responsibility. Regarding levels of government and scales of social organization, discrimination Blacks experience in job and housing markets means they accumulate less income and wealth. In addition, their homes appreciate in market value less quickly than those of Whites. These dynamics create a smaller tax base in PGC than in neighbouring counties, resulting in less tax revenue for government services in Prince George's County.

Curing what ails the United States

As COVID-19's consequences mount, PGC will likely be more susceptible to capitalist practices taking advantage of economically struggling neighbourhoods. In the wake of the foreclosure crisis, communities with concentrations of vacant houses were eventually bought by corporations who rent properties, reducing the stability of neighbourhoods as fewer homes became owner occupied, home turnover frequency increased, and homes became overcrowded (Simms 2019). Residents who move to these communities are likely to be low- and moderate-income households who often exacerbate fiscal strain. And thus, the vicious cycle begins anew.

The faltering fiscal foundation decisionmakers in majority-Black jurisdictions face requires federal and state governments respond to the health and economic crises COVID-19 has wrought, *plus* those that preceded the virus. Majority-Black locales, regardless of class composition, need hundreds of millions of dollars, if not billions, in additional funds to close budget breaches reflecting America's oldest virus that has served the interests of White capitalist elites: anti-Black racism. In addition, legislation must guard against predatory financial practices in Black communities. Finally, there must be better regional coordination of resources and responsibility for low-income households. Black communities deserve resources on the scale of the Marshall Plan the U.S. established to rebuild Europe after World War II. Only in this case, the federal government would not be *re*building, it would be living up to long-overdue debts to its Black citizens.

Acknowledgements

I gratefully acknowledge support from the Columbia Population Research Center (CPRC), which is supported under award P2CHD058486. Special thanks go to Andrew Rundle and James Quinn of CPRC for creating a map of the D.C. region displaying demographic differences.

Disclosure statement

No potential conflict of interest was reported by the author(s).

Funding

I gratefully acknowledge support from the Columbia Population Research Center (CPRC), which is supported under award P2CHD058486. Special thanks go to

Andrew Rundle and James Quinn of CPRC for creating a map of the D.C. region displaying demographic differences.

References

Burd-Sharps, Sarah and Rebecca Rasch. 2015. "Impact of the U.S. Housing Crisis on the Racial Wealth Gap across Generations. Brooklyn, NY: Social Science Research Council." Accessed July 14, 2020. https://www.aclu.org/sites/default/files/field_document/discrimlend_final.pdf.

Darity, William and A. Kirsten Mullen. 2019. *From Here to Equality: Reparations for Black Americans in the Twenty-first Century*. Chapel Hill, NC: University of North Carolina Press.

Drake, St. Clair and Horace Cayton. 1993 [1945]. *Black Metropolis: A Study of Negro Life in a Northern City*. Chicago, IL: The University of Chicago Press.

Du Bois, W.E.B. (William Edward Burghardt). 2007 [1935]. *Black Reconstruction in America: An Essay Toward a History of the Part Which Black Folk Played in the Attempt to Reconstruct Democracy in America, 1860-1880*. New York, NY: Oxford University Press.

Fairfax County. 2017. "Fairfax County, Virginia Adopted Budget Plan: Overview." Fairfax County, VA: Department of Management and Budget. Accessed October 12, 2020. https://www.fairfaxcounty.gov/budget/sites/budget/files/assets/documents/fy2018/adopted/overview.pdf.

Fairfax County. 2020. "FY 2021 Updated Budget Proposal in Response to the Coronavirus Pandemic." Fairfax, VA: Office of Management and Budget." Accessed July 14, 2020. https://www.fairfaxcounty.gov/budget/sites/budget/files/assets/documents/fy2021/fy-2021-updated-budget-proposal-covid.pdf.

Fletcher, Michael. 2015. "A Shattered Foundation: African Americans Who Bought Homes in Prince George's Have Watched Their Wealth Vanish." *The Washington Post*, January 24. Accessed January 11, 2018. http://www.washingtonpost.com/sf/investigative/2015/01/24/the-american-dream-shatters-in-prince-georges-county/?utm_term=.04fe11200088.

Foner, Eric. 1998. *The Story of American Freedom*. New York: W.W. Norton & Company, Inc.

Frey, William. 2014. *The Diversity Explosion: How New Racial Demographics Are Remaking America*. Washington, DC: The Brookings Institution.

Harvey, David. 2007. *A Brief History of Neoliberalism*. New York, NY: Oxford University Press.

Johnson, Valerie C. 2002. *Black Power in the Suburbs: The Myth or Reality of African American Suburban Political Incorporation*. Albany, NY: State University of New York Press.

Katznelson, Ira. 2005. *When Affirmative Action Was White: An Untold History of Racial Inequality in Twentieth-Century America*. New York, NY: W.W. Norton & Company.

Kendi, Ibram. 2016. *Stamped from the Beginning: The Definitive History of Racist Ideas in America*. New York, NY: Nation Books.

Lacy, Karyn. 2012. "All's Fair? The Foreclosure Crisis and Middle-Class Black (In)Stability." *American Behavioral Scientist* 56 (11): 1565–1580.

Logan, John R., and Harvey Molotch. 2007. *Urban Fortunes: The Political Economy of Place*. Berkeley, CA: University of California Press.

Lung-Amam, Willow. 2017. "An Equitable Future for the Washington, D.C. Region?: A 'Regionalism Light' Approach to Building Inclusive Neighborhoods." Presented at

"A Shared Future: Fostering Communities of Inclusion in an Era of Inequality." Cambridge, MA: Harvard Joint Center for Housing Studies. Accessed April 3, 2019. https://www.jchs.harvard.edu/sites/default/files/a_shared_future_equitable_future_washi ngtondc.pdf.

Maryland Association of Counties(a). 2020. "Montgomery Council Approves FY21 Budget, FY 21-26 CIP." Annapolis, MD. Accessed July 14, 2020. https:// conduitstreet.mdcounties.org/2020/05/22/montgomery-council-approves-fy-21-budget-fy-21-26-cip/#:~:text=The%20Montgomery%20County%20Council% 20yesterday,infrastructure%20improvements%20and%20community%20projects.

Maryland Association of Counties(b). 2020. "Prince George's Writes Down Revenue Projection by $134 Million." Annapolis, MD. Accessed July 14, 2020. https:// conduitstreet.mdcounties.org/2020/04/27/prince-georges-writes-down-revenue-projections-by-134-million/.

Maryland Department of Labor. 2020. "Local Area Unemployment Statistics - Workforce Information, and Performance." Baltimore, MD. Accessed July 14, 2020. https://www.dllr.state.md.us/lmi/laus/.

Massey, Douglas S. and Nancy A. Denton. 1993. *American Apartheid: Segregation and the Making of the Underclass*. Cambridge, MA: Harvard University Press.

Minority Business Development Agency. 2016. "Fact Sheet: U.S. Minority-Owned Firms." Washington, DC: United States Department of Commerce, Minority Business Development Agency. Accessed February 25, 2019. https://www.mbda. gov/sites/mbda.gov/files/migrated/files-attachments/2012SBO_MBEFactSheet02 0216.pdf.

Montgomery County. 2017. "Revenue Schedules." Rockville, MD: Office of Management and Budget. Accessed October 12, 2020. https://www.montgomerycountymd.gov/ OMB/Resources/Files/omb/pdfs/FY18/psp_pdf/75-ScheduleC-ALL-FY2018-APPR-Publication-Report.pdf.

Pager, Devah and Hana Shepherd. 2008. "Employment, Housing, Credit, and Consumer Markets." *Annual Review of Sociology* 34: 181–209.

Pattillo, Mary. 2013. *Black Picket Fences, Second Edition: Privilege and Peril among the Black Middle Class*. Chicago, IL: University of Chicago Press.

Perry, Andre, Jonathan Rothwell, and David Harshbarger. 2018. *The Devaluation of Assets in Black Neighborhoods: The Case of Residential Property*. Washington, DC: The Bookings Institution. Accessed July 14, 2020. https://www.brookings.edu/wp-content/uploads/2018/11/2018.11_Brookings-Metro_Devaluation-Assets-Black-Neighborhoods_final.pdf.

Prince George's County. 2017. *Budget at a Glance*. Prince George's County, MD: Office of Management and Budget. Accessed October 12, 2020. https://www. princegeorgescountymd.gov/DocumentCenter/View/17965/Budget-OverviewPDF.

Prince George's County Council. 2017. "Prince George's County Council Blue Ribbon Commission on Addressing the Structural Deficit." Upper Marlboro, Maryland.

Rhodes, Anna, and Siri Warkentien. 2017. "Unwrapping the Suburban 'Package Deal' Race, Class, and School Access." *American Educational Research Journal* 54 (1): 168S–189S.

Simms, Angela. 2019. "Power, Privilege, and Peril: Governing in a Suburban Majority Black and Middle Class County—a Regional Perspective." PhD diss. University of Pennsylvania.

Stepler, Renee and Mark Hugo Lopez. 2016. "U.S. Latino Population Growth and Dispersion Has Slowed since Onset of the Great Recession: Ranking the Latino Population in Metropolitan Areas." Washington, DC: Pew Research Center:

Hispanic Trends. Accessed September 17, 2018. http://www.pewhispanic.org/2016/
    09/08/5-ranking-the-latino-population-in- metropolitan-areas/.

Taylor, Keeaga-Yamahtta. 2019. *Race for Profit: How Banks and the Real Estate Industry
    Undermined Black Homeownership.* Chapel Hill, NC: University of North Carolina
    Press.

The New York Times. 2020. "COVID in the U.S.: Latest Map and Case Count." Accessed
    October 12, 2020. https://www.nytimes.com/interactive/2020/us/coronavirus-us-
    cases.html?name=styln-coronavirus-national&region=TOP_BANNER&label=
    undefined&module=undefined&block=storyline_menu_recirc&action=
    click&pgtype=Interactive&impression_id=29468d00-0cdc-11eb-b1a9-
    c1978b635d95&variant=1_Show.

Urban Institute and the Metropolitan Washington Council of Governments. 2011.
    "Washington, DC. Accessed October 12, 2020. Metropolitan Area Foreclosure
    Monitor – Winter 2011." Washington, DC. https://www.urban.org/sites/default/
    files/publication/26926/1001522-washington-d-c-metropolitan-area-foreclosure-
    monitor-winter-.pdf).

U.S. Census Bureau. 2018a. "New Census Bureau Population Estimates Show Dallas-
    Fort Worth-Arlington Has the Largest Growth in the United States." Washington,
    DC: United States Department of Commerce. Accessed July 14, 2020. https://
    www.census.gov/newsroom/press-releases/2018/popest-metro- county.html.

U.S. Census Bureau. 2018b. "QuickFacts: Prince George's County, Maryland." Suitland,
    MD: United States Department of Commerce. Accessed July 14, 2020. https://www.
    census.gov/quickfacts/fact/table/princegeorgescountymaryland/PST040217.

U.S. Census Bureau. 2019a. *QuickFacts: Prince George's County, Maryland.* Suitland, MD:
    United States Department of Commerce. Accessed December 16, 2020. https://
    www.census.gov/quickfacts/princegeorgescountymaryland.

U.S. Census Bureau. 2019b. *QuickFacts: United States.* Suitland, MD: United States
    Department of Commerce. Accessed December 16, 2020. https://www.census.
    gov/quickfacts/fact/table/US/PST045219.

U.S. Department of Treasury. 2020. "The CARES Act Provides Assistance for State, Local,
    and Tribal Governments." Washington, DC. Accessed July 14, 2020. https://home.
    treasury.gov/policy-issues/cares/state-and-local-governments#:~:text=and%
    20Tribal%20Governments-,The%20CARES%20Act%20Provides%20Assistance%
    20for%20State%2C%20Local%2C%20and%20Tribal,%24150%20billion%
    20Coronavirus%20Relief%20Fund.

Virginia Department of Labor. 2020. "Estimated Labor Components." Richmond, VA.
    Accessed July 14, 2020. https://www.vec.virginia.gov/sites/default/files/news-
    12017-05-2020%20Pre%20%26%2004-2020%20Rev%20%20--%20Estimated%
    20Labor%20Force%20Components.pdf.

How COVID-19 may alleviate the multiple marginalization of racialized migrant workers

Maike Isaac and Jennifer Elrick

ABSTRACT
The COVID-19 pandemic has heightened the visibility of "low skilled" migrant workers in the agricultural and care work sectors, who have been rebranded as "essential" by receiving states in the Global North. Many such workers are from the Global South and experience marginalization due to their overlapping social positions: race, gender, ascribed skill level, and legal status. We assess how COVID-19 can prompt a revaluation of the legal statuses of "essential" migrant workers in countries of the Global North and thereby alleviate their marginalization to a small extent. We present two frames of deservingness – based on work and based on sacrifice – as having the potential to facilitate claims for improved legal status. We argue that deservingness claims stemming from migrants' willingness to sacrifice their health and lives have the greatest potential for success.

Introduction

The COVID-19 pandemic has shed light on society's dependency on workers whose labour covers basic human needs relating to health, transportation, and food supply. Suddenly rebranded as "essential" during the pandemic, these workers have continued to work outside the safety of their homes, thereby exposing themselves to a heightened risk of infection and death. This has been the case especially in the agricultural and care work sectors across the Global North. A significant proportion of workers in those sectors are migrants from the Global South; due to their race, gender, ascribed skill level, and legal status, these workers receive low wages and work under poor conditions. From a political economy perspective, the marginalization of migrant workers along these axes is linked to the dynamics of global capitalism and that system's longstanding practice of exploiting racialized groups as "unfree labour" (Sharma 2012; Zolberg 1987). The relationship between skill and remuneration in sectors marked by the "three Ds" (i.e. involving work that is dirty, demeaning, and dangerous) is broadly determined by racialized hierarchies of worth. A permanent structural demand is met with a labour supply that is predominantly non-White and from the Global South (Ehrenreich and Hochschild 2003; Parreñas 2015). Low remuneration for racialized workers perceived as fundamentally "low skilled" is furthermore facilitated by immigration policies that confer precarious legal status on workers. This status precarity robs migrant workers of the power to push back against exploitative working conditions (Anderson 2010; Bakan and Stasiulis 2012).

In this short debate article, we consider how COVID-19 could potentially prompt a revaluation of the legal statuses of "essential" migrant workers in countries of the Global North and thereby alleviate their marginalization to a limited extent. Since legal status is one of the overlapping social positions that contribute to migrant workers' marginalization, improvements like the granting of temporary foreign worker status to undocumented workers or permanent residency to temporary foreign workers would represent a modest overall reduction in migrant worker marginalization. Race, gender, and "skill" are all defined by deeply rooted cultural schemas (Anderson 2010; Boucher 2016; Romero 2018). These axes of marginalization are therefore unlikely to be susceptible to sudden change. However, historical precedents and current responses to the pandemic suggest that legal status adjustments could result from claims of deservingness in light of COVID-19's effects on working conditions. A change in this one axis of inequality could represent a small amelioration of the multiple marginalization experienced by migrant workers from the Global South.

The article proceeds as follows. We first position the COVID-19 pandemic as a "moment of rupture" that could potentially change perceptions of migrant workers' deservingness of legal status adjustments. We then consider two frames of deservingness offered by the literature on migration and citizenship – deservingness based on work and deservingness based on sacrifice. Either frame could be invoked to promote or realize legal status adjustments. We argue that deservingness claims on the basis of migrants' health sacrifices are more likely to be successful, because such claims would be limited in both time and scope. We point to recent developments in Canada, France, and Italy to substantiate our argument. We conclude with a brief discussion of the limits of legal status adjustments in overcoming multiple, particularly racialized, forms of marginalization.

COVID-19: a moment of rupture?

Labour that covers basic human needs relating to health, transportation, and food supply is critical for any society. Yet, it is often classified as requiring only "low" levels of skill, which in turn justifies poor remuneration (Piore 1979). The COVID-19 pandemic brings to the fore this paradoxical relation between workers' actual societal value, their assigned economic value, and their ascribed skill levels.

Due to the increased risks of illness and death faced by these workers and their importance in providing for basic societal needs, governments in the Global North began, early in the pandemic, to re-brand them as "essential" (rather than "low skilled"). In Canada and in Germany, this re-branding was accompanied by wage subsidy programmes (DW 2020; GoC 2020a). At the same time, the pandemic heightened public awareness about the poor working conditions under which many workers provide "essential" services. This public awareness sparked, across the Global North, public displays of solidarity with, and appreciation for, "essential" workers. In doing so, it has potentially helped propel change. Occupations that had previously been described as "low skilled" and unworthy of high remuneration were suddenly revaluated symbolically and, in some cases, also materially.

Migrants are overrepresented in sectors that have been rebranded from "low-skilled" to "essential". In the midst of a global pandemic that is causing economic decline, states may depend on the cheap labour of migrant workers more than ever. At the same time, the general public in North America and much of Europe now appears to be paying greater attention to the conditions under which migrant workers satisfy the basic needs of citizens (IOM 2020; Triandafyllidou and Nalbandian 2020).

Current public debates in Europe and North America about the remuneration, work conditions, and also the legal precarity of "essential" migrant workers appears to offer what pragmatist social theorists refer to as a "moment of rupture". Established notions and routines are suddenly disrupted, thereby creating the possibility for experimentation and change (Dewey 1991 [1939]; Schneiderhan 2011). In the course of the COVID-19 pandemic, long-established notions and routines that previously promoted the exemption of "low-skilled" racialized migrants from fair working conditions and the rights and privileges held by citizens are being questioned publicly (IOM 2020; Triandafyllidou and Nalbandian 2020). Many countries in the Global North are now considering whether and, if so, to what extent the legal precarity of these foreign workers should be reduced. How *deserving* of legal status adjustments are migrants who provide essential societal services in the midst of a global pandemic?

We argue that there are two possible ways in which the COVID-19 pandemic could change public perceptions relating to "essential" migrant workers' deservingness of legal status adjustments. First, migrant workers could become more deserving of legal status adjustments on the basis of their work that has now been categorized as "essential". Second, the deservingness of "essential" migrant workers could be enhanced due to the heightened risk of death during the pandemic. Each scenario relates to a distinct notion of deservingness that has historically played a major role in the acquisition of citizenship: deservingness through work and deservingness through sacrifice.

Legal status through work

Notions of citizenship are at the heart of the public and political debate on "essential" migrant workers' deservingness of legal status improvements. Legal status is one dimension of citizenship that denotes membership in a political and geographic community and confers on its holder a set of civil, political and social rights (Bloemraad, Korteweg, and Yurdakul 2008). According to Marshall (1950, 96), "the basic civil right is the right to work". With the emergence of the modern welfare state, the worker-citizen who pays taxes has been considered deserving of welfare benefits and other social rights.

There are many examples of migrant workers with a legal status below full citizenship who are granted access to civil and social rights as well as a pathway to improved legal status (Anderson 2015). The position of so-called "guest workers" and their descendants in Germany and other Western European states in the second half of the twentieth century lead scholars like Soysal (1994) to celebrate "denizenship" (or rights based on residency and work) as a good alternative to full citizenship status. Chauvin and Garcés–Mascareñas (2014) show that even "illegal" migrants can enter a pathway to regularization on the basis of "low skilled" work, if they have been faithful to their employer or paid taxes.

However, access to temporary and longer-term legal statuses that grant access to a range of civil and social rights are increasingly being reserved for "high-skilled" migrants (Chauvin, Garcés-Mascareñas, and Kraler 2013). Since the definition of skill as "high" or "low" is fundamentally informed by gender and race, feminized and racialized occupations in the care sector and agriculture are defined as outside the purview of "high skilled" entry streams. These prioritize male-dominated occupations in managerial and professional occupations (Boucher 2016; Romero 2018). Defined as "low skilled", migrant care and agricultural workers are usually subject to temporary migration schemes that do not offer a pathway to a more secure legal status (Anderson 2010). Although they work and pay taxes, their access to social benefits is restricted, both legally and in practice, and their presence as workers and taxpayers does not make them deserving of more advantageous types of legal status.

The rebranding of "low skilled" migrants into "essential" migrant workers during the COVID-19 pandemic might lead to a revaluation of their deservingness of civil and social rights and, therefore, of a legal status that confers such rights. This could mean the extension of temporary legal status to undocumented workers or permeant residency status to those with temporary legal status. If such legal status adjustments were accomplished as a result of the COVID-19 pandemic, they would mark a significant conceptual shift in the political economy of labour migration. Perceived levels of skill would no longer be the sole determinant of the economic worth of migrants and their worthiness of permanent residency. Instead, migrants' worthiness would be evaluated based on their actual societal contributions.

Legal status through sacrifice

Immigration policies, which assign legal status and rights to migrants at the time of entry, are also fundamentally about defining migrants' deservingness of membership in the national collective. As Zolberg (2006, 11), states: "the actual or potential role of [...] migrants as members of society evokes their assessment on a scale of moral value, referring to their impact on regime-maintenance and national integration (...)". Arguably the strongest indicator of an individual's commitment to regime-maintenance and national integration is their willingness to sacrifice their life for the nation. Weber (1998) identifies military service as a key basis for successful claims to citizenship by individuals outside the ruling classes in ancient Greek and medieval European city-states. Theorizing the development of modern nation-states, Anderson (1983, 7) argues that nations are "imagined communities" that connote a "deep, horizontal comradeship" powerful enough to create, among their members, a willingness to die on their behalf. Thus, theoretically, willingness to sacrifice oneself for the receiving nation presents itself as a potential means for migrant workers to make and enforce a claim to improved legal status under immigration policy.

Historical precedents in Canada and the United States show that military service can be used successfully by racialized immigrant groups to press for improved legal status and rights. In Canada, Roy (2008) notes that concerns about subsequent demands for enfranchisement made the Canadian government initially reluctant to draft Chinese residents into the Armed Forces during the Second World War. She also documents how, as anticipated, Chinese community leaders explicitly referenced Chinese service in the Armed Forces during the Second World War in appeals to the government to extend the franchise, which ultimately occurred in 1949. In the United States, Wolgin and Bloemraad (2010) document how the logic of family reunification rights for American soldiers with Asian "war brides" ultimately opened the door for a subsequent large-scale policy shift toward a family-centric, universal immigrant admission policy. COVID-19 could force a re-negotiation of "essential" migrant workers' legal status, because it has something in common with military service: it places workers at risk of death in service to the receiving nation.

Deservingness claims during a global pandemic: work or sacrifice?

It seems unlikely, in our estimation, that the moment of rupture caused by the COVID-19 pandemic will lead to an improvement in the legal status of migrant workers based on work-related deservingness. Countries in the Global North are unable to meet the labour demand in sectors that are notoriously low-paid and marked by poor working conditions. *Because* these sectors are "essential" in any society, states endeavour to maintain a constant labour supply for them, including through migrant labour. "Low skilled" and racialized migrant workers often lack alternative employment options and therefore provide a reliable pool of workers (Zolberg 1987). Thus, agricultural and care work have always been "essential" and, in recent history, largely done by racialized migrants from the Global South. Temporary legal statuses, employment restrictions, and limited access to social rights play an important role in ensuring that migrant workers stay in specific sectors and industries, claim a minimum amount of public goods, and do not overstay their welcome. The legal status of migrants is therefore deeply interwoven into the logic of the political economy of labour migration and a necessity to keep the costs and wages in "essential" sectors such as agriculture and care work at a minimum. Legal status adjustments based on the "essential" nature of migrants' work would threaten the global capitalist system. While the COVID-19 pandemic as a "moment of rupture" may lead to some changes in the treatment of migrant workers, we are doubtful that it will entirely overhaul the dynamics of global capitalism and the position of migrant workers within it.

Racialized constructions of skill provide not only the basis for the material valuation of labour and migrant's long-term societal worth; they are also a means to control the ethnic and racial composition of society (Sharma 2012; Zolberg 1987). They effectively block migrant workers from the Global South from accessing the pathways to permanent residency reserved for "high skilled" workers and select family members. If the "essential" nature of labour was the key determinant of migrants' moral worth as future citizens, a major hurdle to permanent residency and, ultimately, citizenship would be lifted for a large number of non-white migrants. In light of the current surge of anti-immigrant and xenophobic sentiment in countries across the Global North (Golder 2016), we doubt that governments will be willing to take this step.

Deservingness based on sacrifice could be the more viable frame for claiming legal status improvements, for two reasons. *First*, deservingness claims based on migrants' willingness to sacrifice their health and life during the

COVID-19 pandemic can be invoked only for as long as the pandemic is ongoing and an effective medical remedy remains elusive. This limits the time frame, the numeric scale, and the degree of status adjustments to which immigration policy makers would have to subscribe. Concessions under this deservingness frame would link legal status adjustments to the risks to health and life induced by the pandemic and *not* to the "essential" nature of labour. Such concessions would leave unscratched the inherent logic of the political economy and thus reduce the long-term consequences for states when responding positively to deservingness claims.

It appears that the intention to limit legal status concessions in time and scope is behind the Italian government's approach in responding to the legal status precarity of "essential" workers. In May 2020, the Italian government provided a pathway to temporary residence permits to around 200,000 of the approximately 550,000 undocumented migrants in Italy (D'Ignoti 2020). These temporary permits are valid for six months and open only to agricultural and domestic workers. Since they can be rescinded as soon as the pandemic is under control, these temporary permits maintain legal precarity and keep the commitment of the Italian government vis-à-vis undocumented migrant workers at a minimum. Yet, in taking this minimal step, the Italian government arguably appeases voices on the political left *and* right. Striking this balance appears vital in the current, polarized socio-political climate that marks many countries in the Global North.

Second, historic and contemporary precedents for legal status improvements on the basis of sacrifices for the nation show that this frame has been effective. For example, in the United States and Canada, military service can offer a path to naturalization with reduced requirements (GoC 2020b; USCIS 2020). While they are not entering a theatre of war, migrant care and agricultural workers are risking their lives to ensure the well-being of receiving countries by feeding and caring for their citizens. The motivation for doing this, be it self-interest (e.g. economic survival) or altruism (e.g. genuine willingness to ensure the wellbeing of others), is inconsequential even for military personnel. While some individuals enlist in the military for purely patriotic reasons, others enlist to improve their economic situation or to access free education (Helmus et al. 2018). For "essential" migrant workers, the pandemic has created parallels to military personnel that could be leveraged for legal status adjustments.

The notion of migrant workers' sacrifices has already been invoked in response to the COVID-19 pandemic by civil society and governmental actors in Canada and France. As of early July 2020, over 1,000 migrant farm workers in the Canadian province of Ontario alone have tested positive for COVID-19, and three have died. On the basis of this sacrifice, protesters and migrant rights organizations have called for migrant farm workers, who enter on temporary visas, to receive permanent resident status, a stepping-stone to Canadian citizenship (CBC 2020b). In the Canadian province of Quebec, immigration advocates are demanding the extension of permanent resident status to asylum-seekers from the Global South who provide care work in senior citizens residences, where the majority of the provinces' COVID-19 infections and deaths have occurred (CBC 2020a). Whether such calls are successful in Ontario and in Quebec remains to be seen. In France, important steps have already been taken into that direction. In September 2020, the French government announced that groups of foreign workers (incl. care workers), who were at a particularly high risk during the lockdown "in order to fight against the COVID-19 epidemic" should be fast-tracked for naturalization (Willsher 2020). Wrapped into a rhetoric that mirrors situations of combat, government representatives explained that these foreign workers "have shown their commitment to the nation" and "actively participated in the national effort with dedication and courage". The French state therefore "wishes to recognize their commitment" through a speedy naturalization process. It is notable that the French policy response is only directed at migrant "essential" workers who worked during the lockdown. This excludes future "essential" migrant workers from fast-tracked naturalization processes.

The policy responses to the legal status precarity of "essential" migrant workers in Italy and France, and also the organized demands for such policy responses in Canada, might currently be introducing a new category of migrants to the migration regimes of countries in the Global North: that of the "essential" migrant worker who risks life and limb for the well-being of the host country. This recategorization and revaluation of *some* migrant workers harbours the potential of producing new grounds for marginalization and exclusion. If migrant workers' deservingness of legal status improvements becomes based on the type of labour they perform (i.e. "essential" or "non-essential") or the sacrifices they are willing to make, migrants whose labour is not categorized as "essential" or potentially dangerous could be deemed as (even) less deserving of non-precarious status. Especially in the current socio-political climate, where the perceived permanent presence of too many migrants can easily polarize entire societies, concessions to one group of racialized migrants could well be accompanied by heightened barriers for others. Thus, while a door might currently be opening for "essential" workers, another door might be closing for "low skilled", "non-essential" migrant workers.

Concluding discussion: would legal status changes reduce marginalization?

In this short debate article, we identified two potential deservingness frames – work and sacrifice – that could be leveraged during the COVID-19 pandemic to improve the legal status of racialized migrant workers in "essential" sectors of the economy. Of the two, we argued that deservingness claims on the basis of sacrifice are more likely to be successful. Although we believe that an improvement in legal status (and concomitant access to civil and social rights) could slightly alleviate racialized migrant workers' marginalization, we recognize that any improvements would be limited and potentially reversable, especially in contexts where anti-immigrant sentiment is on the rise.

Even full legal citizens benefit unequally from their status, depending on their ascribed social group memberships like race, gender, class, ability, etc. For example, Joseph (2020, 59) shows that "citizens of color" in the United States are regularly treated as "'foreign others' who do not fully belong to the envisioned nation". Similarly, Beaman (2017) documents how descendants of North African immigrants to France remain "citizen outsiders" despite their high level of socioeconomic inclusion in the middle class.

Also, access to the rights attached to legal status may change over time and become contingent on individuals' ascribed social positions, even for full citizens. Glenn (2002), for example, shows how the extension of full legal citizenship to Blacks and women in the United States has, historically, been followed by the narrowing of the social and economic rights that status entails. Bloemraad et al. (2019, 86) show that, while citizenship has symbolically become more inclusive of ethnic and racial minorities across the Global North, "[a]ccess to welfare resources has eroded, or at least become more conditional on deservingness judgments", which disadvantage the poor and racialized minorities. The 2018 Windrush scandal in the United Kingdom demonstrates that citizenship status can even be reversed entirely. There, approximately 500,000 individuals who entered the country as Commonwealth citizens from Caribbean countries prior to 1971 and considered themselves full British citizens were "illegalized". This was due to their inability to fulfil newer documentation requirements arising from the "hostile environment", which they did not know applied to them. Importantly, these individuals had entered the United Kingdom at the invitation of the government to fill labour shortages in the country's National Health Service sector and other essential economic sectors (BBC 2020).

In light of these examples, there is no reason to believe that a small change in legal status – e.g. from undocumented status to temporary foreign worker, or temporary foreign worker to permanent resident – will eliminate experiences of marginalization of racialized migrant workers. Research in Canada confirms this skepticism (see, e.g. Goldring and Landolt 2011; Tungohan et al. 2015). Temporary foreign workers who transition to permanent residence status remain trapped in the low-wage, precarious employment sectors they were originally allotted to under immigration law, due to lack of work experience in other sectors, lack of money to renew qualifications, and truncated social networks. Additionally, poor remuneration leaves them unable to afford the costly process of exercising their right to family reunification.

Nevertheless, we believe that even a limited improvement in the legal status, and related rights, for "essential" migrant workers in response to the COVID-19 pandemic would represent a small step toward reducing their marginalization. Improvements in legal status extend the formal rights of migrant workers and reduce the legitimacy of differences in treatment and remuneration that currently exist between racialized migrant workers and citizens/legal residents. Even if the ability of "low skilled" and racialized "essential" workers to enforce these claims remains contingent on their social group membership and the socio-political context, having a legal basis from which to fight for the enforcement of rights is better than the absence of such a basis. Finally, we would like to echo Chauvin and Garcés-Mascareñas (2014, 426), who argue that "the master frame of the 'deserving migrant' may [...] be reinforced by the multiplicity of its deployments and become more readily available for further uses". In this spirit, we hope that any successful deservingness claims based on "sacrifice" during the COVID-19 pandemic that prompt a revaluation of "essential" migrant workers' legal status can be expanded to and used by a range of "essential" *and* "non-essential" migrant workers in the future.

Disclosure statement

No potential conflict of interest was reported by the author(s).

Funding

Support for this work was provided by an Internal McGill University COVID-19 Rapid Response Social Sciences and Humanities Award & MI4 Emergency COVID-19 Research Funding (ECRF).

References

Anderson, Benedict. 1983. *Imagined Communities: Reflections on the Origin and Spread of Nationalism*. London: Verso.

Anderson, Bridget. 2010. "Migration, Immigration Controls and the Fashioning of Precarious Workers." *Work, Employment and Society* 24 (2): 300–317.

Anderson, Bridget. 2015. "Immigration and the Worker Citizen." In *Citizenship and Its Others*, edited by B. Anderson, and V. Hughes, 41–57. Basingstoke: Palgrave Macmillan.

Bakan, Abigail B, and Daiva Stasiulis. 2012. "The Political Economy of Migrant Live-in Caregivers: A Case of Unfree Labour?" In *Legislated Inequality: Temporary Labour Migration in Canada*, edited by P. T. Lenard, and C. Straehle, 202–226. Montreal: McGill-Queen's University Press.

BBC. 2020. "Windrush Generation: Who Are They and Why Are They Facing Problems?" *The Guardian*. 31 July. Accessed 8 October 2020. https://www.bbc.com/news/uk-43782241.

Beaman, Jean. 2017. "Citizen Outsider: Children of North African Immigrants in France." Oakland, California: University of California Press. Retrieved.

Bloemraad, Irene, Anna Korteweg, and Gökçe Yurdakul. 2008. "Citizenship and Immigration: Multiculturalism, Assimilation, and Challenges to the Nation-State." *Annual Review of Sociology* 34 (1): 153–179. doi:10.1146/annurev.soc.34.040507.134608.

Bloemraad, Irene, Will Kymlicka, Michèle Lamont, and Leanne S. Son Hing. 2019. "Membership without Social Citizenship? Deservingness & Redistribution as Grounds for Equality." *Daedalus* 148 (3): 73–104.

Boucher, Anna. 2016. *Gender, Migration and the Global Race for Talent*. Manchester: Manchester University Press.

CBC. 2020a. "Immigration Advocates Demand Permanent Status for Asylum Seekers Working in Quebec's Long-Term Care Homes," online: *CBC News*. Accessed 8 July 2020. https://www.cbc.ca/news/canada/montreal/asylum-seekers-immigration-covid-19-front-lines-chsld-quebec-1.5601868.

CBC. 2020b. "Protesters Gather at Minister's Office, Demand More Rights for Migrants Workers" *CBC News*, online. Accessed 8 July 2020. https://www.cbc.ca/news/canada/toronto/protesters-immigration-minister-office-1.5637957.

Chauvin, Sébastien, and Blanca Garcés-Mascareñas. 2014. "Becoming Less Illegal: Deservingness Frames and Undocumented Migrant Incorporation." *Sociology Compass* 8 (4): 422–432.

Chauvin, S., B. Garcés-Mascareñas, and A. Kraler. 2013. "Working for Legality: Employment and Migrant Regularization in Europe." *International Migration* 51 (6): 118–131.

Dewey, John. 1991 [1939]. "Theory of Valuation." In *John Dewey: The Later Works, 1925–1953*, Vol. 13, edited by J. A. Boydston, 189–251. Carbondale: Southern Illinois University Press.

D'Ignoti, Stefania. 2020. "Italy's Coronavirus Amnesty: Migrant Rights or Economic Self-Interest?" *The New Humanitarian*. 25 May. https://www.thenewhumanitarian.org/feature/2020/05/25/Italy-coronavirus-migrant-labour.

DW. 2020. "Germany Passes Coronavirus Aid Package for Workers." *Deutsche Welle*. 23 April. Accessed 12 October 2020. https://www.dw.com/en/germany-passes-coronavirus-aid-package-for-workers/a-53213509.

Ehrenreich, Barbara, and Arlie Russell Hochschild. 2003. *Global Woman: Nannies, Maids, and Sex Workers in the New Economy*. New York: Metropolitan Books.

Glenn, Evelyn Nakano. 2002. *Unequal Freedom: How Race and Gender Shaped American Citizenship and Labor*. Cambridge: Harvard University Press.

GoC. 2020a. "Canada's Covid-19 Economic Response Plan." online: Government of Canada. https://www.canada.ca/en/department-finance/economic-response-plan.html.

GoC. 2020b. "Citizenship Grants: Canadian Armed Forces." online: Government of Canada. Accessed 7 July 2020. https://www.canada.ca/en/immigration-refugees-citizenship/corporate/publications-manuals/operational-bulletins-manuals/canadian-citizenship/grant/canadian-armed-forces.html.

Golder, Matt. 2016. "Far Right Parties in Europe." *Annual Review of Political Science* 19 (1): 477–497. doi:10.1146/annurev-polisci-042814-012441.

Goldring, Luin, and Patricia Landolt. 2011. "Caught in the Work-Citizenship Matrix: The Lasting Effects of Precarious Legal Status on Work for Toronto Immigrants." *Globalizations* 8 (3): 325–341.

Helmus, Tood C., Rebecca Zimmermann, Marek N. Posard, Jasmine L. Wheeler, Cordaye Ogletree, Quinton Stroud, and Margaret C. Harrell. 2018. "Life as a Private. A Study of the Motivations and Experiences of Junior Enlisted Personnel in the U.S. Army." Vol. Santa Monica: RAND Corporation.

IOM. 2020. "Standing in Solidarity with Migrants: Supporting Civil Society and Other Stakeholders in Responding to the Covid-19 Pandemic." 7 August. Accessed 15 October 2020. https://www.iom.int/news/standing-solidarity-migrants-supporting-civil-society-and-other-stakeholders-responding-covid.

Joseph, Tiffany. 2020. "Whitening Citizenship: Race, Ethnicity, and Documentation Status as Brightened Boundaries of Exclusion in the U.S. And Europe." In *Routledge International Handbook of Contemporary Racisms, Routledge International Handbooks*, edited by J. Solomos. Abingdon, 55–66. Oxon: Routledge.

Marshall, T. H. 1950. *Citizenship and Social Class, and Other Essays*. Cambridge, England: University Press.

Parreñas, Rhacel Salazar. 2015. *Servants of Globalization: Migration and Domestic Work*. Stanford: Stanford University Press.

Piore, Michael J. 1979. *Birds of Passage: Migrant Labor and Industrial Societies*. Cambridge: Cambridge University Press.

Romero, M. 2018. "Reflections on Globalized Care Chains and Migrant Women Workers." *Critical Sociology* 44 (7-8): 1179–1189.

Roy, Patricia E. 2008. *The Triumph of Citizenship: The Japanese and Chinese in Canada, 1941–67*. Vancouver: UBC Press.

Schneiderhan, Erik. 2011. "Pragmatism and Empirical Sociology: The Case of Jane Addams and Hull-House, 1889–1895." *Theory and Society* 40 (6): 589–617.

Sharma, Nandita. 2012. "The 'Difference' That Borders Make: 'Temporary Foreign Workers' and the Social Organization of Unfreedom in Canada." In *Legislated Inequality: Temporary Labour Migration in Canada*, edited by P. T. Lenard, and C. Straehle, 26–47. Montreal: McGill-Queen's University Press.

Soysal, Yasemin Nuhoğlu. 1994. *Limits of Citizenship: Migrants and Postnational Membership in Europe*. Chicago: University of Chicago.

Triandafyllidou, Anna, and Lucia Nalbandian. 2020. "COVID-19 and the Transformation of Migration and Mobility Globally - "Disposable" and "Essential": Changes in the Global Hierarchies of Migrant Workers after COVID-19." International Organization for Migration, "Think Pieces" series from Migration Research High Level Advisers, 1-13. Geneva: IOM.

Tungohan, Ethel, Rupa Banerjee, Wayne Chu, Petronila Cleto, Conely de Leon, Mila Garcia, Philip Kelly, Marco Luciano, Cynthia Palmaria, and Christopher Sorio. 2015. "After the Live-in Caregiver Program: Filipina Caregivers' Experiences of Graduated and Uneven Citizenship." *Canadian Ethnic Studies* 47 (1): 87–105.

USCIS. 2020. "Naturalization through Military Service." online: USCIS. Accessed 7 July 2020. https://www.uscis.gov/military/naturalization-through-military-service.

Weber, Max. 1998. "Citizenship in Ancient and Medieval Cities." In *The Citizenship Debates*, edited by G. Shafir, 43–52. Minneapolis: University of Minnesota Press.

Willsher, Kim. 2020. "Foreign Covid Workers in France to Be Fast-Tracked for Nationality." *The Guardian*. 15 September. Accessed 12 October 2020. https://www.theguardian.com/world/2020/sep/15/foreign-covid-workers-in-france-to-be-fast-tracked-for-nationality?CMP=Share_iOSApp_Other&fbclid=IwAR1LY4Z8OBKwt6guA-IFDjmk4Ze4XxP7BCablnvH7ZZRzovWwKVyY_syx80.

Wolgin, Philip E., and Irene Bloemraad. 2010. "'Our Gratitude to Our Soldiers': Military Spouses, Family Re-Unification, and Postwar Immigration Reform." *The Journal of Interdisciplinary History* 41 (1): 27–60.

Zolberg, Aristide. 1987. "Wanted but Not Welcome." In *Population in an Interacting World*, edited by W. Alonso, 36–73. Cambridge: Harvard University Press.

Zolberg, Aristide. 2006. "Patterns of International Migration Policy. A Diachronic Comparison." In *The Migration Reader: Exploring Politics and Policy*, edited by A. M. Messina, and G. Lahav, 110–125. Boulder, CO: Lynne Rienner Publishers.

Rethinking refuge in the time of COVID-19

Nasar Meer, Emma Hill, Timothy Peace and Leslie Villegas

ABSTRACT
COVID-19 has profoundly impeded the global movement of people. Two key questions, however, remain unclear. Firstly, what are the possible medium and long-term implications of recent developments and, secondly, do they mark a departure from the existing approaches in state practices toward displaced migration? Using examples limited to Europe, we argue that the first question cannot yet be fully answered but a better understanding can be achieved by considering recent trends. The second question, we maintain, is no easier to gauge but should be facilitated by utilizing conceptual material to theorize current and infolding developments, and specifically to consider which repertoires appear especially suited as these unfold. Two literatures, one drawn from the discussion of displaced migration and the "disease" metaphor, and the other from thinking about asylum and the "racial state", are brought together not to assert any definitive conclusion, but in order to help re-think contemporary developments.

Introduction

COVID-19 has profoundly impeded the global movement of people, illustrated by the roughly 46,000 travel restrictions imposed by individual states and whole regional blocks by early April 2020 (International Organization for Migration (IOM) 2020). While some states have been more cautious than others, in the large majority of cases, a freeze on mobility has included the closure of borders to asylum seekers and refugees (Meer and Villegas 2020). Two key questions, however, remain unclear. Firstly, what are the possible medium and long-term implications of recent changes and, secondly, do they mark a qualitative departure from the existing approaches in state practices toward displaced migration? In this short article, and using examples limited to Europe, we argue that the first question cannot yet be fully answered but a better understanding can be achieved by considering recent trends and developments. The second question, we maintain, is no easier to gauge but should be facilitated by utilizing conceptual material that can theorize current and infolding developments, specifically to consider which theoretical repertoires in a crowded field may appear especially suited as developments continue to unfold in light of the current pandemic. Two literatures, one drawn from the discussion of displaced migration and the "disease" metaphor, and the other from thinking about asylum and the "racial state", are brought together not to assert any definitive conclusion, but in order to help read contemporary developments.

Recent trends and developments

As part of a series of restrictions on the movement of people, the right to seek asylum and refuge was severely curtailed during the early months of the COVID-19 pandemic. At least 57 countries made no exception to their travel restrictions for refugees seeking asylum (UNHCR 2020a), even though the World Health Organisation (WHO) offered clear guidance on the use of quarantines and health screening measures at points of entry for those fleeing persecution. As a result, travel bans and other emergency measures led to a continual decline in asylum applications in the EU compared to pre-COVID levels, with a registered drop of 43% in March and a subsequent decline of 87% in April 2020 following many countries' suspension of asylum procedures for public health reasons (Fundamental Rights Agency 2020).

This move left many people seeking refuge stranded in already precarious conditions, and led Filippo Grandi, the UN High Commissioner for Refugees, to argue that, "the core principles of refugee protection are being put to test" (UNHCR 2020c). In other words, and despite protections enshrined in international law, the UNHCR saw the response to the global public health emergency as posing a novel risk to established conventions. Specifically, and as Villegas and Meer (2020) have summarized,

> since 1951, the United Nations Refugee Convention has protected refugees and asylum seekers from being returned to a place where they would be in danger because of their race, religion, nationality, membership in a particular social group, or their political opinion.

The key point here in the Convention is that it makes the principle of "non-refoulement" a cornerstone of international refugee protection.[1] Presently, the UNHCR has been clear in stating that neither the 1951 Refugee Convention nor EU refugee law provide any legal basis for suspending asylum applications (UNHCR 2020a, 2020b). While stakeholders recognize, and try to mitigate, that it is presently lawful for undocumented migrants to be detained for a short and finite amount of time, it needs to be stressed that

arbitrary detention is prohibited and removal can only be the result of individual determinations, not a blanket application of policy (Human Rights
Watch 2020). These the bare minimal safeguards achieved in near recent
memory of the Holocaust.

In specific cases, however, and well before the COVID 19 pandemic arose,
the European Court of Justice found several EU member states guilty of not
fulfilling their asylum responsibilities by attempting to opt out of EU treaties
that require them to admit asylum seekers. Importantly these cases date back
to 2015 and include how, in its April 2, 2020 decision, the European Court of
Justice Court ruled against Hungary, the Czech Republic, and Poland and their
refusal to relocate asylum seekers from Greece and Italy on the grounds of
maintaining public safety and law and order (Rankin 2020). What the
COVID-19 pandemic has arguably blurred however is the thin line states
can tread between violating the principle of non-refoulement and doing
just enough to stay within its parameters. For example, when it comes to
asylum seekers enroute by sea, international law requires states to disembark
people rescued in a place where they are safe. Despite this, pandemic conditions have allowed actions, such as those undertaken in Cyprus, in which
Cypriot authorities pushed a boat carrying Syrian refugees back out of its ter-
ritorial waters, forcing it to dock in the self-declared Turkish Republic of
Northern Cyprus, and which has no effective asylum system (Connelly
2020). Italy and Malta meanwhile also closed their ports for most boats and
NGOs, and suspended their search and rescue operations at sea to comply
with emergency legislation (Keller, Schöler, and Goldoni 2020).

In one respect, these moves are an escalation of what has gone before,
including Hungary's "chutes and ladders" asylum system which, as Armstrong's (2018) documents, has made it effectively impossible to be
granted asylum. In the context of COVID, while closing borders and ceasing
asylum procedures are therefore not explicit and overt refoulement actions,
they have prevented potential asylum seekers from registering at the
border (Fundamental Rights Agency 2020). A stronger reading, however,
would be to say that case law has extended the scope of Article 33 (1)
whereby today it is commonly understood that:

> It precludes any act of refoulement, of whatever form, including non-
> admittance at the frontier, that would have the effect of exposing refugees
> or asylum seekers to: (i) a threat of persecution on account of race, religion,
> nationality, membership of a particular social group or political opinion; (ii) a
> real risk of torture or cruel, inhuman or degrading treatment or punishment;
> or (iii) a threat to life, physical integrity or liberty (Lauterpacht and Bethlehem
> 2001, 128).

In this reading it may indeed be argued that closing humanitarian borders
and procedures violate the principle by indirectly pushing asylum seekers

into situations where their human rights can be violated. Yet focusing on this matter alone, however, is to overlook the conditions of people seeking asylum who are presently in Europe but prevented from moving on.

Deteriorating conditions for those seeking asylum in Europe

Here there is evidence that displaced migrants have been held in wholly unsatisfactory and overcrowded reception centres in conditions that exacerbate the risk of COVID-19 infections. In several of the Greek hotspots, camps have lacked the most basic sanitation, including soap and clean running water, with thousands forced to sleep in close proximity. Although the authorities announced certain measures to prevent the spread of disease in the hotspots, including restricting residents' movements, such measures also deepened human suffering and increased existing tensions in the camps (Fundamental Rights Agency 2020).

Even before the 8 September 2020 fires that consumed the Moria camp on the Greek island of Lesvos, making it uninhabitable and leaving nearly 13,000 without shelter or basic services, medics on the ground reported horrific conditions where "recommended measures such as frequent hand washing and social distancing to prevent the spread of the virus are just impossible" (MSF 2020). "Siyana Marhroof Shaffi, director of the UK-based charity Kitrinos Healthcare, which runs a medical clinic on Lesvos, reported that many of the camp's residents already had respiratory infections and that, scabies was 'rampant'" (Iacobucci 2020). As Meer (2020) has argued, "these and camps in the other Aegean islands of Chios, Samos, Leros, and Kos, swelled following the EU-Turkey deal (signed in 2016) commenced to prevent onward movement from the camps" (cf Long 2018).

In Cyprus, where the provision of accommodation for those seeking asylum is virtually non-existent (Christodoulou and Michael 2019), asylum seekers living in independent accommodation were forced to move to the Pournara camp in Kokkinotrimithia. Here they were effectively imprisoned as part of a nationwide lockdown and even when national restrictions were eased, residents of the camp were not allowed to leave, leading to hunger strikes and demonstrations (Bennett 2020). Such acts of desperation are not limited to reception facilities in Southern Europe. In Sweden, an inmate at a migrant detention centre died from COVID-19 in April 2020 and hunger strikes have taken place at a number of the Swedish Migration Agency's detention centres. Revolts have also been reported at various reception and detention centres in Italy where living conditions remain precarious. One such protest in the Sicilian town of Caltanissetta occurred after the death of a man from Tunisia seeking asylum and a hunger strike took place at the detention centre of Gradisca d'Isonzo in the north east of the country to protest against the risk of the virus spreading (Fundamental Rights Agency 2020).

Similarly, in Bologna, displaced migrants living in reception centres wrote an open letter to local and regional authorities calling for improvements in living conditions to reduce the chance of transmission of COVID-19. Campaign groups report that in some cases, displaced migrants are forced to labour in jobs where they are openly exposed to the risk of infection:

> Many of us work side by side, day and night, at the Interporto, where in some warehouses the workload has doubled to keep pace with the growing demand provoked by the pandemic. When we have to rest, we go back to the crowded reception centres. In via Mattei, more than 200 of us live and sleep in dorms with 5–10 persons each, with beds very close, one on top of the other (Coordinamento Migranti Letter reported in European Commission (2020).

The political rhetoric of some leaders across Europe, meanwhile, has used the pandemic to re-articulate anti-migrant sentiment. The Hungarian Prime Minister Viktor Orbán, for example, has told the people of Hungary that "Our experience is that primarily foreigners brought in the disease, and that it is spreading among foreigners" (France 24 2020). In Italy, the former Interior Minister Matteo Salvini claimed that a migrant rescue ship should not have been allowed to dock in Sicily due to the supposed health risk posed by those on board (Tondo 2020). In a similar vein, the Governor of Sicily, Nello Musumeci, cited fears of migrants spreading COVID when he ordered an emergency decree, subsequently quashed by the Italian government, to close down all hotspots and emergency reception centres. In Greece, the New Democracy government used COVID to implement closed camps (which are essentially detention centres) for asylum seekers stranded on various Aegean islands. In France, Marine Le Pen cited the spread of the coronavirus to justify her renewed push to close France's border with Italy (Trilling 2020). Alice Weidel, The AfD (Alternative for Germany) leader in the Bundestag, has blamed the spread of the virus on what she called "the dogma of open borders" (Zerka 2020). Elsewhere, Santiago Abascal, head of the Vox movement in Spain has been quoted blaming the Socialist government for the spread of COVID-19, because they are, "so keen to bring down borders it has not even taken the minimum measures dictated by common sense" (Ashfor 2020).

If political rhetoric is relevant then these statements matter in forging norms in public discourse, and in setting agendas more broadly, and of course dovetail with material policy changes. Across the examples discussed above, pandemic conditions have resulted in heightened and tightened curbs on border entry and, in our view, facilitated violations of international human rights law. For asylum seekers and refugees already resident in-country, pandemic conditions have also resulted in increased internal restrictions on their mobility and a swift, enforced decline in living conditions. In some cases, politicians have used the pandemic to advance their agenda on displaced migration, taking the opportunity to put in place enhanced border measures to prevent entry into the state. In others, disease prevention controls – social restrictions, quarantining, lockdown – have coincided with existing border controls such as immobilization, coercive housing and border closures.

Theorizing developments

Within this context, the cases above are particularly striking on two counts: (1) that expressions of anxiety or hostility towards displaced migration and/in pandemic conditions coincide in the language of "disease" and that (2) whilst this language displays open hostility to migrants of all backgrounds, it utilizes frameworks that signal asylum seekers and refugees are at the nexus of this concern. The use of the language of "disease" to talk about displaced migration has particular potency within pandemic. Though it may appear to be specific to the current context, there are ample pre-COVID precedents for mobilizing medicalised racism against asylum seekers and refugees, consideration of which offers frameworks and explanatory starting-points from which to analyse the deterioration of border and living conditions for displaced migrants.

(i) Displaced migration and the "disease" metaphor

The association of immigration with "disease" is a discursive strand with a distinctive genealogy. Evidence from the mid-nineteenth century onwards indicates that migrants of all statuses have been associated with medicalised prejudice, from the association of typhus with Irish refugees in mid-nineteenth century Britain (Darwen et al. 2020; Hickman and Ryan 2020), to the coterminous stigmatization in the US of Irish migrants as the "bearers of cholera" (Kraut 2010, 125), the naming of late-nineteenth century outbreaks of tuberculosis as the "Jewish disease" (ibid), and the blaming of Chinese groups for the San Francisco plague in the early twentieth century (Rosenberg 1962). By the twentieth century, this rhetoric found a specific target, so that in the UK, the Aliens Order (1920), identified refugees as "unsanitary aliens", and sought to restrict their entry on the alleged grounds that their "presence is likely to be a danger to the health of the people of this country" (quoted in Taylor 2016, 520). This is a trend echoed in contemporary examples of politicians representing displaced migrants as "swarms", "swarming", or "swamping" – thereby likening them to insects or unhuman entities who carry disease – whilst calling for more stringent and restrictive border regulations. The language deployed by present anti-immigrant actors above must therefore also be situated within this genealogy.

One way of unpacking the discourse of "disease" in the context of displaced migration is to consider the role of the body politic in sustaining the "disease" metaphor. As Musolff (2004, 437–438) notes, the rhetorical association of refuge with "disease", has allowed political actors to present nation states as analogous to a "body" in need of protection from "invasion, penetration, infection or disease", a rhetoric which has become "[one of] the foundation[s] for the arguments of immigration restrictions" (Kraut 2010, 125). The body politic of the nation-state might therefore be understood to occupy the centre of the "disease" metaphor, whereby the nation is imagined as the representative "body" of its citizens, made in their normative image. In this representational economy, the language of "disease" is used to express the limits of the nation-state, and those outside the body politic are not only considered "foreign" or Other, but also potential "threats" to the well-ness, "purity" and resilience of the body of the nation.

There is precedent for the language of "disease" to be applied to a number of social groups who are considered beyond the body politic (including the unemployed, people living in poverty, LGBTQIA populations, and racialized minority groups more broadly). However, a broad analysis of the relationship between the body politic and the "disease" metaphor does not account for the specificities of its application to displaced migrants. As the examples above indicate, the "disease" metaphor appears to be of particular utility for those wishing to express hostility towards asylum seekers and refugees. Why? What so directs its focus towards displaced migration? One possible explanation is related to asylum seekers' and refugees' distinctive immigration status. Achiume (2019) has argued that in contrast to forms of migration over which they can exert full border controls (such as economic or familial migrants), for signatories of the 1951 Convention, which obliges nation-states to honour human rights commitments, displaced migration represents a loss of border (and national) sovereignty, making asylum and refugee statuses the migrant category over which nation-states have least control. Pandemic imaginaries that associate asylum seekers and refugees as "bringing disease" therefore might in part be explained as an expression of nation-states' perceived loss of control resulting from their international humanitarian obligations. In this framework, and within the disease metaphor, asylum seekers and refugees are imagined as the vessels of disease, of threat to the nation, which, at a time when borders play a central role in pandemic regulation, is able to exert less control over their arrival, and is vulnerable to "infection".

(ii) Asylum and the "racial state"

It is not simply the case, however, that the disease metaphor is utilized to express anxieties about high levels of infection in pandemic conditions. Rather, it is used to perform a political sleight of hand, in which asylum seekers and refugees are framed not simply as *carrying* disease, but *as the disease.* As Darwen et al. (2020), Kraut (1994, 2010) and Taylor (2016) help elaborate, this is a pattern which is well-established, from Jewish and Irish displaced migrants, to post-1990 asylum seekers and refugees from former-colonies in the Global South. It is also a trend readily identifiable in the examples above, including, (for instance) the swift translation of far-right "asylum-seekers-as-disease" rhetoric into actual border and port closures. Yet if this is so, it also requires a consideration of the underlying governmentality in current approaches.

In this regard, a second register that can help continue to theorize present and emerging approaches to refugee in light of COVID is that which comes from theorisations of asylum and the "racial state". This is specifically used to (a) express anxiety over the entry and presence of racialised minorities in the nation state, and (b) technologised control to regulate and discipline their movements. The "disease metaphor" therefore requires further elaboration, with reference to frameworks which theorize the relationship between racial hierarchy and the development of the nation. Of relevance here is David Theo Goldberg's scholarship (2002, 2008), which has argued that modern nation-states are in fact "racial states" (Goldberg 2002), with the purpose of maintaining white hegemony. Theorizing the nation-state as the "racial state" means that race is understood as one of the key organizing forces of the nation-state, and that factors such as citizenship, access to the nation and belonging is hierarchized as such. This offers a framework and motive with which to analyse the representational economy of the "disease" metaphor, as applied to displaced migrants, and sheds further light on European nation-states' approaches to displaced migration. An influential argument, it is taken up by a number of authors to specifically theorize current approaches to migration in ways helpfully summarized by Lentin (2007, 612):

> Through constitutions, border controls, the law, policy making, bureaucracy and governmental technologies such as census categorizations, invented histories and traditions, ceremonies and cultural imaginings, modern states, each in its own way, are defined by their power to exclude (and include) in racially ordered terms, to categorize hierarchically, and to set aside.

As Lentin indicates, border controls, including those enacted upon asylum seekers and refugees, are central to the maintenance of the "racial state". Border controls can be connected to what Goldberg (2002, 43) identifies as the two traditions of the racial state – naturalism and historicism – which perpetuated narratives of racialised populations as "biologically inferior", or "less developed", and positioned border controls as "necessary" measures to "preserve" the perceived white "homogeneity" of European nation-states. Here, we suggest, it is possible to glimpse the roots of the language of "disease" deployed against racialised minorities and displaced migrants, where racist imaginaries of racialised populations as "subhuman" map onto the somatic imagery of the body politic, and have established a means through which immigration can be framed as (racial) "infection".

Elsewhere, scholars including Bhambra (2015, 2017), Mayblin (2017) and El-Enany (2020) insist that for European nations of colonialism, racial hierarchies also had a series of additional functions, including (1) inhibiting movement from the colonies to the imperial centre and then, after independence, (2) delegitimising the claims of residents of ex-colonies – "making migrants" then of otherwise citizens of the ex-imperial nation-state. These functions served the purpose of preserving the wealth of colonial spoils for the (white) citizens of the imperial centre, whilst preventing racialised citizens from accessing the benefits of stolen wealth. As Mayblin (2017) observes, it is not a coincidence that restrictions on asylum controls have developed in parallel with demographic shifts amongst asylum seeking populations, which, once predominantly white European, since 1990, have increasingly been made up of Black and Brown displaced migrants from the Global South.

Some might ask why this is relevant to the discussion at hand, and one answer is that the resulting regime of racialised and colonial border logics has both national and international effects, with distinctly "medicalised" characteristics. For instance, Achiume (2019) suggests that European border regimes have effectively enacted a continental quarantining on states in the Global South. At the same time, within European nation-states, an agenda of what El-Enany (2020, 4) has called "racial (b)ordering" seeks to prevent the entry of racialised populations to the state and subjects the "racialised poor" to the "operation of internal borders [...] to street and state terror".

Outwith pandemic conditions, these internal "everyday bordering" (Yuval-Davis, Wemyss, and Cassidy 2018) practices to which displaced migrants are subject – coerced immobility, enforced impoverishment, precarious and unsafe accommodation, and spatial "dumping" (Hill, Meer, and Peace 2021; Cheshire and Zappia 2016) – might be understood in the now-familiar terms of public health measures – "infection control", social quarantining, social distancing. *Within* pandemic conditions, and following increased public health measures, thinking with "everyday bordering" approaches might at least allow us to consider how current practices can also be understood as (1) compounding existing controls on asylum seekers and refugees, (2) creating conditions in which vulnerability to and likelihood of infection are increased, and (3) creating secondary risks to their everyday survival (i.e. food poverty or increased social vulnerability).

Governing refuge after COVID 19

This short discussion is necessarily limited given the allotted space, but it has at least sought to contribute to an understanding of some medium and long-term implications for refuge in light of COVID 19, including whether present approaches signal a departure from what has prevailed in state practices toward displaced migration. Using examples limited to Europe, we have ela-borated some recent trends and developments which suggest that there is good reason to believe we are witnessing both continuity and novelty.

We note how during the early stages of the pandemic, international pro-tections nominally afforded to asylum seekers and refugees were withdrawn on multiple fronts, and we maintain that it is insufficient to characterize these as merely continuity of what has gone before. This is especially relevant as states have partially eased their lock-down measures, and where it is far from clear that the new normal will be a return to pre-lockdown asylum regimes. Continued analysis is then necessary, but this description of events is not only an empirical matter, however, but is relevant to conceptual considerations and specifically how theoretical repertoires may appear especially relevant as developments continue to unfold.

This allows us to understand how the extended COVID restrictions can be read within an environment in which strategies of immobilization are used to control the movements of asylum seekers and refugees, and are utilized in order to maintain a racial order which discriminates against asylum seekers from the Global South (El-Enany 2020). We have argued that this might also allow us to understand that while, outwith the pandemic, existing "every-day bordering" practices established an infrastructure with necropolitical objectives (Mayblin, Wake, and Kozheni 2019; Mbembe 2003), pandemic con-ditions enable them to be more readily realized. To this end, we have argued that there is virtue is maintaining a focus on the "disease" metaphor in the context of the "racial state". What this reveals is that whilst the increasingly restrictive, negligent and violent conditions to which displaced migrants are subject are implemented in the name of "viral prevention", these measures may provide the means through which "racial infection" controls can be increased.

These are not certainties that will apply universally, but what the concep-tual material offers to our understanding of unfolding developments is that the present racialization of refuge is a key feature of an emerging inter-national refugee settlement, something that must be analysed as both relying on old tropes while developing new ones in approaches to refuge in the time of COVID-19.

Note

1. Enshrined in Article 33 of the 1951 Refugee Convention, this principle insists that "No Contracting State shall expel or return ("refouler") a refugee in any manner whatsoever to the frontiers of territories where his [or her] life or freedom would be threatened on account of his [or her] race, religion, nationality, membership of a particular social group or political opinion." (UNHCR, 1951).

Disclosure statement

No potential conflict of interest was reported by the author(s).

Funding

This work was supported by Economic and Social Research Council: [Grant Number ES/R00451X/1].

References

Achiume, E. T. 2019. "Migration as Decolonisation." *Stanford Law Review* 71 (6): 1509–1574.

Armstrong, A. B. 2018. "Chutes and Ladders: Nonrefoulment and the Sisyphean Challenge of Seeking Asylum in Hungary." *Columbia Human Rights Law Review* 50 (2): 46–115.

Ashfor, J. 2020. "How Populists are Exploiting the Spread of Coronavirus." The Week UK, 27 February. Accessed 27 August 2020. https://www.theweek.co.uk/105909/how-populists-are-exploiting-the-spread-of-coronavirus.

Authors. forthcoming.

Bennett, C. 2020. "Migrants Forced to Stay in Cyprus Camp Despite Easing of Covid-19 Lockdown." *France 24*, 26th May. https://observers.france24.com/en/20200526-cyprus-migrants-camp-pournara-covid-19.

Bhambra, G. K. 2015. "Citizens and Others: The Constitution of Citizenship Through Exclusion." *Alternatives: Global, Local, Political* 40 (2): 102–114.

Bhambra, G. 2017. "The Current Crisis of Europe: Refugees, Colonialism and the Limits of Cosmopolitanism." *European Law Journal* 23: 395–405.

Cheshire, L., and G. Zappia. 2016. "Destination Dumping Ground: The Convergence of 'Unwanted' Populations in Disadvantaged City Areas." *Urban Studies* 53 (10): 2081–2098.

Christodoulou, J., and A. Michael. 2019. *Integration Governance in Cyprus: Accommodation, Regeneration and Exclusion*. University of Edinburgh, GLIMER Project. http://www.glimer.eu/wp-content/uploads/2019/02/Cyprus-Accommodation.pdf.

Connelly, A. 2020. "Cyprus Pushes Syrian Refugees Back at Sea due to Coronavirus." *Al-Jazeera* 30 March 2020 https://www.aljazeera.com/news/2020/03/cyprus-pushes-syrian-refugees-sea-due-coronavirus-200330091614066.html.

Darwen, L., D. MacRaild, L. Kennedy, and B. Gurrin. 2020. "'Irish Fever' in Britain During the Great Famine: Immigration, Disease and the Legacy of 'Black '47'." *Irish Historical Studies* 44: 270–294.

El-Enany, N. 2020. *(B)Ordering Britain: Law, Race and Empire*. Manchester: Manchester University Press.

European Commission. 2020. "Overcrowded Reception Centres and Informal Settlements make Migrants Vulnerable to COVID-19." https://ec.europa.eu/migrant-integration/news/overcrowded-reception-centres-and-informal-settlements-make-migrants-vulnerable-to-covid-19.

France 24. 2020. "Hungary's Orban Blames Foreigners, Migration for Coronavirus Spread." *France 24*, 13 March. https://www.france24.com/en/20200313-hungary-s-pm-orban-blames-foreign-students-migration-for-coronavirus-spread.

Fundamental Rights Agency. 2020. *Migration: Key Fundamental Rights Concerns - Quarterly bulletin 2.* Vienna: FRA. https://fra.europa.eu/en/publication/2020/migration-key-fundamental-rights-concerns-quarterly-bulletin-2-2020.

Goldberg, D. T. 2002. *The Racial State.* Oxford: Blackwell.

Goldberg, D. T. 2008. "Racial States." In *A Companion to Ethnic and Racial Studies,* edited by D. T. Goldberg, and J. Solomos, 233–258. Oxford: Blackwell.

Hickman, M., and L. Ryan. 2020. "The 'Irish Question': Marginalizations at the Nexus of Sociology of Migration and Ethnic and Racial Studies in Britain." *Ethnic and Racial Studies* 43 (16): 96–114.

Hill, E., N. Meer, and T. Peace. 2021. "The Role of Asylum in Urban Gentrification." *Sociological Review,* in press.

Human Rights Watch. 2020. "Greece-Nearly 2,000 New Arrivals Detained in Overcrowded, Mainland Camps: Citing COVID-19, Authorities Arbitrarily Detain New Arrivals." https://www.hrw.org/news/2020/03/31/greece-nearly-2000-new-arrivals-detained-overcrowded-mainland-camps.

Iacobucci, G. 2020. "Covid-19: Doctors Warn of Humanitarian Catastrophe at Europe's Largest Refugee Camp." *BMJ* 368. https://www.bmj.com/content/368/bmj.m1097.

IOM (International Organization for Migration). 2020. "DTM (COVID-19) Global Mobility Restriction Overview." https://migration.iom.int/reports/dtm-covid19-travel-restrictions-output-—-9-april-2020.

Keller, V. M., F. Schöler, and M. Goldoni. 2020. "Not a Safe Place? Italy's Decision to Declare Its Ports Unsafe under International Maritime Law, Verfassungsblog on Matters Constitutional." https://verfassungsblog.de/not-a-safe-place/.

Kraut, A. M. 1994. *Silent Travellers: Germs, Genes and the 'Immigrant Menace'.* New York: Basic Books.

Kraut, A. M. 2010. "Immigration, Ethnicity, and the Pandemic." *Public Health Reports* 3 (125): 123–133.

Lauterpacht, S. E., and D. Bethlehem. 2001. *The Scope and Content of the Principle of Non-refoulement: Opinion.* Accessed 27 August 2020. https://www.unhcr.org/419c75ce4.pdf.

Lentin, R. 2007. "Ireland: Racial State and Crisis Racism." *Ethnic and Racial Studies* 30 (4): 610–627.

Long, O. 2018. "The EU-Turkey Deal: Explained." Help Refugees. https://helprefugees.org/news/eu-turkey-deal-explained/.

Mayblin, L. 2017. *Asylum After Empire: Colonial Legacies in the Politics of Asylum Seeking.* London: Rowman and Littlefield International.

Mayblin, L., M. Wake, and M. Kozheni. 2019. "Necropolitics and the Slow Violence of the Everyday: Asylum Seeker Welfare in the Postcolonial Present." *Sociology* 54 (1): 107–123.

Mbembe, A. 2003. "Necropolitics." *Public Culture* 15 (1): 11–40.

Meer, N. 2020. "Coronavirus: We are Risking a Covid-19 Tragedy in Europe's Refugee Camps". *The Scotsman,* 7 April. https://www.scotsman.com/news/opinion/columnists/coronavirus-we-are-risking-covid-19-tragedy-europes-refugee-camps-nasar-meer-2532139.

Meer, N., and L. Villegas. 2020. *The Impact of COVID 19 on Global Migration.* Edinburgh: University of Edinburgh.

MSF (Médecins Sans Frontières). 2020. "Evacuation of Squalid Greek Camps more Urgent than ever over COVID-19 fears." Médecins Sans Frontières. https://www.msf.org/urgent-evacuation-squalid-camps-greece-needed-over-covid-19-fears.

Musolff, A. 2004. "'The Heart of the European Body Politic: British and German Perspectives on Europe's Central Organ'." *Journal of Multilingual and Multicultural Development* 25: 437–452.

Rankin, J. 2020. "EU Court Rules Three Member States Broke Law Over Refugee Quotas." The Guardian, 2 April. https://www.theguardian.com/law/2020/apr/02/eu-court-rules-three-countries-czech-republic-hungary-poland-broke-law-over-refugee-quotas.

Rosenberg, E. C. 1962. *The Cholera Years: The United States in 1832, 1849, and 1866.* Chicago: University of Chicago press.

Taylor, B. 2016. "Immigration, Statecraft and Public Health: The 1920 Aliens Order, Medical Examinations and the Limitations of the State in England." *Social History of Medicine* 29 (3): 512–533.

Tondo, L. 2020. "Salvini Attacks Italy PM Over Coronavirus and Links to Rescue Ship." *The Guardian*, 24 February. Available at: https://www.theguardian.com/world/2020/feb/24/salvini-attacks-italy-pm-over-coronavirus-and-links-to-rescue-ship.

Trilling, D. 2020. "Migrants aren't Spreading Coronavirus – but Nationalists are Blaming them Anyway." *The Guardian*, 28 February. Accessed 27 August 2020. https://www.theguardian.com/commentisfree/2020/feb/28/coronavirus-outbreak-migrants-blamed-italy-matteo-salvini-marine-le-pen.

UNHCR (United Nations High Commissioner for Refugees). 1951. "The 1951 Convention Relating to the Status of Refugees." UNHCR. https://www.unhcr.org/4ca34be29.pdf.

UNHCR (United Nations High Commissioner for Refugees). 2020a. "UNHCR UK FAQs on COVID-19 in Relation to Refugees and Asylum Seekers." https://www.unhcr.org/uk/unhcr-uk-faqs-on-covid-19-in-relation-to-refugees-and-asylum-seekers.html.

UNHCR (United Nations High Commissioner for Refugees). 2020b. "UNHCR UK Statement on the Situation at the Turkey-EU Border." Accessed 30 September 2020. https://www.unhcr.org/uk/news/press/2020/3/5e5d08ad4/unhcr-statement-situation-turkey-eu-border.html.

UNHCR (United Nations High Commissioner for Refugees). 2020c. "Beware Long Term Damage to Human Rights and Refugee Rights from the Coronavirus Pandemic: UNHCR." UNHCR. https://www.unhcr.org/en-us/news/press/2020/4/5ea035ba4/beware-long-term-damage-human-rights-refugee-rights-coronavirus-pandemic.html.

Villegas, L., and N. Meer. 2020. "Refuge in the time of COVID-19." Emerald Publishing. https://www.emeraldgrouppublishing.com/topics/coronavirus/blog/refuge-time-covid-19.

Yuval-Davis, N., G. Wemyss, and K. Cassidy. 2018. "Everyday Bordering, Belonging and the Reorientation of British Immigration Legislation." *Sociology* 52 (2): 228–244.

Zerka, P. 2020. "Ill Will: Populism and the coronavirus." European Council on Foreign Relations, 5 March. Accessed 27 August 2020. https://www.ecfr.eu/article/commentary_ill_will_populism_and_the_coronavirus.

Has the Covid-19 pandemic undermined public support for a diverse society? Evidence from a natural experiment in Germany

Lucas G. Drouhot ⓘ, Sören Petermann, Karen Schönwälder and Steven Vertovec

ABSTRACT
The Covid-19 pandemic has led to widespread worries that the health crisis is resulting in generalized hostility towards minorities and reduced support for a diverse society. Relying on a large survey of diversity attitudes in Germany fielded before and during the pandemic, we employ a quasi-experimental design to evaluate whether such a trend has occurred among the general public. Past work suggests two competing expectations – one anticipating a rise in hostility grounded in threat theories, and one anticipating stability grounded in public opinion research and theories of longer-term value change. Empirical results reveal generally high assent to socio-demographic diversity and minority accommodation, and remarkable stability during the pandemic period. Additionally, survey vignettes show strong and equally stable anti-discrimination norms that are inclusive of Asian-origin populations. Overall, results suggest that surges in racist incidents during the pandemic do not reflect analogous surges in hostility within the population at large.

Has the Coronavirus pandemic "unleash[ed] a tsunami of hate and xenophobia, scapegoating and scare-mongering" as the United Nations General Secretary warned in May 2020 (UN 2020)? In Germany, as in many other countries, public authorities and media have noted an increase in hate-based incidents and racist attacks targeting, among others, persons perceived as Asian as the alleged spreaders of the virus (Antidiskriminierungs-stelle des Bundes 2020). Such worry for increasing hostility also exists for other minority groups. For instance, the Commissioner for Human Rights at the Council of Europe has expressed concern for the increasingly hostile climate towards LGBT persons (Council of Europe 2020). Are we witnessing a more general shift towards ethnic exclusionism and hostility towards min-orities? Has the pandemic led to reduced public support for societal diversity?

This article presents evidence from a large survey in German cities, fielded before and during the pandemic (Drouhot et al. forthcoming).[1] The timing of our survey allows us to employ a quasi-experimental design to evaluate the effect of the pandemic on attitudes towards and support for diversity in one of Europe's foremost countries of immigration. Our results show generally high assent to socio-demographic diversity and minority accommodation, and remarkable stability of such assent during the pandemic period. Additionally, survey vignettes suggest strong and equally stable anti-discrimi-nation norms that are inclusive of Asian-origin populations, before and during the Coronavirus outbreak. In spite of an increased number of racist incidents during the pandemic period, our results suggest it is unlikely that public opinion towards diversity as well as ethnic and other minorities signifi-cantly changed as a result of the Covid-19 outbreak.

Two competing theoretical expectations

While there exists little work on the effect of the Covid-19 pandemic yet, past social science research suggests two opposite expectations for its effects on attitudes towards socio-cultural heterogeneity and minority groups.

The influence of perceived group threat on prejudice has been firmly established by past scholarship in social psychology (see Riek, Mania, and Gaertner 2006 for a review and meta-analysis). In addition, and building on Blumer's (1958) work emphasizing the significance of large-scale collective events, social scientists have examined the influence of shocks like terror attacks (Bar-Tal and Labin 2001; Legewie 2013), but also sudden financial downturns (Becker, Wagner, and Christ 2011) on hostility towards specific outgroups. "In times of crises", Becker, Wagner, and Christ (2011, 881) suggest, "people deal with this unspecific threat by attributing the cause of the crisis to certain scapegoats in order to reduce uncertainty and to rebuild control". Scapegoating thus occurs when individuals feel threatened and engage in "causal attribution" (Hewstone 1989) of the negative conse-quences of such events to certain groups.

A global disease outbreak may be particularly prone to triggering gener-alized hostility: evolutionary perspectives within political science and social psychology emphasize the central role of the fear of diseases in shaping xenophobia and activating latent prejudice (Aarøe, Petersen, and Arceneaux

2017). They go beyond specific attribution and expect risk-averse, and affect-based responses to perceived health threats to produce generalized prejudice against all minority groups. Extending these approaches to the current health crisis, one might assume that confidence in the benefits of a socio-culturally heterogeneous society will deteriorate and appeals for cohesion through homogeneity (including racist and xenophobic sentiments) will increase.

An alternative theoretical narrative suggests that support for socio-cultural diversity and respect for minority rights will remain stable in the current crisis. Public opinion research shows immigration and other political attitudes among adults are remarkably constant over the life course (Kiley and Vaisey 2020; Kustov, Laaker, and Reller forthcoming; Dennison and Geddes 2018, 2020). In Germany, pre-pandemic, "baseline" diversity attitudes are decidedly positive: past work shows that diversity and the presence of minorities has become an ordinary and much appreciated part of urban life (Schönwälder et al. 2015). Such pro-diversity attitudes are founded in a high valuation of individual freedoms, minority rights and cosmopolitanism (Norris and Inglehart 2019, 33), and are tangible in the strong social norms against prejudice and discrimination now existing in many European countries (Blinder, Ford, and Ivarsflaten 2013, 842). Together, this evidence suggests major attitudinal changes as a result of the Coronavirus pandemic are unlikely.

Data and empirical strategy

To evaluate these competing theoretical expectations, we exploit temporal variation in the fielding of a large-scale survey on diversity attitudes in twenty German cities between November 2019 and April 2020. The survey includes measurement of attitudes towards socio-cultural heterogeneity, experiences of diversity in everyday life, as well as measurement of anti-discrimination norms through a set of vignette questions among other themes. It was administered by telephone on a random sample of 2,917 respondents in twenty German cities.

The administration of the survey occurred in two distinct phases – one between 18 November 2019 and 21 January 2020 (2,135 respondents) and a second between 3 March and 29 April 2020 (782 respondents). We exploit this exogenous variation to formulate a quasi-experimental design where the survey periods correspond to an experiment's control and treatment groups.

Figure 1 shows the time periods when the survey was conducted. The gap between the two survey periods, and the recording of the first cases of Covid-19 infections in between, creates natural control and treatment groups without ambiguity regarding a strict cut-off point. The Coronavirus gained

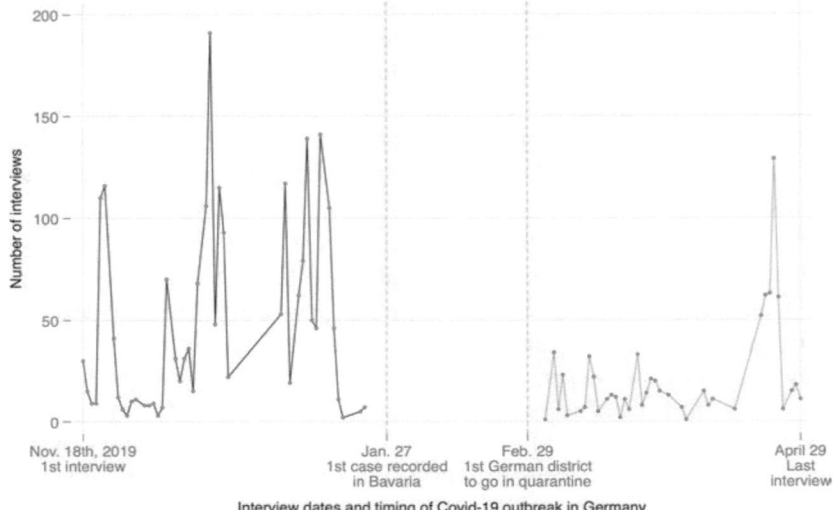

Figure 1. Illustration of control (left, interview completed earlier than January 27th, 2020) and treatment (right, interview completed later than February 29th, 2020) groups around the start of the pandemic in Germany.

ground on German soil in that period, and up to the first closing of schools, and all public life in one west German district in late February.

Our identification strategy of the causal effect of Covid-19 on diversity attitudes rests on two critical assumptions (for an analogous approach, see Legewie 2013). First, compositional differences between the treatment and control groups should be non-existent or along dimensions that can be statistically adjusted for. For instance, older respondents tend be more easily reachable by phone if they are retired and more often at home. Conversely, immigrants are typically harder to reach. This so-called reachability bias can create imbalance between control and treatment groups, and confound results if groups whose diversity attitudes differ are more systematically present in the control group or vice versa.

We control for well-known predictors that influence respondents' reachability, namely age, employment status and migration background. Second, our approach builds on an assumption of temporal stability – namely, that diversity attitudes would not have changed in the absence of the treatment. This assumption guarantees that the measured effect of the treatment is not confounded with a time-varying variable that is causally prior to the treatment – for instance, if diversity attitudes were affected by bad weather and seasonal change, which co-occur with the survey periods in our design. Given this is highly implausible and that there exist no other time-varying confounders to our knowledge, we consider that our design meets this assumption.

Hence, we estimate the average causal effect of the Covid-19 period with regression models controlling for demographic composition across experimental groups and a dummy variable for the treatment status. Formally:

$$y_i = \alpha_i + T_i\theta + \mathbf{X}_i\beta + \epsilon_i \tag{1}$$

In regression Equation (1), we model a diversity outcome y as a function of treatment T – yielding the coefficient θ, the mean difference in y conditional on a set of covariates $\mathbf{X}$ – in our case age, sex, whether or not the respondent holds a job, educational attainment, city of residence, migration background and far right voting for respondent i. θ can be interpreted causally if the temporal stability assumption holds, and if no variable creating a reachability bias is omitted from $\mathbf{X}$. Corresponding coefficients β are not of direct substantive interest, and are not reported on in detail. We dichotomize all outcome variables for comparability across items[2] and express all results for θ as marginal effects (Mood 2010). A table describing the demographic and social composition of our sample is available in Appendix A.

We present our results in two distinct steps. First, we model variation in responses to six questions measuring attitudes to diversity and minority rights (for details see Appendix B). We report results for questions on:

- Whether Germany's cultural life is enriched by immigrants,
- Whether young people benefit from contact with others of different origin or religious belief,
- Whether Muslims living in Germany should have the right to build mosques, even in the respondent's neighbourhood,
- Whether the media should report less about discrimination,
- If too much is being done to meet the specific needs of gays and lesbians or of refugees.

In a second step, we analyse responses to vignette questions measuring the strength of anti-discrimination norms. Each question features a fictitious scenario where a third-party protagonist engages in openly stigmatizing discourse, and in which we randomly manipulate the group being targeted – with one such group being "Asian". Given the reporting of specific increase in anti-Asian stigma as a result of the Covid-19 pandemic, we focus on the vignettes involving hostility towards Asian-origin populations. The number of individuals who received the "Asian" condition when answering vignette questions varies between 264 and 336 across the four vignettes. Here is the wording in one of them:

- Imagine you are attending a family reunion. You sit together, it's nice, the family is enjoying the party. At some point, the conversation turns to politics and you hear a relative say: "I think the main problem is that we have too many Asians in the country. We'd all be better off if this was not the case".

The three other vignettes are based on scenarios involving a conversation with a neighbour, a supermarket cashier, and a person in a waiting room – in each case complaining about an Asian couple present in the interaction (for details see Appendix B). Each vignette was followed by two questions on whether or not the respondent would be bothered by the behaviour he or she witnessed, and what course of action he or she would take – e.g. do nothing, informally signify disagreement, voice a different opinion, and sharply protest. We use responses to these vignettes to study the effect of the pandemic period on the social legitimacy of discrimination against Asian-origin populations.[3]

While the temporal variation in the fielding of our survey affords us a unique research opportunity to gauge the effect of the pandemic, we nevertheless acknowledge that our questionnaire was not designed to directly measure perceptions of threat. Rather, we consider changes in diversity attitudes and toward the legitimacy of discrimination against Asian-origin populations to reflect the extent to which scapegoating occurred – that is, how much societal diversity and specifically people of Asian origin were held responsible for the spread of the virus. Likewise, while our vignettes do not directly measure intergroup threat, it is reasonable to expect that the latter would be associated with an increase in the perceived legitimacy of discrimination against Asian-origin populations.

Results I: attitudes towards diversity and minority groups

Figure 2 shows the estimated causal effect of the pandemic period on responses to questions probing attitudes towards diversity.[4] Overall, we find that the Covid-19 period has had little effect on diversity attitudes among respondents in our survey. This is readily visible in the overlapping confidence intervals between each predicted value, and the quasi-straight lines connecting each predicted value for illustration. If anything, being interviewed during the pandemic has a slightly positive effect on the evaluation of cultural enrichment brought about by immigration, and a slightly negative effect on the probability to agree with the statement that the media should report less on discrimination. In contrast to threat theory and other work emphasizing the influence of fear of disease on hostility towards minority groups, we find that urban dwellers in Germany are generally supportive of diversity – both before and during the pandemic period.

A majority of respondents agrees that Germany's cultural life is enriched by immigrant newcomers, that contact between youths of different origins and religions is generally good, and that Muslims residing in Germany should have the right to build mosques, even in the respondent's

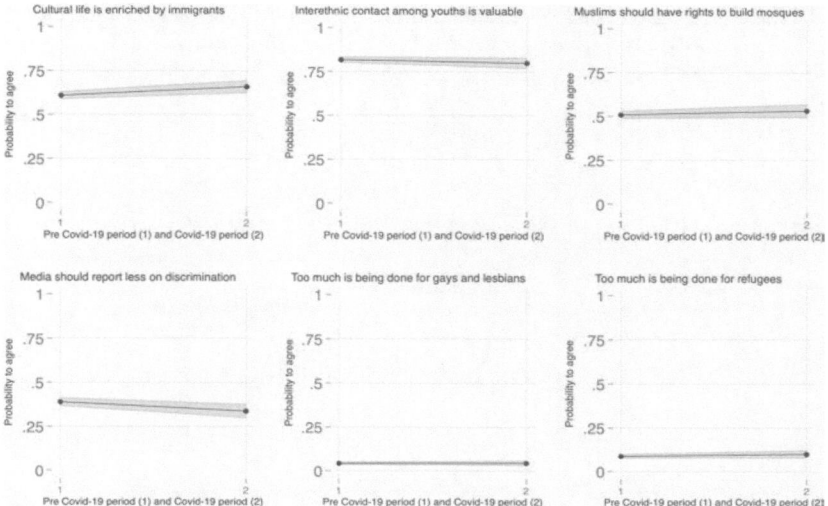

Figure 2. Estimated causal effect of Covid-19 period on diversity attitudes (grey areas are 95 per cent confidence intervals).

Notes: Figure 2 shows change in predicted probabilities for response to questions on diversity among respondents who answered the survey in the control (pre-Covid 19) and the treatment (during Covid-19) groups. Underlying models include controls for age, gender, professional status, migration background, educational attainment, far-right voting, and city of residence – all held at mean/representative values.

neighbourhood. Conversely, only a minority of respondents think that the media should report less on discrimination, and an even far smaller minority thinks that too much is being done for gays and lesbians as well as refugees. Supplementary analyses show similar patterns of stability and high support for diversity across nine other items measuring analogous issues – for instance on parliamentary representation of disadvantaged groups or teaching about all religions in schools.[5]

Results II: social legitimacy of discrimination against Asian-origin populations during the pandemic period

Figure 3 shows the estimated causal effect of the pandemic period on the propensity to be bothered by discrimination events against Asian-origin populations (Panel A), as well as the propensity to engage in informal sanctioning (voicing a different opinion, sharply protesting) when witnessing such events (Panel B). Respondents declare they would be bothered if witnessing a discrimination event against Asians at very high rates – over 90 per cent across all 4 vignettes. Rates of informal sanctioning are also high, hovering between 70 per cent and 87 per cent – with lower intervention rates in scenarios involving interaction with strangers compared to familiar others.

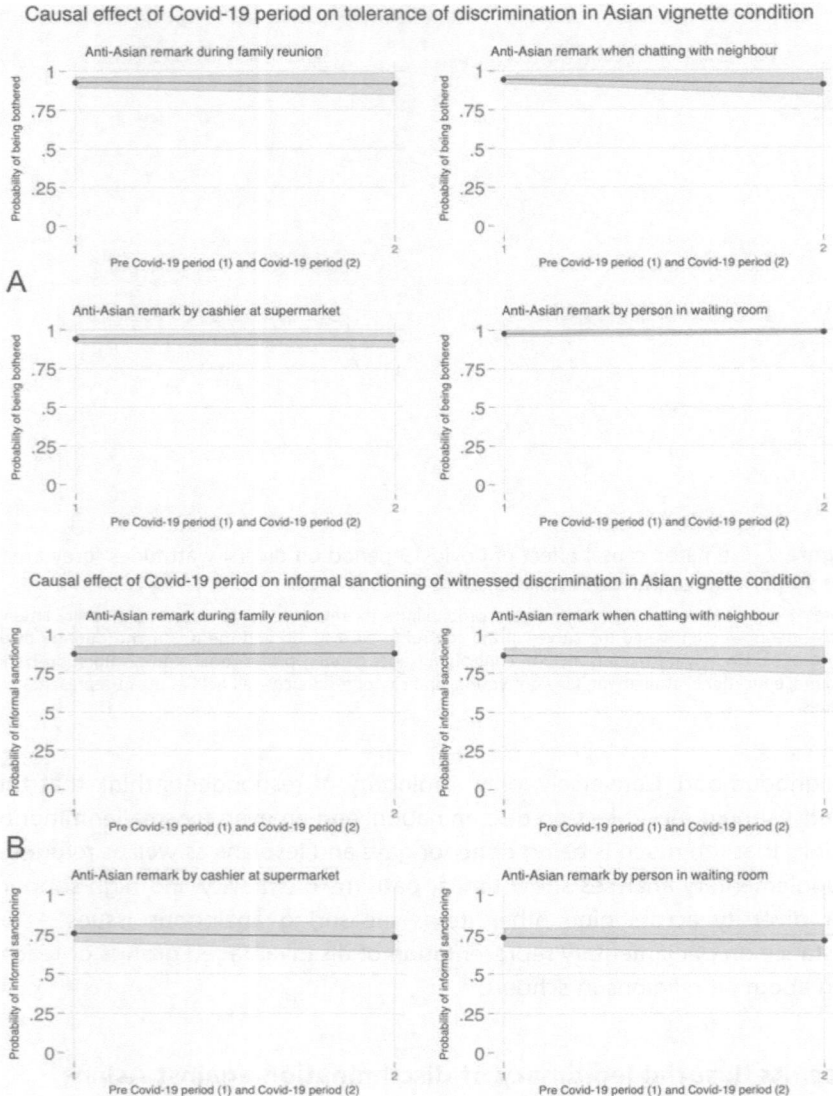

Figure 3. Estimated causal effect of Covid-19 period on antidiscrimination norms in vignette questions involving discrimination events against Asian-origin populations.

Notes: Figure 3 shows change in predicted probabilities for response to vignette questions on reaction (Panel A) and favoured behavioural response (Panel B) to discrimination event against Asian-origin populations in the control (pre-Covid 19) and the treatment (during Covid-19) groups. Underlying models include controls for age, gender, professional status, migration background, educational attainment, and far-right voting – all held at mean/representative values.

Importantly, we observe no change in the pandemic period in responses to our vignette questions designed to measure antidiscrimination norms against Asian-origin populations. Both before and during the pandemic, respondents perceive discriminatory behaviour against Asians as socially ille-gitimate. We observe no relaxation of such social norms in the pandemic period where one might have anticipated a normalization of hostility against Asians due to their perceived association with the Coronavirus. Rather, intervention rates to sanction witnessed discrimination in our ficti-tious scenarios remain high. Asian-origin populations are included in social norms against the expression of prejudice, even during a major health crisis in which hate crimes and hostile behaviour against Asians have been increasing.

Supplementary analyses

We re-ran all analyses based on a cut-off date set at March 19th – after German chancellor Merkel gave a solemn speech on the gravity of the health situation in Germany – for the definition of experimental groups. In other analyses, we added interaction effects for far-right voting and migration background with interview periods, in case the former signifi-cantly depended on the latter. We also replicated the analyses restricting our analytical sample to those without a migration background, those with less than a high school education, and those located in East Germany in case an effect was only present among this subset of respon-dents, and possibly lost in the pooled sample approach we took. Finally, we attempted to identify a temporally heterogeneous treatment effect by interacting experimental groups with interview days, as well as interview months. In all these supplementary analyses, the results we obtained were substantively identical to the ones above pointing to a null effect. We refrain from presenting these results due to space constraints but they are available from us upon request.

Conclusion

Has the Covid-19 pandemic undermined public support for a diverse society? Earlier in this article, we noted two theoretical expectations regarding atti-tudes towards minorities in times of societal crisis. Group threat theory and work emphasizing the fear of diseases suggest that negative attitudes will intensify under conditions in which health and well-being are deemed to be threatened. Meanwhile, past work in public opinion research and theories of longer-term value change suggest that diversity attitudes should remain stable despite this external threat. Our findings clearly support the latter proposition. Employing a quasi-experimental design and exploiting temporal variation in the fielding of a large survey on diversity attitudes, we find that the onset of the Covid-19 pandemic has not lowered the high level of assent to diversity in urban Germany.

What explains the null effect we document? Our study is descriptive, and we can only speculate on the causal processes behind our findings. For instance, it is possible that financial support and intervention from the government helped mitigate feelings of threat due to the pandemic. Likewise, repeated appeals to solidarity made by prominent political leaders may have dampened the backlash expected under the group threat narrative and mitigated causal attributions of the health crisis to particular groups. Future research should investigate the processes underlying the non-effect of the pandemic on diversity attitudes.

In closing, we wish to emphasize that these results do not negate the existence of significant discrimination against different minorities in Germany (Scherr, El-Mafaalani, and Yüksel 2017). Anti-minority violence and acts of outward discrimination during the pandemic period and at other times constitute a severe problem. And yet, we contend that surges in hate crime should not be equated with a more general shift in public opinion. Indeed, positive attitudes towards diversity among the general urban population documented in earlier work (e.g. Schönwälder et al. 2015) appear to be resilient to this societal crisis. Diversity assent may well be a valuable public good helping heterogeneous societies face significant collective challenges.

Notes

1. The dataset will be made available through the GESIS data archive.
2. Supplementary analyses (not shown) using the items' original scales yield identical results.
3. Due to the lower number of observations as the "Asian" condition was one of ten other conditions, we do not include the respondent's city of residence to avoid estimation issues when computing predicted values.
4. The underlying logistic regression models produce log odds, which should be kept as such for the precise estimation of the causal effect. However, here, for ease of interpretation we express the results in probabilities, which remain substantively identical to log odds in their expressing of a non-effect.
5. We omit these results here due to space constraints but they are available from the authors upon request.
6. We used 7 as a cutoff to make our measurement more conservative. Setting the cutoff at 5 or 6 yields substantively identical results, however.

Acknowledgements

We wish to thank Mauricio Bucca, Matthias König, Mario Molina, Benjamin F. Rosche and members of audience at the Sociology Colloquium at the University of Göttingen for helpful comments and criticisms on an earlier version of this article, as well as Margherita Cusmano for helpful research assistance.

Disclosure statement

No potential conflict of interest was reported by the author(s).

ORCID

Lucas G. Drouhot ⓘ http://orcid.org/0000-0001-8080-6212

References

Aarøe, Lene, Michael Bang Petersen, and Kevin Arceneaux. 2017. "The Behavioral Immune System Shapes Political Intuitions: Why and How Individual Differences in Disgust Sensitivity Underlie Opposition to Immigration." *American Political Science Review* 111 (2): 277–294.

Antidiskriminierungsstelle des Bundes. 2020. *Diskriminierungserfahrungen im Zusammenhang mit der Corona-Krise*. Berlin: Antidiskriminierungsstelle des Bundes.

Bar-Tal, Daniel, and Daniela Labin. 2001. "The Effect of a Major Event on Stereotyping: Terrorist Attacks in Israel and Israeli Adolescents' Perceptions of Palestinians, Jordanians and Arabs." *European Journal of Social Psychology* 31: 265–280.

Becker, Julia C., Ulrich Wagner, and Oliver Christ. 2011. "Consequences of the 2008 Financial Crisis for Intergroup Relations: The Role of Perceived Threat and Causal Attributions." *Group Processes & Intergroup Relations* 14 (6): 871–885.

Blinder, Scott, Robert Ford, and Elisabeth Ivarsflaten. 2013. "The Better Angels of Our Nature: How the Antiprejudice Norm Affects Policy and Party Preferences in Great Britain and Germany." *American Journal of Political Science* 57 (4): 841–857.

Blumer, Herbert. 1958. "Race Prejudice as a Sense of Group Position." *The Pacific Sociological Review* 1 (1): 3–7.

Council of Europe. 2020. "COVID-19: The Suffering and Resilience of LGBT Persons Must Be Visible and Inform the Actions of States." https://www.coe.int/en/web/commissioner/-/covid-19-the-suffering-and-resilience-of-lgbt-persons-must-be-visible-and-inform-the-actions-of-states (consulted July 10th, 2020).

Dennison, James, and Andrew Geddes. 2018. "A Rising Tide? The Salience of Immigration and the Rise of Anti-Immigration Political Parties in Western Europe." *The Political Quarterly* 90: 107–116.

Dennison, James, and Andrew Geddes. 2020. "Why Covid-19 Does Not Necessarily Mean That Attitudes Towards Immigration Will Become More Negative." https://hdl.handle.net/1814/68055 (consulted September 10th, 2020).

Drouhot, Lucas G., Sören Petermann, Karen Schönwälder, and Steven Vertovec. forthcoming. "The 'Diversity Assent' (DivA) Survey – Technical Report." Göttingen: Max Planck Institute for the Study of Religious and Ethnic Diversity.

Hewstone, Miles. 1989. *Causal Attribution: From Cognitive Processes to Collective Beliefs*. Oxford, UK: Blackwell.

Kiley, Kevin, and Stephen Vaisey. 2020. "Measuring Stability and Change in Personal Culture Using Panel Data." *American Sociological Review* 85 (3): 477–506.

Kustov, Alexander, Dillon Laaker, and Cassidy Reller. forthcoming. "The Stability of Immigration Attitudes: Evidence and Implications." *Journal of Politics*.

Legewie, Joscha. 2013. "Terrorist Events and Attitudes Toward Immigrants: A Natural Experiment." *American Journal of Sociology* 118 (5): 1199–1245.

Mood, Carina. 2010. "Logistic Regression: Why We Cannot Do What We Think We Can Do, and What We Can Do about It." *European Sociological Review* 26 (1): 67–82.

Norris, Pippa, and Ronald Inglehart. 2019. *Cultural Backlash: Trump, Brexit and Authoritarian Populism*. Cambridge: Cambridge University Press.

Riek, Blake M., Eric W. Mania, and Samuel L. Gaertner. 2006. "Intergroup Threat and Outgroup Attitudes: A Meta-Analytic Review." *Personality and Social Psychology Bulletin* 10 (4): 336–353.

Scherr, Albert, Aladin El-Mafaalani, and Gökçen Yüksel, eds. 2017. *Handbuch Diskriminierung*. Wiesbaden: Springer VS.

Schönwälder, Karen, Sören Petermann, Jörg Hüttermann, Steven Vertovec, Miles Hewstone, Dietlind Stolle, Katharina Schmid, and Thomas Schmitt. 2015. *Diversity and Contact: Immigration and Social Interaction in German Cities*. Basingstoke: Palgrave Macmillan.

United Nations. 2020. Press Release on 8 May: Secretary-General Denounces 'Tsunami' of Xenophobia Unleashed Amid COVID-19, Calling for All-Out Effort Against Hate Speech, www.un.org/press/en/2020/sgsm20076.doc.htm (consulted July 10th, 2020).

Appendices

Appendix A. Descriptive statistics and balance between experimental groups

Table A1. Covariate balance between treatment and control groups.

Proportions	Control group (before Covid-19)	Treatment group (during Covid-19)
with a migration background	0.18	0.40
aged 18–24	0.01	0.03
aged 25–44	0.13	0.21
aged 45–64	0.40	0.44
aged 65+	0.45	0.30
with high school degree (Abitur) or more	0.55	0.54
far right voter	0.03	0.02
female	0.54	0.58
currently employed	0.50	0.61
Bochum	0.06	0.06
Delmenhorst	0.02	0.01
Dormagen	0.02	0.00
Emden	0.02	0.01
Frankfurt	0.19	0.23
Gießen	0.02	0.02
Hamburg	0.21	0.19
Herten	0.02	0.01
Ingolstadt	0.04	0.09
Krefeld	0.05	0.06
Konstanz	0.02	0.01
Leverkusen	0.03	0.12
Lübeck	0.04	0.10
Mannheim	0.06	0.04
Schweinfurt	0.02	0.01
Viersen	0.02	0.00
Brandenburg	0.02	0.00
Dessau-Roßlau	0.02	0.00
Erfurt	0.07	0.05
Neubrandenburg	0.02	0.00
Observations	2,135	782

Table A1 contains frequencies for covariates included in regression models underlying Figures 2 and 3. Following standard expectation of reachability bias in survey research, covariate imbalances are visible between experimental groups in terms of proportion of respondents with a migration background, age structure, professional status, and city of residence. Statistical differences between experimental groups along these lines are confirmed in a logistic model predicting membership in the treatment group (not shown). Our statistical controls adjust for this variation in the regression equation. In fact, and somewhat remarkably, we find very little difference in attitudes when comparing the control and treatment groups without controls. The raw and adjusted results are very close.

The characteristics of our sample reflect our sampling strategy – we focused on twenty randomly selected cities in Germany and stratified city selection by size. Second, we aimed at a share of 25 per cent of respondents with a migration background (see Drouhot et al. forthcoming for details).

Appendix B. Variable construction and survey instruments

For the first series of analysis, we constructed binary response variables, by coding responses of 7 and above as "1" for the cultural life question,[6] and responses of "somewhat" and "fully" agree as "1" for questions regarding the building of mosques and interethnic contact. For the questions on discrimination report by the media, and too much being done for refugees / gays and lesbians, the answer lead to binary response variables by design. Finally, in the case of the vignette questions, we first created binary response variables reflecting the answer to whether or not the respondent would be bothered, and then created a binary response variable for informal sanctioning (whether the respondent would either voice a different opinion of protest sharply, versus choose non-confrontation for those who disapprove and any other option for those who approve of the third party's discriminatory behaviour/discourse).

Below are the exact wordings for the survey questions our analyses focus on, in German (in italics) and in English.

Würden Sie sagen, dass das kulturelle Leben in Deutschland im Allgemeinen durch Zuwanderer UNTERGRABEN oder BEREICHERT wird?

Bitte sagen Sie mir auf einer Skala von 0–10, was Sie denken, wobei "0" bedeutet, dass das kulturelle Leben in Deutschland im Allgemeinen durch Zuwanderer UNTERGRABEN wird, und "10" bedeutet, dass das kulturelle Leben in Deutschland im Allgemeinen durch Zuwanderer BEREICHERT wird. Mit den Werten dazwischen können Sie Ihre Meinung abstufen.

Would you say that Germany's cultural life is generally undermined or enriched by people coming to live here from other countries?

Please tell me on a scale of 0–10 what you think, where "0" means that cultural life in Germany is generally UNDERMINED by immigrants, and "10" means that cultural life in Germany is generally ENRICHED by immigrants. With the values in-between you can scale (gradate) your opinion.

Ich lese Ihnen jetzt einige Aussagen vor. Bitte geben Sie jeweils an, ob Sie zustimmen oder nicht zustimmen.

Die in Deutschland lebenden Muslime sollten das Recht haben, Moscheen zu bauen, auch in IHREM Wohnviertel.

Junge Leute profitieren davon, mit Gleichaltrigen anderer Herkunft oder anderen Glaubens in Kontakt zu sein.

I am now going to read you several statements. Please state whether you agree or disagree with each statement.

- The Muslims living in Germany should have the right to build mosques, including in your own neighbourhood.
- Young people profit from contact with other young people of different origin or religious belief.

Do you fully agree, somewhat agree, neither agree nor disagree, somewhat disagree or definitely disagree?

Nun eine Frage zu Fällen von Diskriminierung etwa von Homosexuellen oder dunkelhäutigen Menschen. Finden Sie:

1. *Die Medien sollten EHER MEHR über Fälle von Diskriminierung berichten. ODER*
2. *Die Medien sollten EHER WENIGER über Fälle von Diskriminierung berichten.*

Now a question on cases of discrimination, for example against homosexuals or dark-skinned people. Do you think:

1. the media should report MORE about cases of discrimination. OR
2. the media should report LESS about cases of discrimination.

In Deutschland wird Einiges getan, um den spezifischen Bedürfnissen einzelner Gruppen gerecht zu werden. Wie ist das bei Schwulen und Lesben [Flüchtlingen]?

Finden Sie, dass hier in Deutschland zu viel, genug oder zu wenig getan wird, um deren spezifischen Bedürfnissen gerecht zu werden?

In Germany, things are being done to meet the specific needs of individual groups. How about Gays and lesbians [Refugees]?

Do you find that here in Germany too much, enough or too little is being done to meet their specific needs?

Vignette questions:
Jetzt wir möchten Ihnen einige Situationen beschreiben, die in Ihrem Alltag auftreten können, und fragen, wie Sie reagieren würden.

Stellen Sie sich bitte einmal vor, Sie besuchen ein Familientreffen. Sie sitzen zusammen, es ist nett, die Familie genießt das Fest. Irgendwann kommt das Gespräch auf die Politik und Sie hören, wie jemand sagt: "Ich finde, das Hauptproblem ist, dass wir zu viele [Asians] im Land haben. Es würde uns allen besser gehen, wenn das nicht so wäre."

Wie ist es mit Ihnen, würde Sie die Aussage des Verwandten stören?

Now we would like to describe some situations that may occur in your everyday life and ask you how you would react.

Imagine you are attending a family reunion. You sit together, it's nice, the family is enjoying the party. At some point, the conversation turns to politics and you hear a relative say: "I think the main problem is that we have too many [Asians] in the country. We'd all be better off if this was not the case."

How about you, would your relative's statement bother you?

Stellen Sie sich bitte einmal vor, Sie stehen vor Ihrer Haustür und plaudern mit einem Nachbarn. Jemand von der Hausverwaltung kommt mit einem [Asian [couple]] Paar vorbei, um die freistehende Wohnung nebenan zu zeigen. Der Nachbar sagt zu Ihnen: "Mir würde es stinken, wenn wir solche Leute als Nachbarn bekommen würden."
Wie ist es mit Ihnen, würde Sie der Kommentar des Nachbarn stören?

Imagine you are standing in front of your front door and chatting with a neighbour. Someone from the property management comes by with a [Asian [couple]] couple to show them the vacant apartment next door. The neighbour says to you: "I would be upset if we had such people as neighbours."
What about you, would you be bothered by the neighbour's comment?

Stellen Sie sich bitte einmal vor, Sie stehen im Supermarkt in der Schlange an der Kasse. Vor Ihnen in der Schlange ist ein [Asian [couple]] Paar. Das Paar braucht eine ganze Weile, um zu bezahlen und die Einkäufe einzupacken. Als sie weg sind und Sie selbst bezahlen, sagt der Kassierer: "Entschuldigen Sie, diese Sorte Leute halten immer den Betrieb auf".
Wie ist es mit Ihnen, würde Sie die Aussage des Kassierers stören?

Imagine you are standing in the checkout-line at a supermarket. A [Asian [couple]] couple is in front of you in the queue. It takes the couple quite a while to pay and pack their groceries. When they are gone and you are paying, the cashier says: "Sorry about that, this kind of people always disturb the flow of business".
How about you, would the cashier's statement bother you?

Und nun stellen Sie sich bitte einmal vor, Sie sitzen in einem Wartezimmer. Es ist voll, mit Ihnen warten noch etwa 15 Personen. Als sie aufgerufen werden, steht ein [Asian [couple]] Paar auf und verläßt das Wartezimmer. Nachdem sie weg sind, sagt ein Mann laut: "Es ist eine Zumutung, dass man sich heute überall hinter solchen Leuten anstellen muss."
Wie ist es mit Ihnen, würde Sie die Aussage des Mannes stören?

And now imagine that you are sitting in a waiting room. It's full, there are about 15 people waiting with you. A [Asian [couple]] couple is called and leaves the waiting room. After the couple is gone, [A] a man/[B] a woman says loudly: "It's unacceptable that everywhere you have to wait behind such people today".

What about you, would you be bothered by the [A] man's/[B] woman's statement?
For each question, the options for chosen behavioural responses read as follows, depending if the respondent declares he/she would be bothered:
Filter: Wenn Ja
Und was würden Sie tun?

3. nichts,
4. Ihre Ablehnung z.B. durch einen bösen Blick oder Kopfschütteln signalisieren,
5. knapp sagen, dass Sie anderer Meinung sind.
6. scharf protestieren.

Filter: Wenn Nein
Und was würden Sie tun?

7. nichts,
8. Ihre Zustimmung z. B. durch Nicken signalisieren,

9. *knapp sagen, dass Sie der gleichen Meinung sind,*
10. *deutlich bekräftigen, dass Sie zustimmen.*

Filter: If Yes
And what would you do?

3. nothing,
4. signal your disagreement, for example with a nasty look or by shaking your head,
5. briefly say that you are of a different opinion.
6. protest sharply.

Filter: If No
And what would you do?

7. nothing,
8. signal your agreement, for example by nodding,
9. say briefly that you are of the same opinion,
10. clearly emphasize that you agree.

Works cited:

Drouhot, Lucas G., Sören Petermann, Karen Schönwälder, and Steven Vertovec. forthcoming. "The "Diversity Assent" (DivA) Survey – Technical Report." Göttingen: Max Planck Institute for the Study of Religious and Ethnic Diversity.

Cultures of rejection in the Covid-19 crisis

Benjamin Opratko, Manuela Bojadžijev, Sanja M. Bojanić, Irena Fiket,
Alexander Harder, Stefan Jonsson, Mirjana Nećak, Anders Neegard,
Celina Ortega Soto, Gazela Pudar Draško, Birgit Sauer and
Kristina Stojanović Čehajić

ABSTRACT
This article offers a collectively developed analysis of the Covid-19 crisis as it
relates to contemporary cultures of rejection, i.e. the socio-cultural conditions
in which authoritarian and right-wing populist politics thrive, in Europe. We
explore how the pandemic and its management reinforces, transforms and/or
overrides existing antagonisms and institutes new ones in Serbia, Croatia,
Austria, Germany and Sweden. We discuss how the Covid-19 crisis affects the
rise of new statisms; gendered patterns of social reproduction; mobility and
migration; digital infrastructures; and new political mobilizations.

This article offers a collectively developed analysis by a transnational research
group (www.culturesofrejection.net) investigating contemporary socio-cultural conditions in which authoritarian and right-wing populist politics
thrive. The authors conduct research in Austria, Croatia, Germany, Serbia,
and Sweden: five states and societies that together constitute a political
space instituted by the migration movements since 2015 and the political
struggles that have emerged with them (Jonsson 2020). The "welcome
culture" (Bojadžijev 2018) that had initially emerged with these movements
and struggles has since been overshadowed by a conjuncture of right-wing
mobilisations and an authoritarian turn in European, and the emergence of

what we term "cultures of rejection". In this contribution, we sketch the multi-faceted impact the Covid-19 crisis has on cultures of rejection.

We have developed the heuristic and deliberately provocative concept of "cultures of rejection" to investigate socio-cultural conditions in which authoritarian and right-wing populist politics have become acceptable. This approach both diverges from and illuminates the existing research on right-wing populism or neo-fascism. We introduce the concept of *cultures of rejection* fully aware of the role "culture" plays in neo-racist discourses (Balibar 1991, 22). We consciously refute any essentialist understanding of "culture" and a de-politicizing "culturalization" of social phenomena (cf. Fornäs et al. 2007; Lentin 2014). Instead, we draw on the critical tradition of Cultural Studies which "insists on a 'deep' understanding of culture, which looks 'up and out' at the structures of power, history and economics, but also 'down and in' at the structures of feeling which animate it" (Alexander 2016, 1434). Thus, we consider cultures as conditions of "concrete social life", assembling, as Fredric Jameson (1971, 16) put it, "words, thoughts, objects, desires, people, places, activities," in which subjects navigate terrains of contradiction and antagonism. Our desire is to research the material and everyday conditions of existence, both in the ways in which we live it, and in ways in which we feel they ought to be lived (Cole 2020). Supplementing well-established terms such as "othering" and "exclusion", the notion of *rejection* provides us with a focus on attitudes and practices in the everyday life of workers, that combine and articulate well-known cultural operations of othering and exclusion (Balibar 2005) with the rejection of *apparatuses of authority*, such as state institutions or established media outlets. In all five countries, our research has shown that the objects of rejection may vary and combine differently, but often include immigration, domestic political elites, institutions of civil society and media, shifting gender relations, and racialised or culturalised Others. If we address so many "varieties of reality" and think of them as more than just a composite, it is because we believe our time demands "archaeologies of the future" (Jameson 2005). Thinking the current conjuncture through the notion of cultures of rejection helps us understand the modality in which experiences of transformation and crisis are lived across Europe today (cf. Hall et al. 1978, 394).

Cultures of rejection and multiple crises

Long before the COVID-19 pandemic plunged our world(s) into an exceptional global crisis, scholars have identified elements of an ongoing "multiple crisis" (Houtart 2010). More recently, informatization of labour processes (Raj-Reichert, Zajak, and Helmerich 2020) and the logistification and digitalization of migration regimes (Altenried et al. 2018) have added new dimensions to these dynamics of change and crisis. It is within this specific literature that the concept of *cultures of rejection* has emerged. In our empirical investigations (Harder and Opratko 2020), we have encountered a number of themes that indicate how subjective investments in cultures of rejection are articulated with experiences of crisis. These include a wider detachment from discourses and institutions of authority, such as state institutions and "politics" in the broadest sense, shifting gender relations, which were both in turn linked to the rejection of migrants and "non-belonging" Others, and a rejection of news media. We highlight these topics because they are currently re-negotiated, re-articulated and reinforced under the conditions of the Covid-19 pandemic. We have used the current situation to jointly reflect on our initial findings under the conditions of the global pandemic. While our discussion remains inevitably sketchy, we believe that we can provide valuable observations on how the Covid-19 crisis is affecting cultures of rejection by reinforcing, transforming or overriding existing antagonisms, but also by instituting new ones. With wide-ranging quarantine measures affecting people's everyday lives in unprecedented ways, shedding light on the state of public health systems, and a pandemic-induced global economic crisis, questions of ethical and political authority, of trust in and consensus with moral and political leadership, have come to the fore. In this light, this contribution, written in Summer 2020, focuses on five selected fields that play an imminent role in our research: (1) The re-articulation of the role of the state during the pandemic, and the rise of new statisms; (2) the re-negotiation of the domestic sphere and gendered patterns of social reproduction; (3) practices of mobility and migration and political attempts at their regulation; (4) the role of digital communication infrastructures; and (5.) new political mobilizations against anti-COVID measures.

(1) The rise of Covid-19 statisms

The Covid-19 crisis has reinforced some longer-term tendencies in the way European states act (and are perceived to act), particularly in the context of deeply entrenched neoliberal policies (Standring and Davies 2020). At the same time, we observe indications of new ruptures in the relationship between state, society and economy. Three dimensions are particularly important in relation to cultures of rejection. First, in an acute crisis like the current one, executive powers gain the upper hand over parliamentary and judicial procedures. It is the proverbial "hour of the executive" (a formula often attributed to Carl Schmitt). In many European countries, governments suspended the decision-making power of parliaments and ruled by means of decrees. While the introduction of a "state of emergency" may seem as extraordinary as the pandemic itself, the disempowerment of parliaments and the introduction of authoritarian elements within formally democratic structures has recent predecessors, for example in France and Spain (Oberndorfer 2020).

Secondly, many European states relied heavily on policing and military aid in their crisis management. Quarantine and social distancing measures were or are punishable by law. The often invoked call for "solidarity" was flanked by coercive measures, some of which, as in the case of Austria, turned out not to be covered by law. In Vienna alone, 3,300 administrative criminal proceedings were appealed against, according to the City authorities, and the Constitutional Court ruled that some of the restrictions put in place by the Federal Government in March 2020 were unconstitutional (Ehs 2020). These dimensions of state action have long been familiar elements of an "authoritarian neoliberalism" (Bruff and Tansel 2019), i.e. a focus of state action to punitive and disciplinary measures, or what Bourdieu (2000) called the "right hand" of the state. Thirdly and finally, many European states and the European Union rediscovered Keynesian forms of governing – i.e. deficit spending in times of crisis. Even neo-liberal political actors and governments advocated that the state should be the institution to lead the way out of the economic crisis by providing financial support to the economy or offering compensations to businesses and the unemployed. In our pre-crisis research, building on interviews with workers in the retail and logistics sector in five countries, we have encountered wide-spread rejection of the welfare state among workers who considered it "too generous", subsidizing lazy do-nothings while taking away money from hard workers such as themselves. Now, with a dramatic rise in unemployment and majorities welcoming the "left hand" of the state, we expect changing antagonisms in this field. Sweden appears to be an interesting outlier here, with policy responses emphasizing consent and voluntary precaution rather than enforced lockdowns. While the health-related and epidemiologic results of this are debatable, the political outcomes so far indicate increased public trust in government (Novus 2020a, 2020b). But this trust meets with increased tendencies of rejection and insubordination in certain parts of the political landscape, in terms of, at least in the symbolical sense insurgent, movements, mainly in Germany and Serbia, albeit in different ways (see below) that re-articulate the rejection of state institutions in new ways.

(2) Social reproduction and the renegotiation of the home

The imperative to "stay at home" was perhaps the strongest state message during the first phase of the pandemic. In the states' dominant interpellation, to remain cloistered was framed as an act of solidarity and prevention, both an act of self-care and a way of caring for others, not least elderly loved ones. Here, we witness a renegotiation of the role and function of the home as a material and symbolic place. While the home is supposed to be a safe haven, a place of comfort and protection, it is at the same time a place of work. During the pandemic, official and dominant discourses reinforce both aspects at the same time. The home becomes the place of protection par excellence, but also, through home office and the introduction of new technologies, it needs to be *productive*. Both aspects become problematic in their own ways. Recent numbers show that productivity rates remained relatively stable, indicating that public and private spheres could easily be integrated in the production process at no or little cost. Subjectively, for some segments of the populations, this was certainly the case. At times, we could witness a "romantization of the quarantine", when staying at home was portrayed as free time and a chance for personal growth. The less loud voices soon started stating the obvious: that quarantine is a class privilege for the non-migrant population (Altenried, Bojadžijev, and Wallis 2020). Not only could the majority of workers not actually work from home, but the digital divide affects even one's access to healthcare (Ramsetty and Adams 2020). And even for the ones who could work from home, inequalities appear on various levels. The overlap of public and private gets complicated when there is additional work to be done, such as care for children or elderly relatives. With kindergartens and schools closed, the care and education services are taken away from the institutions and placed back to the private sphere, which of course is heavily gendered. Patriarchal patterns in the division of domestic labour and gendered modes of subjectivation acted, once again, as a resource in crisis management (Hajek and Opratko 2016; Allmendinger 2020). One early indicator for this in our own academic context, albeit of limited explanatory value, is the fact that there are significantly lower numbers of women appearing as single authors in peer reviewed journals (Dolan and Lawless 2020; Flaherty 2020). While the "productive" aspect of the home becomes problematic in this way, the "protective" one does so, too. For many people, staying in the private sphere is not. There is mounting evidence of an increase of gendered domestic violence across the globe during lockdowns (Bao 2020; Bradbury-Jones and Isham 2020; Campbell 2020; Usher et al. 2020).

This renegotiation of the role of the home, and in a wider sense of the relationship between the public and the private sphere, is highly relevant for the study of cultures of rejection. Many of our informants experience the public sphere as an annoyance, as overwhelming and stressful, and centre their lives around a rather restricted space of the private home. When this very home becomes a point where government techniques, public health strategies, economic imperatives, and patriarchal structures intersect in novel ways during the pandemic, we expect new social tensions to arise.

(3) Migration and mobility

Since 2015, authoritarian and right-wing movements and parties have successfully translated issues of national identity and nationalist discourses into a "question of migration" (Bojadžijev 2018). This has been the case regardless of the actual numbers of migrants or patterns of movement in different European countries. The "question of migration" was a decisive contributing factor in the deepening crisis of the European Union itself, exacerbating an inner conflict between nationalist and sovereignist forces on the one hand, and "Europeanist" or cosmopolitan ones on the other. This constellation has been at least temporarily broken by the pandemic. With the closure of the EU's external borders as well as many of the internal ones, the suspension of the right to asylum and restrictions on freedom of movement within the Schengen area, the far right's core issues regarding the "question of migration" were undercut and their old demands for closing EU and national borders sounded like an echo from a distant past. At the same time, COVID-related scapegoating and hate crimes have reinforced various, racisms, and extreme violence and human rights violations in Europe's "borderlands" continue and are even exacerbated during the current crisis. In Croatia, the Border Violence Monitor Network continues to report illegal push-backs, involving the use of electric discharge weapons and fire arms, arbitrary detention in substandard facilities, and humiliating treatment such as forceful undressing and spray tagging (Border Violence Monitoring Network 2020a). Inequality has been sharpened further for migrants since the onset of Covid-19 lockdowns, limiting access to asylum, healthcare, adequate accommodation, and safety from brutal collective expulsions (Border Violence Monitoring Network 2020b). Similar observations are reported in all countries of our study from Sweden to Serbia, where the "left hand of the state" has not only failed to assist the migrant populations most vulnerable to the pandemic but has openly ignored their human rights.

In interviews with workers in the retail and logistics sectors in Croatia conducted during the pandemic, we also witnessed the growing influence and rapid spread of anti-migrant sentiment on social media across the Balkan countries, as well as covert racism towards co-workers of different ethnic backgrounds among Croatian informants. This contrasts with recent quantitative data from the European Social Survey (ESS) on attitudes towards immigration, where 60% of the population in Croatia believe the state should allow immigration from the poorer non-European countries (European Social Survey 2020). This result places the country among the European nations most open to migration, even in comparison to their neighbouring countries (Italy: 51%; Serbia: 45%; Austria: 39%; Hungary: 8%). Even though the ESS fieldwork was done during 2018 and 2019, the numbers are surprising giving the ongoing reports of human rights violations in treatment of migrants coming to or transiting the territory of Croatia during 2019 and 2020. However, we should be vary of these results, given the problems conventional cross-cultural quantitative studies are prone to (Buil, de Chernatony, and Martínez 2012). The ESS numbers have been portrayed by media in Croatia as unquestionable evidence of Croatian general openness – triggering reactions in the population questioning not only the validity of the data, but the integrity of scientific and educational institutions in general. We read this as another example of a conflict emerging on the basis existing cultures of rejection. In this case, a number of crucial antagonisms – against migrants/migration, against "mainstream media", and against scientific institutions – intersect to produce a new and potentially volatile constellation.

(4) Digital infrastructures in the Covid-19 Crisis: Public broadcasting, networked publics, private networks?

The pandemic has been a catalyst for digital infrastructure in terms of media use, political authority, and demand for technology providers. These developments impact both processes of labour (e.g. remote work, virtual consulting, digital surveillance) and social reproduction (e.g. online retail, delivery services, streaming). Protest mobilizations relied on digital infrastructures for spreading information and making sense of the crisis, and deepened contradictions between public broadcasting channels and digital communication platforms. YouTube, Twitter and Facebook increased their content moderation to curb the dangers of an "Infodemic" – misinformation and mass confusion (Ghebreyesus 2020). At the same time, German public broadcasting saw record numbers in viewership and trust during the crisis (ZDF 2020). In Germany and Sweden, the necessity to render the pandemic understandable and to justify state interventions propelled experts in epidemiology and virology into the public spotlight, commenting on current developments in daily podcasts, talk shows or on Twitter. A conjuncture of state policies, expert knowledge, broadcast and social media turned virologists into prominent figures. If and how this development actually solidifies public broadcasting regimes remains to be seen. Early interviews in Germany stress the ubiquity of instant messaging services like WhatsApp or Telegram for conducting relationship with pre-existing private networks of friends, colleagues and neighbours. During the crisis, platforms facilitating individual and group conversations outranked public platforms like Facebook for sharing information and making sense of politics during the pandemic, chiefly among friends or colleagues (Nielsen et al. 2020, 13). Fatigue regarding online publicity (cf. Lupinacci 2020), media overstimulation (Nicholson 2020) or the paralyzing effects of endless negative headlines (Watercutter 2020) might contribute to the increase of political discussions on instant messengers, instead of Facebook. WhatsApp and Telegram can serve as means for the deliberate disconnection from broader publics (Swart, Peters, and Broersma 2018) and serve as a crucial vectors for nationalist, conspiracist and racist content that eludes regulation (Holnburger and Welty 2020). The intensified – and understudied – role the these more opaque, private and personal platforms play in the circulation of information complicates and, in the case of right-wing groups and channels, explicitly counteracts the constellation of state policy, expert knowledge and media broadcasting, which is framed as authoritarian, technocratic and overbearing. Simultaneously, political mobilizations focusing on the risks for vulnerable populations and issues of inequality eclipsed by the state of emergency, employed digital infrastructures in a different manner. Protests against the mistreatment of refugees, the impending climate crisis or structural racism mobilized primarily through social media and utilized the platforms' global scope to highlight the transnational dimension of these struggles. Live-streaming, hashtags and videoconferencing allowed the creation of public congregations that linked diverse digital and physical environments. Use of digital infrastructure was less a rejective act against specific media constellations than a strategic tool for the choreography of assembly (Gerbaudo 2012). By digitally directing, instructing and framing public congregations, physical protests were both in line with pandemic measures and connected to global issues of migration, police brutality or wage inequality.

(5) New political mobilisations

While far-right and authoritarian populist parties in most European countries initially struggled to find their place during the pandemic (Katsambekis and Stavrakakis 2020), right-wing movements did find new issues and means to mobilize under new circumstances. In Germany, despite the fact that assemblies were officially prohibited and social distancing rules ordained, more than 10.000 people attended protests nationwide in May. Protesters demonstrated their rejection of protective measures against the pandemic and their general sentiment of rejection, and often did so in the name of democracy and the rule of law. A number of demonstrators held up copies of the Constitutional Law of the Federal Republic of Germany during their manifestations, protesting against the alleged "abolition" of fundamental rights, against the "outdated elites", the "bringing into line" ("Gleichschaltung") of the media as well as the "abolition of public discussion" because of the Corona pandemic measures. The protest movements were a heterogeneous mixture of predominantly right-wing extremist movements and parties, esoterics as well as anti-vaccination activists. On a symbolic level, an "info war" took place: a disturbing play with symbols (LGBTQI flags, "No one is Illegal"-banner, anti-fascist symbols) of the "other side", reversing their meanings and integrating symbols of democracy and anti-fascism into an authoritarian mobilization. One striking example was the framing of anti-pandemic measures as an "Enabling Act", alluding to the historical Enabling Act of 1933 which brought Adolf Hitler to power. Because the Infection Protection Act, passed by the Federal Parliament on 22 March, included limitations and restrictions on the right to assemble, protesters called it a "de facto dictator-ship" and compared it to the Nazi regime, notwithstanding the fact that a sig-nificant number of the protesters came from Neo-Nazi milieus themselves (Vieten 2020).

Civil activism expressing other demands, for example for justice, equality and democratic empowerment, have also emerged during the C19 pandemic. These protests largely accepted the restrictions imposed by the Corona measures and included an international "online demonstration" by the Fridays for Future movement, as well as numerous manifestations against the conditions in refugee camps and shelters and for the reception of refu-gees in Germany, which were often broken up by the police and led to arrests. The largest demonstrations took place on the weekend of Pentecost in several European cities in solidarity with the Black Lives Matter movement.

The largest and perhaps most momentous mobilisations took place in Serbia, where huge protests took place against the government's mismanage-ment of the Covid-19 crisis. The mobilisations were triggered by the govern-ment's zig-zag course, from neglecting the challenges of the "funniest virus in the world" (February 2020) to imposing the strictest lockdown measures in Europe (April 2020) to an early return to "normalcy" in May 2020. Protesters included members of left and liberal groups as well as a large number of sup-porters of the far-right. Police reacted violently and significantly increased its presence in the city of Belgrade. In the following few days, after one day of peaceful protests with the slogan "Sedi, ne nasedaj" ("Sit, don't be deceived") – perceived as a liberal response to state violence – police started firing teargas and randomly arresting protesters. Groups aligned to the political left were visible in the protests from July 4, attempting to raise the voice and attract attention among citizens against the very loud and organized right-wing groups. The protests revealed the impotence of the oppositional parties and groups to construct a coherent narrative and develop common demands. They also revealed an authentic rage and dissatisfaction among the Serbian population. They often articulate a desire to return to a "pre-political state", evi-dence of a culture of rejection directed against politics and politicians in general, coupled with a deep dissatisfaction with social conditions in the country. Many attempts on social media to formulate demands on behalf of the citizens faced negative response and didn't produce any substantial result. At the time of writing, it seems like the far-right has been able to capi-talize on the protests, becoming more visible and entering the public main-stream more easily, with potentially dramatical long-term consequences.

Conclusion: new contradictions

The pandemic has created the perspective of a global threat through latent and increasingly economic-ecological contradictions – in regard to climate change and viral spread – while simultaneously creating the desire to return to a pre-pandemic state, open businesses and the democratic pretension that the way of doing economy is and was valid. Caught between a deep rupture in the self-evidence of the economic and social order and the inability to find feasible political alternatives, feelings of inescapabilty or being "locked in" can arise. In his 1944 crisis drama *Huis Clos* – translated as "No Exit" in English, but literally meaning "Locked Gates" – Jean Paul Sartre prefigures the fundamentally rejective reaction to this pandemic: "Hell is other people".

As we have shown above, the Covid-19 crisis has multiple and deep impacts on the various aspects of cultures of rejection. In some cases, existing antagonisms – such as those instituted around the figure of the "migrant" or the "asylum seeker", or against established media and scientific institutions and discourse – are being reinforced and charged with new layers of "viral" meaning. Other antagonisms – such as the rejection of the welfare state as "too generous" may be weakened by the experience of a deep public health crisis and mass unemployment. And finally, new antagonisms – such as those articulated by protests against quarantine measures, social distancing and the wearing of face-masks – arise and link up with existing ones, creating new potential lines of conflict and, perhaps, solidarity. Future research will have to take account of how the new contradictions arising from the pandemic and its management affect cultures of rejection in different locations and over time.

Disclosure statement

No potential conflict of interest was reported by the author(s).

Funding

This work was supported by Volkswagen Foundation: [Grant Number 94 765].

Bibliography

Alexander, Claire. 2016. "The Culture Question: A View from the UK." *Ethnic and Racial Studies* 39 (8): 1426–1435.
Allmendinger, Jutta. 2020. *Der lange Weg aus der Krise. Corona und die gesellschaftlichen Folgen: Schlaglichter aus der WZB-Forschung.* Berlin: WZB. Research Report. https://www.econstor.eu/handle/10419/223169 (November 20, 2020).
Altenried, Moritz, et al. 2018. "Logistical Borderscapes." *South Atlantic Quarterly* 117 (2): 291–312.
Altenried, Moritz, Manuela Bojadžijev, and Mira Wallis. 2020. "Platform (Im)Mobilities: Migration and the Gig Economy in Times of COVID-19." *Routed. Migration & (Im)mobility Magazine.* https://www.routedmagazine.com/platform-immobilities.

Balibar, Etienne. 1991. *"Is There a "Neo-Racism"?"* In *Race, Nation, Class. Ambiguous Identities*, edited by Balibar, Etienne, and Immanuel Wallerstein, 17–28. London/ New York: Verso.

Balibar, Etienne. 2005. "Difference, Otherness, Exclusion." *Parallax* 11 (1): 19–34.

Bao, Hongwei. 2020. "'Anti-Domestic Violence Little Vaccine': A Wuhan-Based Feminist Activist Campaign During COVID-19." *Interface: A Journal for and About Social Movements* 12 (1): 53–63.

Bojadžijev, Manuela. 2018. "Migration as Social Seismograph: an Analysis of Germany's 'Refugee Crisis' Controversy." *International Journal of Politics, Culture, and Society* 31 (4): 335–356.

Border Violence Monitoring Network. 2020a. "Illegal Push-Backs and Border Violence Reports. Balkan Region April/May 2020." https://www.borderviolence.eu/wp-content/uploads/Balkan-Region-Report-May-2020.pdf.

Border Violence Monitoring Network. 2020b. "Special Report: COVID-19 and Border Violence along the Balkan Route." https://www.borderviolence.eu/wp-content/uploads/COVID-19-Report.pdf.

Bourdieu, Pierre. 2000. "The Abdication of the State." In *The Weight of the World: Social Suffering in Contemporary Society*, edited by Bourdieu, Pierre, et al. 181–205. Stanford: Stanford University Press.

Bradbury-Jones, Caroline, and Louise Isham. 2020. "The Pandemic Paradox: The Consequences of COVID-19 on Domestic Violence." *Journal of Clinical Nursing* 29 (13–14): 2047–2049.

Bruff, Ian, and Cemal Burak Tansel. 2019. "Authoritarian Neoliberalism: Trajectories of Knowledge Production and Praxis." *Globalizations* 16 (3): 233–244.

Buil, Isabel, Leslie de Chernatony, and Eva Martínez. 2012. "Methodological Issues in Cross-Cultural Research: An Overview and Recommendations." *Journal of Targeting, Measurement and Analysis for Marketing* 20 (3): 223–234.

Campbell, Andrew M. 2020. "An Increasing Risk of Family Violence During the Covid-19 Pandemic: Strengthening Community Collaborations to Save Lives." *Forensic Science International: Reports* 2: 100089.

Cole, Andrew. 2020. "The Dialectic of Space. An Untimely Proposal." *South Atlantic Quarterly* 119 (4): 811–832.

Dolan, Kathleen, and Jennifer L. Lawless. 2020. "It Takes a Submission: Gendered Patterns in the Pages of AJPS." *American Journal of Political Science*. Accessed July 14, 2020. https://ajps.org/author/mpsa1939/.

Ehs, Tamara. 2020. *Krisendemokratie. Sieben Lektionen Aus Der Coronakrise*. Vienna: Mandelbaum.

European Social Survey. 2020. "Integrated File, Edition 2.0 Round 9 [Database]." http://www.europeansocialsurvey.org/download.html?file=ESS9e02&y=2018.

Flaherty, Colleen. 2020. "No Room of One's Own." *Inside Higher Ed*. Accessed July 14, 2020. https://www.insidehighered.com/news/2020/04/21/early-journal-submission-data-suggest-covid-19-tanking-womens-research-productivity.

Fornäs, Johan, et al. 2007. *Culture Unbound: Dimensions of Culturalisation*. Linköping: Linköping University.

Gerbaudo, Paolo. 2012. *Tweets and the Streets: Social Media and Contemporary Activism. 1. Publ.* London: Pluto Press.

Ghebreyesus, T. A. 2020. "Munich Security Conference." https://www.who.int/dg/speeches/detail/munich-security-conference.

Hajek, Katharina, and Benjamin Opratko. 2016. "Crisis Management by Subjectivation: Toward a Feminist Neo-Gramscian Framework for the Analysis of Europe's Multiple Crisis." *Globalizations* 13 (2): 217–231.

Hall, Stuart, et al. 1978. *Policing the Crisis. Mugging, the State, and Law and Order*. London: Macmillan.

Harder, Alexander, and Benjamin Opratko. 2020. "Cultures of Rejection. Insights from Anthropological Research into the Acceptability of Authoritarian Populism." In Lisbon.

Holnburger, Josef, and Ute Welty. 2020. "Warum Telegram so Attraktiv Für Extremisten Ist. Josef Holnburger Im Gespräch Mit Ute Welty." *Deutschlandfunk Kultur*. https://www.deutschlandfunkkultur.de/verschwoerungsmythen-im-messenger-dienst-warum-telegram-so.1008.de.html?dram:article_id=477326.

Houtart, François. 2010. "The Multiple Crisis and Beyond." *Globalizations* 7 (1–2): 9–15.

Jameson, Fredric. 1971. "Metacommentary." *PMLA* 86 (1): 9–18.

Jameson, Fredric. 2005. *Archaeologies of the Future: The Desire Called Utopia and Other Science Fictions*. London: Verso.

Jonsson, Stefan. 2020. "A Society Which Is Not: Political Emergence and Migrant Agency." *Current Sociology* 68 (2): 204–222.

Katsambekis, Girogos, and Yannis Stavrakakis, eds. 2020. *Populism and the Pandemic. A Collaborative Report*. POPULISMUS Interventions No. 7 (Special Edition). Thessaloniki: Aristotle University of Thessaloniki.

Lentin, Alana. 2014. "Post-Race, Post Politics: The Paradoxical Rise of Culture After Multiculturalism." *Ethnic and Racial Studies* 37 (8): 1268–1285.

Lupinacci, Ludmila. 2020. ""Absentmindedly Scrolling Through Nothing": Liveness and Compulsory Continuous Connectedness in Social Media." *Media, Culture & Society* 0 (00): 1–18.

Nicholson, Jill. 2020. "What Happens When Coronavirus Fatigue Sets in? Our Latest Traffic and Engagement Analysis." *Chartbeat*. https://blog.chartbeat.com/2020/04/08/coronavirus-data-news-traffic-trends/.

Nielsen, Rasmus Kleis, et al. 2020. "Navigating the "Infodemic": How People in Six Countries Access and Rate News and Information about Coronavirus." *Reuters Institute*. https://reutersinstitute.politics.ox.ac.uk/infodemic-how-people-six-countries-access-and-rate-news-and-information-about-coronavirus.

Novus. 2020a. *Coronastatus 20200318*. https://novus.se/coronastatus-20200318/.

Novus. 2020b. *Coronastatus 0427*. https://novus.se/coronastatus-0427/.

Oberndorfer, Lukas. 2020. "Between the Normal State and an Exceptional State Form: Authoritarian Competitive Statism and the Crisis of Democracy in Europe." In *The State of the European Union: Fault Lines in European Integration, Staat – Souveränität – Nation*, edited by Stefanie Wöhl, Elisabeth Springler, Martin Pachel, and Bernhard Zeilinger, 23–44. Wiesbaden: Springer.

Raj-Reichert, Gale, Sabrina Zajak, and Nicole Helmerich. 2020. "Introduction to Special Issue on Digitalization, Labour and Global Production." *Competition & Change*. 1024529420914478.

Ramsetty, Anita, and Cristin Adams. 2020. "Impact of the Digital Divide in the Age of COVID-19." *Journal of the American Medical Informatics Association* 27 (7): 1147–1148.

Standring, Adam, and Jonathan Davies. 2020. "From Crisis to Catastrophe: The Death and Viral Legacies of Austere Neoliberalism in Europe?" *Dialogues in Human Geography* 10 (2): 146–149.

Swart, Joëlle, Chris Peters, and Marcel Broersma. 2018. "Shedding Light on the Dark Social: The Connective Role of News and Journalism in Social Media Communities." *New Media & Society* 20 (11): 4329–4345.

Usher, Kim, et al. 2020. "Family Violence and COVID-19: Increased Vulnerability and Reduced Options for Support." *International Journal of Mental Health Nursing* 29 (4): 549–552.

Vieten, Ulrike M. 2020. "The "New Normal" and "Pandemic Populism": The COVID-19 Crisis and Anti-Hygienic Mobilisation of the Far-Right." *Social Sciences* 9 (9): 165.

Watercutter, Angela. 2020. "Doomscrolling Is Slowly Eroding Your Mental Health." *Wired*. https://www.wired.com/story/stop-doomscrolling/.

ZDF. 2020. "Die Gesellschaftliche Relevanz des Öffentlich-Rechtlichen Rundfunks in Corona-Zeiten." *ZDF.de*. https://www.zdf.de/zdfunternehmen/medienforschung-studien-corona-berichterstattung-100.html.

Race, immigration and health: the Hostile Environment and public health responses to Covid-19

Giorgia Donà

ABSTRACT

This paper examines the impact of governmental management of the pandemic on the morbidity and mortality of migrants, gendered and racialized groups by focussing on the relation of its public health message campaign to accommodation, health and survival. The Hostile Environment immigration policies have restricted the ability of these groups to adhere to Government's public health guidelines, increasing risks of their contracting coronavirus. These policies exacerbate existing health inequalities in intersectional ways. The Covid virus, in its socially reproductive capacity, can thus be understood as a biological descriptor for a political crisis of intersectional inequality in the politics of health.

Introduction

Dispelling the public "myth" that coronavirus is the great equalizer, growing evidence points to the disproportionate impacts of Covid-19 on the health, survival and livelihoods of ethnic, migrant and marginalized communities (Atchison et al. 2020; Platt and Warwick 2020; Rosenthal et al. 2020). Whereas these racialized direct impacts are rightly considered, the indirect consequences of the government's response to the pandemic on racialized and gendered individuals have received less attention (Devakumar, Bhopal, and Shannon 2020). The government's management of its Covid-response can also be discriminatory: unequal distribution of resources determines not only who is at greater risk of contracting or dying from the virus but also the ability of individuals to follow the recommendations to control the pandemic (Van Bavel et al. 2020). This paper argues that Covid-19 has not only directly impacted on the morbidity and mortality of migrant and ethnic communities in the UK, but also disproportionally prejudiced their ability to adhere to the Government's public health guidelines, thus putting them doubly at increased risk from coronavirus than the general population. This amounts to a form of structural violence (Devakumar, Bhopal, and Shannon 2020).

The detrimental outcomes of the pandemic, and its management, are experienced differently along intersectional lines of class, gender, ethnicity and generation (Bhala et al. 2020; Paton et al. 2020). These intersectional lines are intertwined and are given presence, force and shape by past inter-sectional histories of discrimination. Similarly to the ways in which during the pandemic the "vulnerable", the "at risk" patients and the elderly occupy an ambiguous place in social and medical hierarchies (Moore 2020), the position of gendered and racialized individuals and communities relates to complex histories whose place in social and medical hierarchies at the time of the pandemic is intricate and ambiguous. In addition to its biomedical properties, Covid must thus be understood as a profoundly social and political pathogen (Fagan 2020). This paper shows that in addition to the literal reproductive capacity of the virus, which is biological, the virus has a secondary repetition, which is social: it reproduces and amplifies the scale and intensity of existing structural and intersectional inequalities in public health, thus differentially impacting the most vulnerable groups. The pathogen must therefore also be understood as a biological descriptor for a political crisis of intersectional inequalities in the politics of health, in which a constellation of agencies of liberal society generate relations of multi-faceted hosting through which the virus registers its effects differentially. Thusly understood, the force and effect of the pathogen is intersectional with reference to categories of migration, race and gender. Not only the virus but also the Government's response to the pandemic is likely to increase existing socio-economic differ-ences and to intensify racial and ethnic discrimination that exacerbate health inequalities (Chouhan and Nazroo 2020). This is because the same living and working conditions experienced by members of ethnic and racial minorities that lead to chronic ill health are the same ones that persist to make it difficult for these individuals to protect themselves from the virus (Meer et al. 2020). This is particularly significant for migrants, asylum seekers and racialized non-citizens who are subjected to the Government's Hostile Environment immigration policies.

The Hostile Environment and public health responses to Covid-19

Recent changes in UK immigration policy have created an intentionally "hostile environment" for irregular migrants. The impact of this environment has spilled into other categories of non-citizens. The 2014 and 2016

Immigration Acts have restricted access to housing, healthcare, banking and legal representation, limited access to services, facilities and employment by reference to immigration status and increased penalties for unauthorized working (Lewis, Waite, and Hodkinson 2018; Targarona and Doná 2021). These punitive measures, aimed at irregular migrants, have negatively impacted upon other categories of migrants, such as individuals in the asylum system and migrants with precarious status (Meier and Doná 2021). They have also affected long-term residents, most notably the Windrush generation of Caribbean migrants who arrived in the UK between 1948 and 1973. As Commonwealth citizens, these migrants have the right to indefinitely reside and work in the UK. However, hundreds of them have been wrongly placed in detention centres, deported to countries that many left as children, and denied legal rights to remain or return to the UK (de Noronha 2019). New restrictions for European citizens were introduced in November 2020, when the Immigration and Social Security Co-ordination (EU Withdrawal) Act was passed into law. The Act has ended free movement for European migrants and paved the way for the government's new Points-Based Immigration System.

The Hostile Environment has become an explicit immigration strategy of the UK Conservative government since it took power in 2010. It has become a major "governmental technology in the control and disciplining of diversity and discourses on migrants and racialised minorities" (SSAHE 2020, 1). However this approach marks a rhetorical rather than qualitative shift away from anti-immigrant policies of previous governments (Weisz 2018) that have longer histories than the Coalition/Conservative governments (SSAHE 2020). Racism is implicit in UK immigration policies, which disproportionately impact people of colour (Goodfellow 2018).

Covid has exposed the ways in which the Hostile Environment interacts with the pandemic and its management to exacerbate existing health inequalities for racialiszed, gendered and citizenship-based categories. Individuals in the asylum system, migrants with insecure immigration status and residents without the "right" papers suffer not only the direct impacts of Covid-19 on their health, lives and livelihoods (Mleya 2020) but also see that opportunities to access health services, availability of information and eligibility for welfare support are restricted by immigration status (Rosenthal et al. 2020). Additionally, their ability to adhere to the public health guidelines implemented by the Government to respond to the pandemic are constrained (Meer et al. 2020; Paton et al. 2020). Thus, the UK Government's Hostile Environment immigration policies serve as a means of further diminishing health equalities for racialized, gendered and non-citizens' groups at the time of the pandemic. These increased health inequalities are detrimental not only to the well being of racialized migrants and minorities but also to a broader national public health agenda for recovering from Covid-19.

On March 23, 2020, Prime Minister Boris Johnson announced a new set of guidelines to delay the Covid pandemic. Lockdown was introduced, requiring the public to stay at home except for absolutely necessary trips to buy food or medicine, to go to work or exercise. The government's announcement was captured by the slogan "STAY HOME – PROTECT THE NHS – SAVE LIVES". Yet, this message presumes that accommodation is safe for all, admission to health services is accessible and free at point of use, and that all residents in the country can follow the guidelines to reduce mortality rates. On May 10, 2020, the message changed to the more ambiguous "STAY ALERT – CONTROL THE VIRUS – SAVE LIVES", in line with the easing of the lockdown. While the content of this message is partially new it also relies on continuities with the rules of lockdown, including social distancing and self-isolation, to avoid the recurrence of another spike. Since the easing of restrictions in June and July, local actions were put in place to contain the spread of the virus where infection rates were high. On October 14, the Government announced a 3-tier system, which saw areas with the highest number of cases being placed in tier three and subjected to the tightest measures. On November 5, a second national lockdown was announced that lasted till December 2 when it was followed by the return of a tiered system of restrictions, and the new message "wash HANDS, wear a MASK, and keep social DISTANCE". As the vaccination programme got underway, with the first vaccination taking place on December 8, a new and more easily transmissible variant of the virus was identified as the cause of the sharp rising of infections in the latter part of 2020. This discovery led the Government to put into place a third national lockdown on January 6 2021. This measure also saw the re-introduction of the previous STAY HOME – PROTECT THE NHS – SAVE LIVES slogan.

Focussing on the government's key public health message "STAY HOME-PROTECT THE NHS-SAVE LIVES", and to a lesser extent on ensuing related communication messages, this piece examines the impact of the Hostile Environment on compliance with public health guidelines in three areas - accommodation, health, and survival. These interrelated spheres are chosen because they are at the core of the government's public health call to stay home during lockdown, to maintain hygiene to protect the NHS and to maintain social distance and other measures to save lives. An overview of these intersections show the pervasive impacts of the Hostile Environment on the ability of racialized and gendered individuals to adhere to public health guidelines during the pandemic that highlight the relationship between race, immigration and health inequalities.

"STAY HOME": accommodation

The government's guideline to "STAY HOME" is predicated on a number of assumptions: that home is a safe space for all, that individuals residing in the UK have a home to stay in, and that the public has autonomy in the decision to stay home. The Institute for Race Relations published a report in which it criticizes the dreadfully overcrowded and unhygienic housing that is provided to asylum seeking families and their children, which increases their risk of contracting Covid-19 (Institute for Race Relations 2020). Asylum seekers who reside in temporary accommodation have to share their spaces with strangers during lockdown, and its easing, in breach of strict measures to contain coronavirus. Speaking on Radio 4's Today programme about the accommodation he has been staying in for the past four months, where people share rooms with two or even three others, John says: "This is risky. In this Covid-19 pandemic my life is at risk. I cannot control their movements. I might bring the infection to them, they might bring it to me. We are very scared. Every day we have new people coming. From where we do not know."(BBC Radio Four 2020) Similarly, individuals subjected to the Hostile Environment in asylum detentions, which have been identified as likely hotspots for spikes following the easing of the lockdown, continue to share their cells with strangers in overcrowded conditions, where they have limited agency on preventing infections, placing everyone there at risk (Gardner 2020).

The government asks individuals exhibiting symptoms and those who have had contact with infected individuals, to self-isolate. The Test, Track and Trace programme relies on individuals, even those with no symptoms, to self-isolate for between ten and fourteen days. While asylum seekers and other migrants in precarious conditions are willing to follow the guidelines, self-isolation and social distancing are unfeasible in over-crowded accommodation shared with strangers.

The gendered impacts of the coronavirus pandemic are ongoing and crises exacerbate pre-existing gender inequalities. Domestic violence in the home has worsened during lockdown (Norris 2020). Yet, for women whose immigration status is linked to that of their partner, the likelihood of leaving an unsafe home is further restricted because of the additional fear of putting their immigration status at risk due to Hostile Environment policies. Asylum-seeking women fleeing domestic abuse are also blocked from accessing help when services are in lockdown (Norris 2020), and fear for their safety in over-crowded refuges for asylum seeking-women (Mleya 2020a).

Children who entered the country as unaccompanied minors and those in refugee families are entitled to formal education, which during lockdown has become "home schooling". Unsuitable accommodation and limited access to technology (internet access is not provided in temporary accommodation), together with language barriers and other challenges regularly faced by newcomers, constitute significant obstacles to "home schooling" as well as children's engagements with blended learning platforms in the foreseeable future (Nanton 2020).

Migrants with no recourse to public funds, asylum seekers living below the poverty level, and those with precarious status are at high risk of being or becoming destitute as a result of the Hostile Environment. A situational analysis conducted by Refugee Action with forty organizations indicates that a key challenge faced by people seeking asylum, refugees and other migrants during lockdown is destitution, as "many city centre hotels have refused to support asylum seekers or homeless. They'd rather close and receive government support" (Refugee Action 2020). Refugee Action's partners continue to encounter problems, and they call attention to areas of real concern for increased risks of rough sleeping, which they attribute to recurrent delays in the legal system, on-going changes of rules and constant uncertainty around immigration status. These migrants, who are already in extremely vulnerable circumstances, are unlikely to be able to follow the government's advice to "stay at home". To not be able to stay in a regular place during lockdown, and its easing, has public health consequences for all.

On Thursday evenings during the first lockdown, the public clapped to celebrate the front line staff in the health and care services. Many of the new sung and unsung heroes in the health, social care, public transport, delivery and other sectors, who kept the economy going during lockdown and continue to do so, are migrants or come from migrant backgrounds (Bhala et al. 2020). For Fagan (2020) the "opportunity to work from home is, one might say, a particular privilege which Covid-19 has underlined. Many others, of course, do not enjoy this privilege" (154). Covid has made visible the existence of societal and structural inequalities that have existed in the country for a long time. Not only do these racialized and gendered migrants risk their lives every day when using public transport and working in unsafe environments, but their efforts to follow public health guidelines are hindered when social distancing is not practiced and protective equipment is not available (Thomas 2020).

Migrants such as domestic workers, outsourced cleaners and security guards, who are in low-paid and insecure jobs, are not in a position to refuse to do non-essential work for fear of losing their jobs and those employed in the gig economy have no sick pay (Mason and Booth 2020), while migrants working in the undocumented sector where many are subjected to modern day slavery conditions cannot afford to "stay home". These gendered and racialized migrants have no rights, including the right to "home", and they do not have the autonomy to follow the guideline to "STAY HOME".

The transition from the "STAY HOME" message to the more ambiguous "STAY ALERT" message is equally problematic for migrants with insecure status and those in the asylum system. For the reasons outlined above, Hostile Environment regulations force migrants to maintain a heightened sense of awareness – to stay extra "alert" while thwarting their rights to levels of protection experienced by the rest of the population and constraining migrants' ability to follow the guidelines like the general public.

"Protect the NHS" – access to health

During the pandemic, the general public was reminded of its responsibility to follow the message, "PROTECT THE NHS". However, this message has different meanings and implications for individuals subjected to Hostile Environment practices. The Hostile Environment policy created barriers to accessing the health service, such as the data sharing of a patient's non-clinical information from the NHS to the Home Office (Hiam, Steele, and McKee 2018). Another Hostile Environment policy that the government introduced in 2018 is the NHS charge, whereby non-EU patients are made to pay fifty per cent more than it costs the NHS to treat them and hospital staff are required to demand proof of entitlement to free healthcare (Bulman 2020a). Defaulting on the payment of bills has serious consequences for migrants and asylum seekers, who can be reported to the Home Office and have their application for settled status rejected due to non-payment. The system of immigration enforcement, which continued during the pandemic, threatens migrants' ability to remain in the country and thus actively discourages them from seeking healthcare (Puntis 2020). Such hostile environment measures undermine the government's response to the pandemic in different ways: they not only have a detrimental effect on the health, welfare and wellbeing of migrants but they also undermine the ethical standards and professional responsibilities of health staff and negatively impact on the national health system more generally (Mahrasingam 2020).

The government has attempted to adapt the immigration system to the realities of the Covid emergency. However, these concessions are conditional. It has made testing for Covid-19 exempt from charges usually payable by migrants for using the NHS, but it maintains charges for other health conditions. The Home Office has scrapped the surcharge for health professionals but not for others. Similarly, it automatically renews the visas of doctors and nurses for a year but other stuff whose visa expire, including those occupying essential roles, are not given extensions. These conditional changes not only reproduce existing inequalities but reinforce downward equality, lifting restrictions for some groups but not others.

Personal hygiene is another core element of the campaign to protect the NHS. A key public health message during the easing of the second lockdown was to "wash HANDS". Yet, soaps and sanitizers are not made available for many migrants in vulnerable circumstances. For example, these essential items are not automatically provided to individuals in immigration detention facilities, who must purchase them using vouchers earned by working under exploitative conditions. The same applies to the wearing of masks and face coverings that were made compulsory in shops and other public places in

England on 24 July with £100 fines for non-compliance (Sparrow 2020). The wearing of masks has become central to the public health communication strategy during the second lockdown. Yet, people in the asylum system who live on £5.39 per day, a rate that is below the national poverty level, cannot afford the costs of these extra items, creating a "support gap" (Bulman 2020b) that disadvantages them in their ability to adhere to public health guidelines.

The pandemic and the government's response to the crisis are taking a toll on the mental health of the nation. Mental health charities have seen a spike in the number of requests for support since the lockdown (BBC 2020). Many individuals seeking asylum have experienced war and displacement, and have been exposed to multiple losses. In the UK they face loneliness, concerns about the status of their application process and ongoing worries about their survival (Doná 2010). Anxieties caused by the Hostile Environment towards non-citizens are exacerbated by the impossibility to follow government's guidelines such as social distancing and self-isolation. According to Refugee Action, mental health is a key issue, and "there are real issues for people in Houses of Multiple Occupancy. If others don't observe the rules, it creates tensions." (Refugee Action 2020).

The Hostile Environment has fostered a milieu in which migrants wishing to follow public health guidelines to protect the NHS are subjected to exclusionary policies. The government's change of message, from "PROTECT THE NHS" to "CONTROL THE VIRUS", is perplexing. A major impact of the Hostile Environment rests in its restriction of individual autonomy. To control an invisible parasite may not resonate closely with those subjected to stringent regulatory requirements and punitive monitoring mechanisms that constrain their ability to have control over their lives.

While waiting for the vaccine, the country relies on widespread testing, contact and tracing to reduce the impact of the second wave of Covid-19. For this programme to be viable, all sections of the population must be willing to be contacted by the NHS or public health staff (Dropkin 2020). Doods and Fakoya (2020)'s detailed investigation among black Africans and community health professionals has uncovered mistrust of self-sampling technologies. Historic and contemporary discrimination and racial inequality are generally associated with distrust in social institutions, including the healthcare system (Van Bavel et al. 2020). Members of these communities are likely to be wary about the public health information they receive, less able to understand the messages because of language proficiency and less willing to adopt recommendations. As new treatments are developed and vaccines are rolled out, there is a need to collect information on ethnic minorities, who are usually inadequately represented in clinical trials and longitudinal health cohort investigations (Bentley 2020). Inclusive policies that guarantee equal access for everyone to the care system, including to testing, new therapies and vaccines are vital for the welfare of the population as a whole.

"Save Lives" – mortality

As of February 2021, the UK death toll has risen to more than 100,000, the highest number of confirmed coronavirus fatalities in Europe and one of the highest in the world (Johns Hopkins University 2021). The government's policies and public health guidelines put in place to respond to the pandemic have all increased the risk of poor health and the gravity of the illness for migrants and black, Asian and minority ethnic people (Devakumar, Bhopal, and Shannon 2020). Increased mortality risks are linked not only to intersectional variables such as race, poverty and immigration status but equally important housing conditions, ability to access health care and to survive below poverty levels, all of which are seriously constrained by the Hostile Environment. The Trussell Trust, which coordinates a network of food banks, has documented an 89 per cent rise in the number of deliveries of emergency food parcels and a 107 per cent increase in parcels donated to children since the inception of the pandemic (Sandhu 2020). Individuals living below the poverty level in the asylum system, migrants with no recourse to public funds, and those heavily reliant on welfare support are at higher risk of coronavirus-related food starvation than the general population. This of course has implications on their ability to contribute to the government's message to "SAVE LIVES", when their own lives are at risk.

The intersectionality of gender, class and occupations is a risk factor in mortality rates, with males working in low paid occupations being at higher risk of losing their lives due to Covid-19 (Aljazeera 2020). Migrants with insecure status and those working in the undocumented sector are disproportionally represented in low paid occupations and have limited rights and protections. Migrants, especially those without documents, are also less likely to report symptoms, go to the hospital, seek help, or may seek help later, with the onset of more advanced disease (Devakumar, Bhopal, and Shannon 2020), putting them at higher risk of getting ill and dying of Covid-19 and non Covid-19 illnesses.

As the UK continues to fluctuate between total and partial lockdowns, it is even more vital for the population to continue to follow public heath guidelines in order to "SAVE LIVES", the third component of the government's slogan. It is then fitting to ask whose lives the government has in mind when urging the nation to "SAVE LIVES" while its Hostile Environment policies are responsible for destroying lives and constraining asylum seekers' and migrants' ability to follow public health guidelines. As one migrant said: "While I've tried to follow government guidance, the asylum system isn't set up to protect our health" (Mleya 2020). One could argue, by extension, that government guidance is not set up to save migrant, gendered and racialized lives. While charities and activists have longed called for the Hostile Environment policies to be scrapped, this imperative is even more relevant to the government's strategy to "SAVE LIVES" during and after the pandemic. This is important not only for racialized migrants and minorities but also for a broader national public health agenda for recovering from Covid.

Conclusion

Covid is not just a viral disease but also a social and political pathogen in the politics of health. Most researchers examine the direct effects of Covid on the morbidity and mortality of migrants and racialized groups. This paper focused on the indirect impact of governmental management of the pandemic through an analysis of the Hostile Environment, and the ways in which immigration policies have restricted the ability of racialized, gendered and citizenship-based categories to adhere to the Government's public health guidelines. The analysis of accommodation, health and survival unravelled the interactions between race and migration, and governance and public health by showing that the Covid virus, in its social reproductive capacity, can be understood as a biological descriptor for a political crisis of intersectional inequality.

Disclosure statement

No potential conflict of interest was reported by the author(s).

References

Aljazeera. 2020. "Male Security Guards at Highest Risk of Dying from COVID-19:ONS". *Aljazeera News*. 11 May https://www.aljazeera.com/news/2020/5/11/male-security-guards-at-highest-risk-of-dying-from-covid-19-ons.

Atchison, C. J., L. Bowman, C. Vrinten, R. Redd, P. Pristera, J. W. Eaton, and H. Ward. 2020. "Perceptions and Behavioural Responses of the General Public during the COVID-19 Pandemic: A Cross-sectional Survey of UK Adults". *MedRxiv*. https://www.medrxiv.org/content/10.1101/2020.04.01.20050039v1.

BBC. 2020. "Lockdown Causes Spike in Wiltshire Anxiety Support Requests" *BBC News*. 27 April. https://www.bbc.co.uk/news/av/uk-england-bristol-52445121.

BBC Radio four. 2020. https://www.bbc.co.uk/sounds/play/live:bbc_radio_fourfm

Bentley, G. R. 2020. "Don't Blame the BAME: Ethnic and Structural Inequalities in Susceptibilities to COVID-19." *American Journal of Human Biology* 32 (5): e23478. https://onlinelibrary.wiley.com/doi/full/10.1002/ajhb.23478. doi:10.1002/ajhb.23478

Bhala, N., G. Curry, A. R. Martineau, C. Agyemang, and R. Bhopal. 2020. "Sharpening the Global Focus on Ethnicity and Race in the Time of COVID-19." *The Lancet* 395 (10238): 1673–1676. doi:10.1016/S0140-6736(20)31102-8

Bulman, M. 2020(a). "Undocumented Migrants Dying of Coronavirus because They're Too Afraid to Seek Help, MPs and Charities Warn". *The Independent*. 17 April. https://www.independent.co.uk/news/uk/home-news/coronavirus-undocumented-migrants-deaths-cases-nhs-matt-hancock-a9470581.html.

Bulman, M. 2020(b). "'5£ a Day is Not Enough': Asylum Seekers Surviving on 'Scandalously Low' Financial Support During the Pandemic". *The Independent* 4 May.   https://www.independent.co.uk/news/uk/home-news/coronavirus-job-losses-laid-domestic-workers-carers-homeless-visa-a9498581.html.

Chouhan, K., and J. Nazroo. 2020. "Health Inequalities." In *Ethnicity, Race and Inequality in the UK – State of the Nation*, edited by B. Byrne, C. Alexander, O. Khan, J. Nazroo, and W. Shankley, 73–92. Bristol: Policy Press.

de Noronha, L. 2019. "Deportation, Racism and Multi-Status Britain: Immigration Control and the Production of Race in the Present." *Ethnic and Racial Studies* 42 (14): 2413–2430. doi:10.1080/01419870.2019.1585559

Devakumar, D., S. S. Bhopal, and G. Shannon. 2020. "COVID-19: The Great Unequaliser." *Journal of the Royal Society of Medicine* 113 (6): 234–235. doi:10.1177/0141076820925434

Doná, G. 2010. "Rethinking Wellbeing: From Contexts to Processes." *International Journal of Migration, Health and Social Care* 6 (2): 3–14. doi:10.5042/ijmhsc.2010.0606

Doods, C., and I. Fakoya. 2020. "Covid-19: Ensuring Equality of Access to Testing for Ethnic Minorities". *British Medical Journal*, 369. May 22. https://www.researchgate.net/publication/342393542_Covid-19_and_ethnic_minorities_an_urgent_agenda_for_overdue_action.

Dropkin, G. 2020. "Covid-19: Contact Tracing Requires Ending the Hostile Environment". *British Medical Journal*, 368, March 31. https://www.bmj.com/content/368/bmj.m1320.

Fagan, A. 2020. The Politics of Identity in the UK: Before, During and After Covid-19. https://repository.essex.ac.uk/28035/1/020.pdf.

Gardner, Z. 2020. "Punishing Migrants: Stubborn Home Office Covid Response puts Everyone at Risk". *Politics.co.uk*. https://www.politics.co.uk/comment-analysis/2020/04/09/punishing-migrants-stubborn-home-office-covid-response-puts.

Goodfellow, M. 2018. "'Race'and Racism in the UK." In *New Thinking for the British Economy*, edited by L. MacFarlane, 150–159. Open Democracy Publishing. https://democracycollaborative.org/sites/default/files/2020-02/New Thinking for the British Economy.pdf#page=150

Hiam, L., S. Steele, and M. McKee. 2018. "Creating a 'Hostile Environment for Migrants': the British Government's use of Health Service Data to Restrict Immigration is a Very bad Idea." *Health Economics, Policy and Law* 13 (2): 107–117. doi:10.1017/S1744133117000251

Institute of Race Relations. 2020. Asylum in the Time of Covid-19. http://www.irr.org.uk/news/asylum-in-the-time-of-covid-19/.

Johns Hopkins University of Medicine. 2021. *Covid-19 Dashboard by the Center for Systems Science and `Engineering at Johns Hopkins University*. https://coronavirus.jhu.edu/map.html.

Lewis, H., L. Waite, and S. Hodkinson. 2018. "'Hostile' UK Immigration Policy and Asylum Seekers' Susceptibility to Forced Labour." In *Entrapping Asylum Seekers. Transnational Crime, Crime Control and Security*, edited by F. Vecchio, and A. Gerard, 187–215. London: Palgrave Macmillan.

Mahrasingam, A. 2020. *Coronavirus: Home Office Urged to Suspend "hostile environment" Amid Fears Infected Migrants Won't Seek Treatment* Medact, March 16.

https://www.independent.co.uk/news/uk/home-news/coronavirus-uk-immigrants-hostile-environment-home-office-nhs-healthcare-treatment-a9404796.html.

Mason, R., and R. Booth. 2020. Coronavirus UK: Unions Warn over Lack of Sick pay for Gig Economy Workers". *The Guardian*, March 3. https://www.theguardian.com/world/2020/mar/03/coronavirus-uk-unions-warn-over-lack-of-sick-pay-for-gig-economy-workers.

Meer, N., K. Qureshi, B. Kasstan, and S. Hill. 2020. The Social Determinants of Covid 19 and BAME Disproportionality." *Discover Society. April*, *30*, 2020. https://discoversociety.org/2020/04/30/the-social-determinants-of-covid-19-and-bame-disproportionality/.

Meier, I., and G. Doná. forthcoming, 2021. "The Politics of Time: Asylum Regimes, Temporalities and Power." In *Stealing Time: Migration, Temporalities and State Violence*, edited by M. Bhatia, and V. Canning. Basingstoke: Palgrave.

Mleya, V. 2020. "Coronavirus is Leaving Asylum Seekers like me More Vulnerable than Ever." *HuffPost*, April 20. https://www.huffingtonpost.co.uk/entry/coronavirus-asylum-seekers_uk_5e998e92c5b62f4a2df53fb4?guccounter=1&guce_referrer=aHR0cHM6Ly9kdWNrZHVja2dvLmNvbS8&guce_referrer_sig=AQAAANxqpl2wbRJ6rz49Rfd2BXvEllSS1ktbt7cEqcbaqWUW0fNrUl-o4KnTVdYi90EyuaEQY-IRdhc4ONi7ov95rT7vmgyQt1yAQmBsKcbl9adkBciBFjwpPwa9TZ4B68BW22invKjPyhWgOnyH13L6fC9rDUhPLdzoyNE86cdkp5gR.

Moore, M. D. 2020. "Historicising 'Containment and Delay': COVID-19, the NHS and High-risk Patients". *Wellcome Open Research*, 5(130) https://wellcomeopenresearch.org/articles/5-130.

Nanton, R. 2020. *Covid-19 & Unaccompanied Asylum Seeking Children*. London: Social Scientists Against the Hostile Environment. https://acssmigration.wordpress.com/2020/05/21/covid-19-unaccompanied-asylum-seeking-children-in-the-uk/.

Norris, S. 2020. "Lost in the Covid Emergency: Migrant Women Escaping Domestic Violence Blocked from Help". *Politics.co.uk*. May 13. https://uk.news.yahoo.com/lost-covid-emergency-migrant-women-075014488.html?guccounter=1&guce_referrer=aHR0cHM6Ly9kdWNrZHVja2dvLmNvbS8&guce_referrer_sig=AQAAAKjkhZ5ZMUWScktTkiXWtHrKyPC3bjf77rlVPmmM9akQmbCakaJMhFSs5lRkYk48KES9qHAIntuMrF_IHLtyYGzTZKqcabkFY2PtUYRcGMdpTDDdBdgeEXwO-yHLamPdaEOYv-rLTqzKusMrhKAYMml99KwcKK-brsJ95WjeL_e2.

Paton, A., G. Fooks, G. Maestri, and P. Lowe. 2020. "Submission of Evidence on the Disproportionate Impact of Covid 19, and the UK Government Response, on Ethnic Minorities and Women in the UK". Aston University Publication. https://publications.aston.ac.uk/id/eprint/41460/.

Platt, L., and R. Warwick. 2020. *Are Some Ethnic Groups more Vulnerable to COVID-19 than Others*. London: Institute for Fiscal Studies.

Puntis, J. W. 2020. "COVID-19: Children on the Front Line". *Archives of Disease in Childhood*. https://adc.bmj.com/content/early/2020/06/28/archdischild-2020-319671.

Refugee Action. 2020. *The 5 Biggest Challenges Covid-19 Poses to Refugees and People Seeking Asylum*. https://www.refugee-action.org.uk/the-5-biggest-challenges-covid-19-poses-to-supporting-refugees-and-people-seeking-asylum/.

Rosenthal, D., M. Ucci, M. Heys, A. Hayward, and M. Lakhanpaul. 2020. "Impacts of Covid-19 on Vulnerable Children in Temporary Accommodation in the UK." *The Lancet* 5 (5): 241–242.

Sandhu, S. 2020. "Food Banks give Twice as Many Emergency Parcels to Children during UK Coronavirus Pandemic Compared to Last Year". *INews*, June 13. https://inews.co.uk/news/food-banks-uk-coronavirus-pandemic-emergency-parcels-children-432943.

Sparrow, A. 2020. "Face Masks to be Compulsory in Shops in England: UK Death Toll Raises by 128 – as it Happens" *The Guardian*, July14. https://www.theguardian.com/world/live/2020/jul/14/uk-coronavirus-live-news-updates-boris-johnson-face-masks.

SSAHE - Social Scientists against the Hostile Environment. 2020. *Migration, Racism and the Hostile Environment: Making the Case for the Social Sciences*. London: Academy of Social Sciences Special Interest Group on Migration, Refugees and Settlement. https://acssmigration.wordpress.com/report/.

Targarona, N., and G. Doná. 2021. "Forced Unemployment or Undocumented Work: The Burden of the Prohibition to Work for Asylum Seekers in the UK." *Journal of Refugee Studies*, feaa090. https://doi.org/10.1093/jrs/feaa090.

Thomas, D. 2020. "Coronavirus: 'We are Not Working in Safe Conditions'". *BB News*, March 26. https://www.bbc.co.uk/news/business-52052580.

Van Bavel, J. J., K. Baicker, P. S. Boggio, V. Capraro, A. Cichocka, M. Cikara, et al. 2020. "Using Social and Behavioural Science to Support COVID-19 Pandemic Response." *Nature Human Behaviour* 4: 460–471. doi:10.1038/s41562-020-0884-z

Weisz, A. 2018. "Preventative or Performative? Assessing the Role and Intention of the UK's 'Hostile Environment' Since 2010." Doctoral dissertation, Columbia University.

Index

Note: Figures are indicated by *italics* and tables by **bold** type. Endnotes are indicated by the page number followed by "n" and the endnote number e.g., 57n50 refers to endnote 50 on page 57.